Oregon Ice Creams
and The Inside Scoop on Fun Things to See and Do

by Gail Hoffnagle

Oregon Ice Creams and the Inside Scoop on Fun Things to See and Do

Copyright © 2011 by Gail Hoffnagle

All rights reserved. No part of this book may be reproduced in any form or by any electronic or mechanical means, including information storage and retrieval systems, without permission in writing from the publisher, except by a reviewer who wishes to quote brief passages in connection with a review written for inclusion in a magazine, newspaper, or broadcast. Although every attempt has been taken in the preparation of this book, the publisher and author assume no responsibility for errors or omissions.

Credits

Editor
Jill Kelly

Book Design/Layout
Amy Livingstone, Sacred Art Studio
www.sacredartstudio.net

ISBN-13:978-1463606947
ISBN-10:146360694X

Printed in the United States of America

Table of Contents

INTRODUCTION 1-6

SECTION 1: PORTLAND 7

Portland Ice Cream 8
Alpenrose Dairy 8
BluePlate Lunch Counter and Soda Fountain 10
Cool Moon Ice Cream 12
Fairley's Pharmacy and Soda Fountain 14
Fifty Licks 16
Lovely's 50-50 17
Peculiarium 18
Piece of Cake 20
Pix Patisserie 22
Pope House Bourbon Lounge 23
Roses Restaurant 25
Ruby Jewel Ice Cream 26
Scoop Ice Cream 28
Sundae in the Park 30
Tonalli's Donuts and Ice Cream 31
Two Tarts Sweets for the Soul 32

Portland Things to See and Do 33
Eastbank Esplanade 33
The Hat Museum 34
International Rose Test Garden in Washington Park 35
Kidd Toy Museum 36
Lloyd Center Ice Rink 37
Oaks Amusement Park 39
Oaks Roller Skating Rink 40
Oregon Museum of Science and Industry (OMSI) 41
Oregon Zoo 42
Pier Park (Disc Golf) 44
Portland Aerial Tram 45
Portland Ukulele Association 46
Powell's Bookstore 47
Rose City Classic Dog Show 48
Rose Festival Grand Floral Parade 50
Saturday Market (and Sunday too) 51
Stark's Vacuum Cleaner Museum 52
3-D Center of Art and Photography 52
Vaux's Swifts at Chapman Elementary School 53
Westmoreland Milk Carton Races 55
World Forestry Center 56

SECTION 2: NEAR PORTLAND 59
Near Portland Ice Cream 60
(near) Carver	Lavender Festival 60
Lake Oswego	Lake Oswego Ice Creamery and Restaurant 62
(near) Lake Oswego	Mt. Hood Ice Cream Company 63
McMinnville	Alf's Ice Cream and Burgers 64
	Serendipity 65
Newberg	Jem 100 Ice Cream Saloon 67
North Plains	Elephant Garlic Festival 68
Woodburn	Paleteria El Paisanito 70

Near Portland Things to See and Do 72
(near) Banks	Oregon Miniature Aircraft Squadron (OMAS) Annual Show 72
(near) Gaston	Tree to Tree Adventure 73
Gladstone	The Children's Course 75
(near) Hillsboro	The Rice Museum of Rocks and Minerals 76
McMinnville	Evergreen Aviation and Space Museum 78
North Plains	Horning's Fishing and Picnic Hideout 80

SECTION 3: THE COLUMBIA RIVER GORGE AND I-84 84
Columbia River Gorge and I-84 Ice Cream 84
Boardman	C & D Drive-In and Bakery and Poppy's Pizza 84
Hood River	Apple Valley Country Store and Bakery 86
	Mike's Ice Cream 87
La Grande	Hought's 24 Flavors 89
Pendleton	Mission Market 91
Troutdale	Troutdale General Store, Ice Cream Parlor & Confectionary 92

Columbia River Gorge and I-84 Things to See and Do 94
(near) Baker City	Oregon Trail Interpretive Center 94
Bonneville	Bonneville Fish Hatchery 95
(near) Bonneville	Eagle Creek Hike 96
Bridal Veil	Multnomah Falls 98
(near) Hood River	Hood River Fruit Loop 100
Hood River	Windsurfing and Kiteboarding 100
LaGrande	Eastern Oregon Fire Museum & Learning Center 101
Pendleton	Charmin' Pendleton 102
	Correction Connection 103
	Hamley and Company 10
	Pendleton Woolen Mill 105
	Pendleton Underground Tour 105

SECTION 4: OFF THE BEATEN I-84 TRACK 107

Off the Beaten I-84 Track Ice Cream 108
Heppner	Sweet Productions Ice Cream Parlor & Diner 108
Joseph	Mad Mary's Soda Shop 110

Off the Beaten I-84 Track Things to See and Do 111
Joseph	Valley Bronze of Oregon 111
	Your Country Store 112
Wallowa Lake	Wallowa Lake 113
	Watch Kokanee Salmon Spawn 114
	Wallowa Lake Tramway 116

SECTION 5: I-5 FREEWAY 118

I-5 Freeway Ice Cream 118
Ashland	Zoey's Café 118
Eugene	Prince Puckler's Ice Cream 119
	History of Oregon Ice Cream Company 121
Grants Pass	Grants Pass Pharmacy 123
Jacksonville	Bella Union Restaurant and Saloon 124
Junction City	History of Lochmead Dairy 125
Keiser	Thai Lotus 127
Oakland	Tolly's Restaurant & Soda Fountain 128
Rice Hill	K-R Drive In 130
Roseburg	History of Umpqua Ice Cream 132
Silverton	The Silverton Coffee Station 134

I-5 Freeway Things to See and Do 135
Albany	Albany Brass Ring Historic Carousel & Museum ...135
Ashland	4th of July in Ashland 137
Cave Junction	Oregon Caves National Monument 13
Central Point	Crater Rock Museum 139
Eagle Point	Butte Creek Mill 140
Gold Hill	House of Mystery at the Oregon Vortex 141
Grants Pass	The Glass Forge 143
Medford	Harry and David Tour 144
Merlin	Wildlife Images Rehabilitation & Education Center ...145
Silverton or Sublimity	Silver Falls State Park 147
Wilsonville	Family Fun Center and Bullwinkle's Restaurant 149

SECTION 6: OFF THE BEATEN I-5 FREEWAY 151

Off the Beaten I-5 Freeway Ice Cream 152
Adair	Jamocha Jo's Java and Ice Cream 152

Off the Beaten I-5 Freeway Things to See and Do 154
Crater Lake	Crater Lake 154
(near) Veneta	Oregon Country Fair 155

SECTION 7: NORTH COAST HIGHWAY 101..159

North Coast Highway 101 Ice Cream... 160
Cannon Beach	Osburn's Ice Creamery 160	
Gearhart	Gearhart Junction Café 162	
	Pop's Sweet Shop Ice Cream............................163	
Manzanita	The Coffee Shop 164	
Oceanside	Brewin' in the Wind.......................................166	
Seaside	Flashback Malt Shoppe, Collectibles & Gifts..................167	
	Zinger's Ice Cream...16	
Tillamook	Tillamook Cheese Factory 170	

North Coast Highway 101 Things to See and Do... 172
Astoria	Columbia River Maritime Museum....................172
Cannon Beach	Cannon Beach Sandcastle Day........................173
(near) Hammond	Fort Stevens State Park 175
(near) Manzanita	Kayak Building on the Oregon Coast.............176
Seaside	Seaside Wheel Fun Rentals............................178
(near) TillamookBay	Ocean Spit.. 179
(near) Tillamook	Tillamook Air Museum 180
(near) Tillamook	Tillamook Forest Center 181

SECTION 8: OFF THE BEATEN NORTH COAST HIGHWAY 101 183

Off the Beaten North Coast Highway 101 Ice Cream 183
Westport	The Berry Patch Restaurant..183

Off the Beaten North Coast Highway 101 Things to See and Do 186
Westport	Westport Ferry... 186

SECTION 9: CENTRAL COAST HIGHWAY 101 187

Central Coast Highway 101 Ice Cream...188
Lincoln City	Eleanor's Undertow Café and Ice Cream Parlor.......... 188
	Wildflower Grill 189
Newport	Bay Latte 190
	Flashbacks Café...191
	Newport Candy Shop & Ice Cream Parlor 192

Central Coast Highway 101 Things to See and Do...193
Lincoln City	Finder's Keepers Glass Float Hunt............................... 193
	Jennifer L. Sear's Glass Art Studio............................... 194
	Mor Art 196
Newport	Oregon Coast Aquarium...197

SECTION 10: SOUTH COAST HIGHWAY 101 199

South Coast Highway 101 Ice Cream 200
Brookings	Slugs 'n Stones 'n Ice Cream Cones 200
Florence	B.J.'s Ice Cream 202
Gold Beach	Cone Amor 203
Seal Rock	Indulge Sweets 204

South Coast Highway 101 Things to See and Do 206
(near) Bandon	Game Park Safari 206
(near) Florence	Sea Lion Caves 208
(near) Florence	Sand Master Park 209
Gold Beach	Jerry's Jet Boats and Rogue River Mail Boat Trips 210
(near) Langlois	Floras Lake Windsurfing and Kiteboarding 212
Port Orford	Port Orford Lifeboat Station 214
Seal Rock	Seal Rock State Recreation Site 216

SECTION 11: MT. HOOD/SHANIKO/KAH-NEE-TA TRIANGLE 217

Mt. Hood/Shaniko/Kah-Nee-Ta Triangle Ice Cream 218
Maupin	Imperial River Company 218
	LLC Whitewater Photo and Ice Cream 219
Shaniko	Shaniko and Goldie's Ice Cream Parlor 220

Mt. Hood/Shaniko/Kah-Nee-Ta Triangle Things to See and Do 222
Government Camp	The Adventure Park at Skibowl 222
(near) Government Camp	Hawk Watch International at Bonney Butte 223
	Trillium Lake 225
Kah-Nee-Ta	Kah-Nee-Ta Resort 226
Timberline	Timberline Lodge 227
Maupin	Rafting on the Deschutes River 229

SECTION 12: BEND AREA 231

Bend Area Ice Cream 232
Bend, Redmond, Prineville, Sunriver	Goody's Soda Fountain & Ice Cream 232
Bend	Hardy's Burgers, Salads, and Ice Cream 235
	Pine Tavern 236
Redmond	History of Eberhard Ice Cream 237
Sisters	B.J.'s Ice Cream 238
	Sno Cap Drive-In 239

Bend Area Things to See and Do 240
(near) Bend	High Desert Museum 240

SECTION 13: SOUTHEASTERN OREGON 243

Southeastern Oregon Ice Cream 244
Fields   The Fields Station...244

Southeastern Oregon Things to See and Do 246
(near) Burns   Crystal Crane Hot Springs..246
(in the Field's area)   Alvord Desert 247
                         Alvord Hot Springs 248
Frenchglen   Frenchglen Hotel 249
Frenchglen area   The Round Barn and Visitor Center...............................251
                         The Sage Grouse Strut and Bird Watching in
                         the Malheur National Wildlife Refuge............................252

SECTION 14: ICE CREAM AND ATTRACTIONS IN MULTIPLE LOCATIONS 255

Ice Cream in Multiple Locations..255
Burgerville..255

Attractions in Multiple Locations 256
Covered Bridge..256
Oregon Lighthouses 257
Oregon Rodeos..262
Live Theater and Musical Venues 263

Acknowledgements... *268*

Index.. *270*

Introduction

I have always loved ice cream. For the last two years I have traveled around Oregon looking for shops that either make their own ice cream or serve an Oregon brand of ice cream. It isn't that I have anything against national brands. In fact, I like some of them quite a bit. However, I decided that I wanted to become an Oregon ice cream expert, in the same way that some people become connoisseurs of wine. I like finding places that are not cookie-cutter replicas of other shops selling a particular brand of ice cream. And I decided that I would focus on good old ice cream as opposed to, say, gelato, frozen yogurt, sorbets, and other spin-offs of the classic American dessert.

My brother, John, hopefully suggested that I pair up the ice cream stops with nearby gyms in Oregon on the outside chance that maybe I could work off a few calories after my strenuous "research." I decided that no one would ever be interested in that book, but I did decide to include "fun things to see and do" in Oregon. Originally, I was going to pair each ice cream stop with one or two activities but that became too unwieldy. I will leave it to you to find a scoop shop and activity that fit together.

Choosing ice cream spots

It has been a great adventure looking for ice cream shops throughout Oregon. I am sure I probably missed a few good scoop shops. I also did not include places that only occasionally serve ice cream as a dessert. I also told the person I spoke with at each location I visited that my rule was clear: "If I can't say something nice, I won't include your business in my book." So a few shops and restaurants were left out of the book because the service was glacially slow. In one case, although the spot was wonderful, the teenage waitress was so extremely rude that I nixed that location too. And some spots simply lacked any charm. My aim has not been to be critical. After all, these businesses are trying to make a living, and who am I to say they are not worth visiting.

Nor did I rate the ice cream at the places I visited. Tastes are so different among ice cream lovers that one person's favorite flavor or brand will differ from another's favorite. It may be simply because one person grew up eating a particular brand rather than another brand. People also have such individual preferences when it comes to flavors. I chose each ice cream location that I included for the quality and uniqueness of the ice cream as a whole, because of the atmosphere of the place, and because of the people I met at each location. I loved talking with most of the servers. What an interesting set of people!

Choosing fun things to see and do
As a native Oregonian, I took the opportunity writing this book to revisit some of my favorite Oregon sites and to find some new favorites. This personal collection may seem an odd hodgepodge of things to see and do. I hope there is a little something for everyone. Oregon is a big place and it would be almost impossible to visit every place worth seeing in the state. However, any visitor to Oregon will get a good overview of the state by using even a few of the suggestions from this book. Use my ideas as starting points for your journey. I hope you have a wonderful time exploring.

One last disclaimer: This book is not meant to be an exhaustive travel guide to everything worthwhile to see and do in Oregon. There are other travel guides that are much more comprehensive. In fact, some of the others are so detailed that for me it takes the fun out of exploring, which is an integral part of any adventure. I want to point you in the right direction and then let you make discoveries on your own. If you want specific directions, Google maps will certainly help you. For those who want to find places the low-tech, old-fashioned way, get an Oregon map. If and when you get close to a spot, stop and ask for directions if you get lost. You will find most Oregonians are a friendly bunch and will be happy to help you find your way. Meeting new people should always be part of any adventure.

The History of Ice Cream
Ice cream has been served in one form or another since before the time of the Romans, but it has not always been a dessert enjoyed by the masses. In the United States, ice cream was found in colonial times when George Washington served ice cream to his guests. Thomas Jefferson was fond of ice cream and brought vanilla ice cream recipes home from his travels to France. Most writing on the history of U.S. ice cream starts with the East Coast. Nothing much is documented about early ice cream production out here in the West.

I found some old, now defunct, Oregon ice creameries listed in old phone books, but that information only told me the company had been in business sometime during that year. It did not reveal the history of the people, the flavors of ice cream, or the company behind the ice cream.

Oregon used to have many more small dairies than you will find today. Many eventually went out of business or merged with other dairies. Ice cream seems to have been added to dairy production long after milk products and butter were established commodities. Many of the stories about the oldest dairies in Oregon are lost to history.

It is easy to take ice cream for granted. After all, today we can go to any grocery store and choose one of many brands and flavors. In some large grocery chain stores, the ice cream section takes up rows and rows of freezer space. But it has not always been so easy to get this frozen treat. Before modern refrigeration, and before the advent of iceboxes, ice, which was needed to make ice cream, was a rare commodity. People could not easily manufacture their own ice at home. Instead, it was harvested from frozen lakes and ponds. Anne Cooper Funderburg, in her book Chocolate, Strawberry, and Vanilla: A History of American Ice Cream, noted that Alaska first shipped ice to California in July 1850. Subsequently, an ice industry developed. The frozen ice was shipped and then stored in specially insulated buildings called icehouses. Consumers could buy blocks of ice to take home and put in their "ice box" to keep perishables chilled (or to make ice cream). Even in an icebox though, the ice slowly melted. In Oregon's ice cream industry development, it may not be a coincidence that the Umpqua ice cream plant was located near a railroad line, where ice could have been shipped directly to the plant. Until recently there was also an icehouse near the Umpqua ice creamery and railway station.

Refined sugar, used in making ice cream, was also a rarity in early America. Vanilla, used as a flavoring in most ice cream, was difficult to buy in the early years of America. Perhaps these commodities slowly made their way to the West Coast like hot fudge slowly sliding down a sundae and our ice cream history simply lagged behind the East.

Ice cream making became easier for the masses with Nancy Johnson's 1843 invention of an "artificial freezer" that consisted of a tub with a cylinder inside and a dasher with removable crank It became the first modern ice cream making machine in America. Other important events in the emergence of American ice cream were the introduction of the ice cream cone during the 1904 World's Fair in St. Louis. Later, Prohibition helped boost ice cream sales as the soft drink and soda fountain industry blossomed, and modern refrigeration led to mass production of ice cream because it could be stored. Today, anyone can make ice cream with just a few ingredients and an electric or hand cranked ice cream maker.

Where to Find Oregon Ice Cream

Today, each Oregon ice cream brand tries to find a niche for its product. Some Oregon ice creams are most easily found in the area of the state where the ice cream is produced. Lochmead, in Junction City, sells most of its ice cream in the Eugene/Corvallis area, although they are now expanding as far north as Portland and as far south as Ashland. Eberhard's sells its product mainly on the east side of the Cascades. Smaller-scale homemade ice cream companies with one to five ice cream shops tend to sell their brand of ice cream even more locally, like Cool Moon in Portland and B.J.'s in Florence.

Then there are the big Oregon ice cream companies who have expanded across the state and beyond. It used to be that customers would find Tillamook ice cream in northern Oregon and Umpqua ice cream in southern Oregon. Now, Tillamook and Umpqua brands, as well as the Ice Cream Company's Cascade Glacier, Julie's Organic Ice Cream, and Alden's Natural and Organic Ice Cream can be found throughout the state and across the region. In addition, some of the big Oregon ice creameries make ice cream for other labels besides their own label. Alpenrose, a local Portland dairy, makes ice cream for Baskin-Robbins. Sunshine Dairy, also in Portland, makes ice cream for Burgerville's delicious milkshakes. The Oregon Ice Cream Company makes ice cream bars for Costco and other products for Jamba Juice and Ciao Bella.

Some of the larger creameries make the "base" ice cream for Oregon brands that sell "homemade" ice cream. The base is made to the specifications of each brand. This partnership helps the smaller labels keep their ice cream affordable for consumers.

The People behind the Ice Cream

I have loved meeting people in the Oregon ice cream business. Several of the large Oregon ice cream companies have been family-owned for several generations, and family pride is clearly evident. Each family generation strives to produce the finest ice cream possible. I also liked the gutsiness of the people who are opening new, smaller homemade ice cream companies. They are innovative entrepreneurs who happily experiment with new flavors and taste sensations. They bring a new zest to the industry. It isn't just chocolate, strawberry, and vanilla anymore.

As for why people get into the ice cream business, the majority say they wanted to be in a job where they could make people happy. For many scoop shop owners, ice cream vending is a second career. They are friendly, outgoing, and very personable. They are also an incredibly hardworking group of individuals.

What I Have Learned

Before I started this project, I was a raging chocoholic. It would have seemed just plain wrong to order an ice cream flavor that did not have at least a little chocolate hidden somewhere in the scoop. But then I began to branch out and it paid off. There are wonderful surprises awaiting those willing to be bold and brave in choosing flavors. Each Oregon brand has some that are simply heavenly. Huckleberry Cheesecake, Kulfi, Grandma's Cookie Batter, Licorice, Mint Stracciatela, and Swamp Thing are just a few of my new favorites.

Vanilla was a flavor I rarely chose at the beginning of my adventure, even though I knew that it is the best-selling flavor for most brands. After all, vanilla is so, well, vanilla. I didn't think it tasted like much of anything. Yet when I asked ice cream owners which flavor they were most proud of, many pointed to one of their vanilla flavors. Notice I said flavors. Some companies have four or more variations of vanilla, like Vanilla, French Vanilla, Vanilla Bean, and Country Vanilla. Each is slightly different from the rest. French Vanilla is yellow because it has eggs in the mixture. Vanilla Bean has little black flecks of the bean.

There had to be something I was missing in all this. So I read Vanilla: Travels in Search of the Ice Cream Orchid, by Tim Ecott. To my amazement, I discovered that vanilla beans are not easy to grow. Most are produced in Madagascar and some are produced in Mexico. Vanilla is a valuable crop and vanilla beans are expensive. Plus the quality of the beans makes a huge difference in the final product. Oddly, vanilla is an ingredient in a lot of chocolates. I have developed a new appreciation for the taste of this finicky flavor.

I have also learned a few things about eating ice cream.

Ice cream tastes best when it is very slightly thawed. It is only then that the flavors burst forth. Ice cream that is too frozen simply tastes cold with no flavor. So be sure to give your ice cream a few minutes to thaw. Hot fudge sundaes are at their best when a little hot fudge is poured in the bottom of the cup before the ice cream is added. The ice cream then melts to a perfect consistency for eating.

When it comes to milkshakes, there seem to be two preferences. Some like their milkshake so thick that you can go cross-eyed trying to sip it from a straw. Others like milkshakes that are thin and easily sipped. I belong to the branch that does not like to work hard to sip the frothy mixture through a straw., though sometimes what is really needed is simply a fatter straw.

Prices

The prices listed in this book may well change. Due to volatile gasoline prices and the price of butterfat, which has, believe it or not, jumped astronomically lately, be ready for increases. Each vendor is fighting to keep their products affordable. At some point they will be forced to raise prices just to stay in business. But don't let that spoil your trip.

Oregon is full of delightful spots to see and explore. Have fun on your adventure and eat lots of Oregon ice cream.

Section 1
Portland

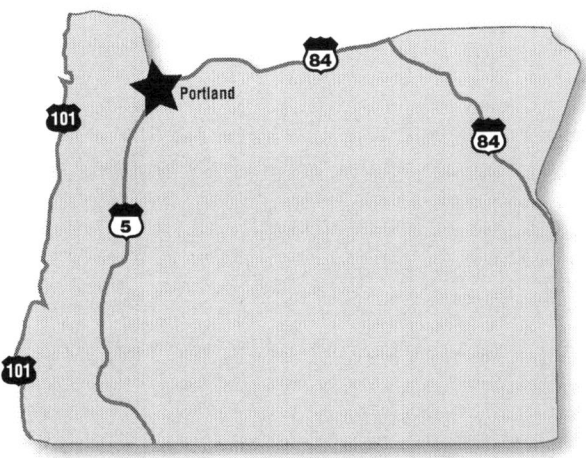

Kidd Museum

Portland
Ice Cream

Alpenrose Dairy

Ice cream plus fun things to do equals a recipe for a good time. No one knows this better than the Cadonau family, originators of Alpenrose Dairy. A family owned and operated business since 1916, this community-oriented Portland-based dairy has built sports facilities and sponsors a variety of noteworthy events that draw thousands of participants to their Southwest Portland location. All Alpenrose events are free for the general public. Alpenrose considers their facilities and events as a way for them to give back to the community.

Take baseball, for instance. Henry Cadonau started out building a humble ball field for his grandkids to play on. The field and grounds were improved and is now known as Alpenrose Stadium. Besides the main stadium, there are two additional baseball fields. The fields are used each year in the spring, summer, and fall by Little Leaguers. In the summer the field is used for a local baseball camp for kids. In August, the field is home to the Little League Softball World Series.

The Easter egg hunt at Alpenrose for 3-8 year olds has been a tradition at the dairy for forty-nine years. Thousands of people come to this event, so if you are planning on attending make sure to get there early. It is amazing how fast kids can clear out Easter eggs when the official says, "Go!"

For those who love the thrill of racing there are two choices at Alpenrose. You will find a quarter midget races organized by the Portland Quarter Midget Racing Association. To be involved in this sport, kids need to be between five and sixteen years old. If you are interested in more information about quarter midget racing, contact the organizers at **www.pqmra.wordpress.com**.

Bike racers will be challenged by Alpenrose's velodrome, a banked racetrack for bikes. This exciting sport is fun for spectators as well as participants. If you would like more information about this action-packed sport go to **www.obra.org/track**.

Alpenrose is also home to a 600-seat theater, known as the Alpenrose Opera House. It is used by a variety of local community groups and schools. Inside the Alpenrose Opera House, there is also a massive organ that was purchased and restored when the Portland Civic Theater was remodeled. The organ was originally built in 1916. It has 4000 pipes and four keyboards.
Dairyville is a series of false-front buildings that replicate an old western town. There is an old-fashioned ice cream parlor, the Opera House, and more. It is also home to a functioning horse stable, 4-H club, 2 model train clubs, and more. During the Christmas season, Dairyville is transformed into Storybook Lane, complete with live animals, a gift store, bakery, and Santa's house. You can also have your picture taken with Santa.

Oh, yes, and then there is the ice cream. Alpenrose ice cream comes in 31 flavors. You can buy it in 3-gallon tubs directly from the dairy. It is also served in many restaurants and scoop shops in Oregon.

Address: 6149 SW Shattuck Road Portland, OR 97221-1044
Phone: 503-244-1133
Web: www.alpenrose.com
Hours: Call for dates and times of events
Restrooms: ADA accessible

FUN FACT

Hazelnuts

Oregon produces 99% of the hazelnuts (also known as filberts) grown in the United States. Chopped hazelnuts are a wonderful topping on ice cream.

BluePlate Lunch Counter and Soda Fountain

Located in a beautifully restored historical building in the heart of downtown Portland, just blocks away from Pioneer Place, the BluePlate is a modest lunch counter that offers good old-fashioned cooking at reasonable prices. The owner, Jeff Reiter, says that he wanted to bring back healthy home-cooked food to those in their 30s and 40s who have grown up without culinary skills due to their hurry-up lifestyle and reliance on fast food and pre-prepared foods. The BluePlate Lunch Counter opened in October 2006.

The lunch menu is divided into two sections. The first section is for daily specials, offering a sandwich of the day ($8) or a "blue plate special" ($10), which is a main dish such as chicken and grits, pot roast with potatoes and carrots, bacon mushroom macaroni and cheese, beef stroganoff, or chicken fried steak and mashed potatoes. The second section of the menu offers dishes available every day, such as a grilled cheese sandwich and tomato soup ($6), BTL salad ($8), classic Caesar salad ($7), and side green salad ($3).

Then there are the special shakes. The BluePlate Lunch Counter uses Cascade Glacier ice cream in its fountain. The P.R. Nelson shake is huckleberry ice cream with homemade purple haze hibiscus syrup. It is one of the best shakes I have ever tasted! Also available is "The 44th," listed as "a shake fit for a healthy President" made of pistachio-almond crunch ice cream.

The soda fountain menu is extensive. Milkshakes are $4. There are many flavors, including arctic chai, chocolate and filbert butter, and cowboy coffee (made with Stumptown beans). More traditional flavors, like chocolate, vanilla, and strawberry, are also crowd-pleasers. Sundaes come in one scoop ($3), two scoops ($5), and three scoops ($7) using vanilla, chocolate, or strawberry ice cream. The ice cream is topped with marshmallow, whipped cream, chopped nuts, sprinkles, and a cherry. A banana split is $8.

One thing that makes this soda fountain special is the variety of sodas created from scratch using cane sugar and natural ingredients. Mr. Reiter says that the hardest part of having a soda fountain has been getting his younger clientele to understand the concept of "from-scratch" sodas. Called "house sodas," flavors such as orange, strawberry, pineapple, lemon, neon lemon, ginger spice. and vanilla honey are available. These sodas cost $2 or if you prefer an ice cream float, $3.50. For the same price, Chef Jeff also can whip up one of his specialties, like Purple Haze, Hawaiian Sunset, Chai Bomb, Karl Marks, or Eastern Connection.

For those who prefer more traditional sodas and floats, "guest sodas" featuring Coca Cola, Barq's root beer, and IBC root beer can be had for slightly more money.

Enjoy fountain "classics" like chocolate malted milkshakes ($4/$6) or cows ($4 float) that come with root beer or cola, chocolate syrup, and ice cream. Old-fashioned egg creams ($2) and ATL Frosted Orange ($4/$6), a soda blended with vanilla ice cream, round out the delightful treats offered at this cute retro urban diner.

Address:	308 SW Washington St., Portland, OR 97204
Phone:	503-295-2583
Web:	www.eatatblueplate.com
Hours:	Monday-Thursday 11 a.m.-5 p.m.
	Friday-Saturday 11 a.m.-9 p.m. The restaurant is busiest from about noon-1:30 p.m. During those times there may be a 10-minute wait to be seated. At all times the food service is slow so be patient. It is worth the wait.
Restrooms:	ADA accessible

Cool Moon Ice Cream

Cool Moon Ice Cream is the brainchild of Eva Bernhard, a native Oregonian raised in Eugene and transplanted to Portland as an adult. When she was 16, her parents sent her to France for cooking lessons. After returning to Eugene, Eva practiced her cooking skills and worked in restaurants during high school. At first she was reluctant to cook for large groups. Her father said, "If you can cook for 4 people, you can cook for 80. Just do the math."

Bernhard took a break from cooking after college and worked as a landscape architect. Then she worked for five and a half years at the Oregon Historical Society. By then, she wanted to start her own business, a gutsy move for anyone. Bernhard says that her dad greatly influenced this life-changing decision because he was always optimistic and sure that things would work out for the best. Bernhard put much thought into creating a business plan that would fit her personality and have a chance of financial success. Her one main criterion: she wanted a job where she could make people happy. An ice cream store seemed the perfect fit: she could use her cooking skills and be creative. Either people came in happy or they would leave feeling better. With the type of business settled, Bernhard looked through literary references and songs for a catchy name for her new shop. Her stepdad suggested "Cool Moon" and the name stuck. The store opened in December 2007.

The ice cream at Cool Moon is made on the premises in small batches. Bernhard uses several different types and sizes of freezers, and each has its own special job in the secret process that makes Cool Moon ice cream unique.

The ice cream flavors are both exotic and wonderful at this cute shop across from Jamison Square Park. The folks at Cool Moon are not afraid to experiment and "go where no ice cream has gone before." They are constantly listening to customers and trying out new recipes. Some flavors are seasonal. Some flavors are unique to Cool Moon and are not found in any other Oregon brand. Bernhard's background in French cooking has given her an exquisite palate that makes eating Cool Moon ice cream a sensual pleasure. One of my favorite flavors is called Kulfi. It is made from rose water, cardamom, and pistachios. It has a fresh, unusual taste that is addictive. Another favorite is cherry almond chip. It has a rich flavor with a satisfying little crunch. Cool Moon ice creams use all-natural ingredients. They also make dairy-free sorbets.

Micro (kid's) cups and cones are $2.90, a regular cone is $3.75, a large cup or cone is $4.75. 20-oz. shakes are $5.85. Floats are $5.50. Sundaes start at $6. If you order a sundae, be sure to have them include the almerano cherry on top. It is heavenly all by itself!

Cool Moon offers creative special deals. Pre-packed Happy Hour pints are available from 4 p.m.-6 p.m. every day for $4. During the Winter Pint-O-Rama sale, if you buy a cone or cup, you can take home a pint for $4. My favorite deal is the Geological Dig, a $4 gamble. These pints contain a minimum of two flavors and a maximum of four flavors. Only when you open the container and "dig in," will you discover which flavors your pint contains.

Whether you stop by for a cone, a classy sundae, a luscious shake, or a pint-to-go, you will be in for a treat at Cool Moon. It is a special stop during any phase of the moon!

...

Address:	1105 NW Johnson St., Portland, OR 97209
Phone:	503-224-2021
Web:	www.coolmoonicecream.com
Hours:	Winter: Sunday-Thursday noon-10 p.m., Friday-Saturday noon-10:30 p.m.
	Summer: Sunday-Thursday 11:30 a.m.-10:30 p.m., Friday-Saturday 11:30 a.m.-11 p.m.
Restrooms:	New public restrooms across the street from the shop

Fairley's Pharmacy and Soda Fountain

Soda fountains in drug stores became the rage in the late 1800s. People would go to their local druggist to have them concoct an energy-boosting drink. Some of the drinks contained cocaine and other stimulants, which were not illegal to use in drinks at the time. Dr. Pepper was created by Charles Alderton in his drug store in 1885. Coca Cola became a fountain drink in 1886, and Pepsi was invented in 1898 by a pharmacist named Caleb Bradham, who called his original drink, Brad's Drink.

In 1888, along came Jacob Baur, who invented a way to store carbon dioxide in tanks. The gas could be added to these energizing drinks to give them a bubbly kick and, voilà, sodas were born! Eventually the more potent drugs like cocaine were taken out of the mixes and the new drinks became known as "soft drinks." Ice cream was added to make "floats."

Over the years, with new ways to bottle and distribute soft drinks, people no longer had to depend on pharmacies for their sodas and the heyday of soda fountains ended, most disappearing by the 1970s. Today only a few original drug store soda fountains remain.

Fairley's Pharmacy and Soda Fountain is one that has stood the test of time. It is in a bright, cheerful, well-lit building.

The soda fountain consists of a bar with 11 stools, each with ample legroom. There are two small tables and chairs in the area. One tall table with a couple of movable stools completes the room that looks out onto Sandy Blvd.

Just as in the old days, there are many options at the soda fountain. For those who don't want ice cream there are old-fashioned drink favorites like egg creams ($1.75), green river or banana phosphates ($1.65-$2.05), flavored sodas ($1.60-$2.20), and cremosas ($1.65-$2.05).

Fairley's serves ten flavors of Tillamook and Sunshine ice creams, sorbets, and sherbets in a variety of forms. Try ice cream in a dish or cone with one or two scoops ($1.50/$2.), one- or two-scoop sundaes with choice of two toppings and a cherry on top ($2.75/$3.75), milkshake ($2.95), malt ($3.25), espresso shake ($3.50), or root beer float ($2.50-$3).

Then there are the special shake flavors ($2.95) that Fairley's has created using ice cream and flavored syrups. They offer chocolate banana, strawberry banana, mango-mind freeze (nondairy), raspberry sherbet shake, Oreo cookie shake, root beer shake, strawberry-cherry shake, raspberry-lime shake, and spumoni shake. The shakes are made using an old-fashioned milk shake machine and served with a tin of extra shake on the side.

The soda fountain does not serve sandwiches or other food items.

Address: 7206 NE Sandy Blvd., Portland, OR 97213
Phone: 503-249-0023
Hours: Monday-Friday 9 a.m.-6 p.m., Saturday 9 a.m.-3 p.m.
Restrooms: No

Fifty Licks Ice Cream

Chad Draizin, then a real estate agent, faced a dilemma when the housing market in Oregon faltered three years ago. He wanted a new career. His criteria for finding a new vocation were simple. Draizin wanted to have a job that he considered fun. He wanted to have a job that created something tangible. Finally, Draizin dreamed of a job where he would be able to express his creativity. Making his own ice cream seemed like the perfect match.

Draizin realized from the beginning that it would be impossible to compete with the major national brands. He knew his ice cream and flavors had to be unique so he tried out dozens of recipes looking for just the right combination of flavors. Today Fifty Licks regularly churns four flavors of ice cream and one flavor of sorbet. The two bestsellers are Maple with Bacon ice cream and Coconut Lemon Saffron sorbet. My current favorite is Caramel Apple ice cream. Tahitian Vanilla and Stumptown Coffee complete the list of ice creams. A unique quality of Fifty Licks is that the ice cream contains much less air than traditional ice cream, just 15%. During the summer months, look for some new seasonal ice cream flavors.

The single-serve ice cream comes in the cutest packaging in the state. The six-ounce square container is made of recyclable cardboard. The lid overlaps the box on three sides. Inside the box is a layer of waxed paper to keep the ice cream fresh. On top of the waxed paper is a flat wooden spoon, like the spoon that used to come with Dixie Cups. Let the ice cream melt slightly before eating to enhance the natural flavors.

You will find Fifty Licks ice cream in pint containers at New Seasons for $5.99. Single servings are available at several locations in Portland for $3.50-$4. You will find them at the Hollywood Theater, the Living Room Theaters, and the Clinton Street Theater. Several restaurants in Portland also serve Fifty Licks.

Starting April 1, 2011, Fifty Licks will have a food cart at SE 43rd and Belmont. They also have an ice cream truck that makes the rounds to special events in the Portland area. The truck is available for weddings and other catered events.

To contact Fifty Licks, call 954-294-8868 or email Chad@fifty-licks.com

For info about three great places to watch movies in Portland:
Hollywood Theater, 4122 NE Sandy Blvd., Portland, OR 97212, 503-281-4215
Living Room Theaters, 341 SW Tenth Ave, Portland, OR 97209, 503-222-2010
Clinton Street Theater, 2522 SE Clinton St., Portland, OR 97202, 503-238-8899

Lovely's 50-50

Mississippi Street in Portland is a happening kind of place. New stores mix in with the old and together are renewing the spark in this part of town, making it a good neighborhood for shopping or an afternoon stroll.

Several years ago, sisters Jane and Sarah Minnick opened an upscale restaurant in the neighborhood called Lovely's. In 2010 they changed their focus. They moved into the space next door and began selling their two favorite-things-in-the-world to eat, ice cream and pizza. It seemed only natural to call the new restaurant Lovely's 50-50. In their new restaurant they have perfected the perfect pizza, and their ice cream is amazingly wonderful.

The sisters make their own ice cream, including the base. They usually have 6 flavors plus 1 sorbet. One scoop is $3.50 and two scoops are $5. Their best-selling ice cream, salted caramel, is always available. The other flavors vary at the whim of the makers. Jane says her favorite flavor is mint stracciatella. I thought the honey lavender was...well, more than lovely. It was heavenly.

On sunny summer days, customers can buy ice cream starting at 2 p.m. even though the restaurant does not open until 5. Twelve-inch pizzas sell for $12-$17 depending on the type. The marguerita pizza is excellent. Sodas are on the menu. Unusual dry sodas (not as sweet as regular sodas) are also for sale in flavors such as rhubarb.

Address:	4039 N Mississippi St., Portland, OR, Suite #101, 97227
Phone:	503-281-4060
Web:	www.lovelysfiftyfifty.com
Hours:	Tuesday-Sunday 5 p.m.-10 p.m.
Restrooms:	ADA accessible

Peculiarium

This place takes the cake-cone for most unusual ice cream sundaes in the state. Maybe unusual isn't the word. Maybe downright creepy fits better. We'll get to that part later.

I read about this new place in Portland that was such an odd combination of things that it had been named the Peculiarium. Boy, did they get that part right. Mike Wellins, Eric Bute, and Lisa Freeman have teamed up to open a new attraction that has only been in business for three weeks. Part snack shop, part fake museum, part art gallery, and part gag gift emporium for the person-who-has-it-coming, it is indeed a mixture of things that make it hard to describe. When I asked Mike and Lisa, "what is this place," they both just started laughing. Let's start with the "museum."

If you have ever wondered what the Northwest sasquatch we call BigFoot might look like, you can see a 10 foot tall version as you enter the store. It will give you an idea of why running in Oregon has become such a big sport. You will be mesmerized by Portland's largest kaleidoscope. If ventriloquist's dummies give you nightmares, you will be happy to see the fate of one that did in his human counterpart.

The art gallery has a number of provocative but well-done drawings on the cartoonish spectrum for adults. But put one of these in your child's room and you will be paying therapist bills for years.

You will find gag gifts (at least I hope that is how they are meant) that cover a lot of bases. From candy with ants in it to old-fashioned paper fish fortune-tellers you will find a smorgasbord of oddities that you will be hard-pressed to lump into one category.

And then there are the ice cream sundaes. Starting with perfectly good Cascade Glacier ice cream, the folks at the Peculiarium have dreamed up some doozies. The tamer sundaes have names like Cookie Dough-Car Wreck ($5), Banana Split Personality ($5), and Alien Smorgy ($5), and Crime Scene Massacre ($6). Then there is the Bug Eater's Delight ($4). Imagine 2 scoops of ice cream with Carmel and Choco ooze, ant cookie, bug larvae (meal worms, and they are big ones), whipped cream, nuts, sprinkles, and a cherry. I asked if anyone ever actually ordered the Bug Eater's Delight and was told that someone had ordered it earlier in the day. They said there was a lot of gagging involved, but the fellow did get it down his throat. If this sundae doesn't sound like your cup of tease, just wait. There is a new sundae in the works with crickets involved. Oh, boy.

Address:	2234 NW Thurman St, Portland, OR 97210
Phone:	503-227-3164
Web:	www.peculiarium.com
Hours:	Thursday-Sunday, 11 a.m.-9 p.m.
Additional Information:	Not suitable for young children. PG-10 is recommended.
Restrooms:	ADA accessible

FUN FACT

Marionberries

George F. Waldo bred the first marionberry at Oregon State University in 1945. Marionberries are a cross between two hybrids, the Chehalem and Olallie berries. After testing the berry for several years, marionberries became available to the public in 1956. Marionberries are named after Oregon's Marion County. The berries ripen in July and August. Try marionberry ice cream, an Oregon specialty.

Piece of Cake

Sometimes I get hungry for a GOOD piece of cake. Just any cake won't do. It has to be a GREAT piece of cake. When that mood hits, I walk (so I can justify the calories) to a store in Sellwood called Piece of Cake to choose from a selection of cakes and cupcakes that are in a cake league all their own.

The owner of the store, Marilyn DeVault, started her cake business in 1978. Originally she planned to make just carrot cakes and nothing else, but she soon discovered that she could not make a living selling only one item, so she started expanding her repertoire. Now, not only does she make a variety of cakes, pies, tortes, and cupcakes, she also offers items that are gluten-free, wheat-free, and sugar-free! Voted Best Cake in Portland is the Fantasy Cake ($6.75/slice), a layer of cheesecake on top of a layer of chocolate cake iced in cream cheese frosting and sided with chocolate curls. I tried a Chantilly cupcake ($3.50) that was rich, moist, and wonderful. Chantilly was voted Best Birthday Cake in the city. It is a moist chocolate cake iced in cream cheese frosting and topped with a lacy chocolate design.

If you happen to stop by when the cakes are being decorated, you're in for a special treat. The cake decorators are true artists. They wield their cake spreaders, frosting bags, and knives effortlessly, but with conviction, creating perfect patterns on the cakes, with even, artistically shaped drips on the sides and playful curly cues on top. By the time they are done, the cake practically screams, "Eat me!"

I happily discovered that Piece of Cake also makes homemade ice cream, usually two or three flavors at a time. The flavors change throughout the year. You might find chocolate, strawberry, vanilla, or caramel ice cream available. Maybe you will discover their cherry, peanut butter, or seasonal berry flavor. The ice cream is made of pure cream and tastes rich and satisfying. It goes well with cakes and cupcakes, and what is better than a good piece of cake?...cake AND ice cream! Because homemade ice cream can be difficult to scoop, Piece of Cake only sells ice cream in pre-poured dessert cups for $3.25 per scoop.

Marilyn DeVault thinks there must be magic in her cakes. Perhaps she is correct. One taste of one of her delicious delicacies and you will be enchanted. People have been known to drive straight to the bakery from the airport so they can sample a dessert. Folks who move out-of-state have cakes mailed to them from the bakery. Is the magic in the cake? Is it in the frosting? I think maybe it comes from the loving hands that craft these wonderful treats. Try one and see what you think.

Address:	8306 SE 17th, Portland, OR 97202
Phone:	503-234-9445
Web:	www.pieceofcakebakery.net
Hours:	Monday-Thursday 9 a.m.-8 p.m.
	Friday 9 a.m.-10:30 p.m.
	Saturday 10 a.m.-10:30 p.m.
	Sunday 1 p.m.-4 p.m.
Restrooms:	One restroom in store.
	It would be difficult to get a wheelchair to the restroom because of the furniture in seating area.
Additional information:	If you would like ice cream, call ahead to see what flavor(s) are available.

FUN FACT

Maraschino Cherry

In 1931 Ernest Wiegand, a horticulturist at Oregon State University, perfected a new method to preserve maraschino cherries, using Oregon Royal Anne cherries. Oregon cherry growers today are the biggest producer and processor of cherries in the world. Half of all Oregon cherries are made into maraschino cherries.

Pix Patisserie

The baked desserts at Pix Patisserie are so magnificently presented that it is almost a shame to bite into one...notice I said ALMOST. The real difficulty is deciding which dessert to choose. Each one is a true artisan masterpiece. Besides selling these baked epicurean delights, Pix also offers homemade ice cream and sorbets. A single scoop is $2.50 and a double scoop is $3.50. To make any dessert à la mode, add $1.50. Pints are $6 and quarts are $12. Usually there are up to eight flavors to choose from. I tried vanilla and mocha and loved both. The vanilla tasted just like the homemade ice cream I have made at home. The mocha had a wonderful rich taste.

Pix offers two alcohol and ice cream-based drinks. Pix's beer float ($8 or $9 with an extra beer) is made from Rogue Chocolate Stout with homemade mocha ice cream. Lambic floats combine Lindeman's Framboise and vanilla ice cream for $10.25. Both are popular sellers.

Pix has an ice cream social during the Division Street fair in July. During the event they offer sundaes, shakes, ice cream sandwiches, beer floats, a spicy habanero ice cream, and a concoction called The Foghorn, consisting of 22 scoops of ice cream and toppings, served in a watermelon. Ah, summer!

Address:	3402 SE Division, Portland, OR 97202
Phone:	503-232-4407
Web:	www.pixpatisserie.com
Hours:	Monday-Thursday, 2 p.m.-midnight
	Friday 2 p.m.-2 a.m.
	Saturday noon-2 a.m.
	Sunday noon-midnight
Restrooms:	Yes

Pix has a second location in North Portland.

Address:	3901 N Williams Ave, Portland, OR 97227
Phone:	503-282-6539
Web:	www.pixpatisserie.com
Hours:	Sunday-Thursday 10 a.m.-midnight
	Friday-Saturday 10a.m.-2 a.m.
Restrooms:	Yes

Pope House Bourbon Lounge

Inspiration sometimes comes when you least expect it. Tim Croghan was on duty as a kitchen manager at Pope House Bourbon Lounge in 2010 when he got some horrific news. His best friend had just been murdered. Because he was at work, he had to bottle up his feelings and continue his shift. He was distraught. For several days he could not eat. He could not keep anything down in his stomach except ice cream. He finally went across the street to a grocery store and came back to the lounge with ingredients to make ice cream. He added some cream de menthe. The result was an amazing taste sensation. Patrons in the lounge went crazy for his new concoction and clamored for more. From tragedy came the beginning of Croghan's new adventure into making homemade ice cream with alcohol. It is a taste sensation like none other. Croghan loves the smiles that he gets when people sample his ice cream.

Most of the alcohol is cooked out of the ice cream mixture, but the alcohol lowers the freezing temperature. The result is an ice cream with a wonderfully smooth texture that is simply heavenly. And the taste! Croghan is a wizard at mixology. His ice creams, which are $4 a scoop, are novel combinations of flavors that are ingenious.

There are usually one or two flavors available at Pope House Bourbon Lounge on any day. You never know what Croghan will come up with next. So far, he has created 27 flavors of his magical ice cream. He makes all of his ice cream bases from scratch. You might be able to try his Dynamite ice cream, which combines chocolate with chipolte and pepper vodka for an ice cream with a kick. The Professional is a mixture of Guinness Espresso Stout, another espresso, and Bailey's. The Sarah Connor on Fire is a concoction of French Vanilla ice cream infused with fire-roasted habanero chilis and a second Navar's French Vanilla liqueur for a spicy ice cream. I tried a sorbet called After Moon Delight. It is a mixture of blood oranges and raspberries with Mud Puddle Chocolate Vodka and Aztec Chocolate Bitters. It is a perfect sorbet for people who are milk-intolerant. I also tasted Swamp Thing. It is made with bourbon and an orange-chocolate creole shrubb. If you love the chocolate-covered candy oranges that are popular during the Christmas season, you may well like this flavor. I also loved The Hog's Bollocks, a bourbon-molasses-praline-bacon ice cream that Croghan had on hand. The texture and flavor is superb.

How does Tim Croghan decide what liqueurs to use in his ice cream? He stares at the myriad bottles of alcohol on the walls of the bar. When he sees a bottle he likes, he tastes what's in the bottle. Then he lets his mind imagine the possibilities. The result is an ice cream that is pure genius.

Tim Croghan's advice is to live in the moment. You will know what he means the minute you try his ice cream.

Address: 2075 NW Glisan St., Portland, OR 97209
Phone: 503-222-1056
Web: www.popehouselounge.com
Hours: Monday closed
Tuesday-Thursday 4 p.m.-midnight
Friday-Saturday 4 p.m.-1 a.m.
Sunday 4 p.m.-midnight
Restrooms: Pope House Bourbon Lounge is up a long flight of stairs. There are restrooms upstairs, but it would be difficult to get a wheelchair into the lounge.
Additional information: Pope House Bourbon Lounge serves good food. Their happy hour menu offers lots of choices at reasonable prices.

Roses Restaurant

Roses Restaurant, not to be confused with the OTHER Rose's (with an apostrophe) that is famous for their giant donuts, cakes, and deli items, is well known for its delicious ice cream. Originally opening in 1950, it was purchased in 1968 by Lew and Marian Evans. The venture quickly became a family affair. Lew masterminded making the ice cream. He and his six kids picked seasonal berries, fruits, and nuts to add to the ice cream base. The kids also helped run the store. Marian worked at the store and made candies to sell. One of the daughters took over the business in 1979. She continued the family tradition until she sold the store in 1994. Three years later the business folded and the store was demolished. Then in 2007, Lew and Marian's daughter and son, Jeanne and Lew Evans Jr. teamed up to reopen a new ice cream store. They bought a Chinese restaurant and remodeled it into an ice cream parlor and restaurant, located on N.E. 42nd, where they serve wonderful ice cream treats year round.

One of the oddities of this ice cream store is that it still houses the lottery concession from the Chinese restaurant days. Observing customers coming and going is great people-watching. It is like watching two sets of people in a parallel universe. One set walks in and heads straight for the swinging doors of the video lottery room while the other set heads straight for the ice cream counter to pick out a flavor of ice cream. The groups don't seem to acknowledge that the other one exists. While one customer goes to the counter to get more change for the machines, the other group talks about local politics and how their kids are doing while their ice cream is being scooped.

Besides 35 flavors of ice cream, including three sherbets (two lactose-free and one sugar-free), Roses serves an assortment of burgers, sandwiches, and daily specials. One scoop of ice cream in a cone or dish sells for $2.75, a single-scoop sundae is $3.95, and a hot fudge sundae is $4.25. Six percent-butterfat milkshakes are $3.95 and extra rich 14% butterfat milkshakes are $4.95. Just like in the old days, you will probably see some of the Evans clan's 12 nieces and nephews working behind the counter, scooping out yummy ice cream treats, made with the freshest ingredients available. It is a fun, family-friendly ice cream parlor you will surely enjoy time and time again.

Address:	5011 NE 42nd Ave, Portland, OR 97218
Phone:	503-256-3333
Hours:	Winter Monday-Saturday 11 a.m.-9 p.m.,Sunday noon-9 p.m.
	Summer Monday-Saturday 11 a.m.-10 p.m., Sunday noon-9p.m.
Restrooms:	Not ADA accessible

Ruby Jewel Ice Cream

Ruby Jewel was created by Lisa Herlinger. As a child growing up in California, Lisa lived near an ice cream shop that specialized in ice cream sandwiches that sold for $1 each. Fond memories of those days inspired her to enter a contest in 2004 sponsored by Oregon State University and the Food Innovation Center, located in Portland, to find an innovative product that had the most potential as a startup business. Herlinger entered the contest by making ice cream sandwiches using homemade ice cream and homemade cookies. She won the contest and was awarded permission to use a commercial kitchen to start her enterprise. The contest sponsors also directed her to marketing people who could help make her dream of starting a business a reality.

Soon Ruby Jewel ice cream sandwiches could be found at the farmer's market at Portland State University. As the popularity of the ice cream sandwiches grew, Ruby Jewel products expanded into three other farmer's markets in the Portland area. From there, Ruby Jewel ice cream sandwiches became a regular item in several retail chains. New Seasons, Fred Meyer, and Whole Foods are just a few of the chain stores where Ruby Jewel treats can be found. You can choose from six or seven different combinations of ice cream and cookies, including honey lavender ice cream between lemon cookies, a heavenly fresh mint ice cream between dark chocolate cookies, espresso ice cream with cinnamon chocolate cookies, peanut butter ice cream with double chocolate cookies, vanilla bean ice cream with chocolate chip cookies, and coming soon will be salted caramel ice cream with double chocolate cookies. Sometimes there is also a seasonal flavor. Each ice cream sandwich costs about $3.50 and is a filling, satisfying dessert. The ingredients for Ruby Jewel products come from local suppliers. Even the fresh mint and lavender in the ice cream are grown by a local farmer.

In 2010, Lisa and her sister Becky Burnett teamed up to open the first Ruby Jewel Scoop Shop located on N Mississippi Avenue in Portland. Becky runs the scoop shop, where you will find 12 flavors of ice cream. Each batch of ice cream at the store is made fresh in a small quantity. Six flavors are always available and the other six flavors rotate. Without the sweetness of the cookie, the ice cream by itself tastes less sweet than any other ice cream I have tasted in the state. With the cookie added, the combination is wonderful.

The sisters experiment with new flavors all the time. The best selling flavor is Carmel with Salted Dark Chocolate. Also popular are Fresh Mint Flake and Singing Dog Vanilla Bean. Kid scoops are $2. A regular single scoop is $3. A double scoop is $5 and a sundae is $6. If you want your scoop in a cone instead of a cup, add $1. Also add $1 for a topping or sauce. Lemonade is $3 and bubbly water costs $2. For the best taste treat, create your own ice cream sandwich for $4. The ice cream sandwiches ARE the Ruby Jewel.

Address: 3713 N Mississippi St., Portland, OR 97227
Phone: 503-505-9314
Web: www.rubyjewel.net
Hours: Sunday-Thursday noon-10 p.m.
Friday-Saturday noon-11 p.m.
Restrooms: ADA accessible

Scoop Organic Ice Cream

Standing in the cold, with rain drizzling just enough to make me put up the hood of my jacket, I started to wonder if I had finally gone completely nuts. Why was I standing out here? I had to admit to myself that it was mostly because this food cart was only going to be open from 5 p.m.-7 p.m. on this particular day due to the lousy spring weather that was breaking records in Portland for most wet days. Who in their right mind would come out in this weather for ice cream?

A man and woman were in line ahead of me. Finally, I tipped my head back so I could peer out from under my hood and I said, "Great day for ice cream." The two turned around to face me. "You know, this is the only place in the world I would stand out in the cold like this for ice cream," the woman said. "Scoops hasn't been open a lot lately because of the weather, and we ran out of ice cream last week…" and her words trailed off. I thought I detected just a hint of panic in her voice. Then she seemed to get hold of herself. "Anyway, we are so happy they are open today." "What's your favorite flavor?" I asked. The woman looked at me quizzically. "Is this your first time here? I nodded and she turned to her companion. "Can you believe it, this lady has never been here before." The woman continued, "Salted Caramel is my favorite flavor." The man chimed in, "I think the Chocolate is the best. Sometimes, though, I let the Chocolate and the Salted Caramel kind of melt together and then I get this extraordinary combination flavor…" We were interrupted by the sound of the window opening in the food cart. Three pints of ice cream ($6.50/pint) were plunked down on the counter. The couple paid and then quietly, but happily, disappeared into the mist.

I tried several flavors ($2.75 single scoop, $3.75 double scoop, and $4.75 triple scoop) and I liked them all, but my favorite was Apricot Almond Cardamon. It had a fruity, fresh flavor that made me smile.

Scoop is one of several food carts located at the site of an old gas station. I found a dining area for food cart customers inside the gas station. The dining area has overhead heat lamps to take away the weather's chill, so I was able to eat my ice cream in comfort.

Now I know why people would brave the weather to get this ice cream. I would definitely go back to Scoops. Amanda Rhoads has owned this business for one year. She is churning out ice cream that is already getting rave reviews from customers.

Address:	2730 N Killingsworth St, Portland, OR 97217
Phone:	503-928-2796
Web:	www.scooppdx.com
Facebook:	www.facebook.com/scoopicecream
Hours:	Go to Facebook for current days and times
Restrooms:	not ADA accessible

Sundae in the Park

For over 30 years, on the first Thursday of August, Sundae in the Park has been a tradition in Portland's Sellwood neighborhood. Held under the tall trees in beautiful Sellwood Park, the yearly event draws hundreds of participants to a day of free musical concerts and neighborhood entertainment. One of the highlights of the event is the ice cream sundaes that sell for 50 cents. Other vendors sell cotton candy, snow cones, hot dogs, sodas, and other kinds of food with a percentage of the profits benefiting Loaves and Fishes. Sponsored by Sellwood's neighborhood association, Sellwood Moreland Improvement League (SMILE), the event is manned by neighborhood volunteers and community organizations. Face painting, crafts, and other free activities are a special treat for kids. Sellwood Park also has a family friendly swimming pool that is open to the public for $4/adult, $2.50/kids 3-17. Ages 2 and under are free.

Address: Sellwood Park is at 7951 SE 7th St., Portland, OR
Phone: For pool times and swim info: 503-823-3679
Web: www.sellwood.org
Hours: 1st Sunday in August, noon-4 p.m.
Admission: FREE to the event. Charges for food.
Restrooms: ADA restroom in pool area. Primitive restrooms in two separate buildings in park, one for men and one for women. Port-a-potties are there for the one-day event.

FUN FACT

National Ice Cream Month

Ronald Reagan designated July as National Ice Cream Month in 1984. The third Sunday of July is National Ice Cream Day.

Tonalli's Donuts and Ice Cream

What could be a better combination than donuts and ice cream? At Tonalli's you can eat your cake (donuts) and have your ice cream too! The donut section has 12 types of donuts. These "basics" can be frosted with one of several tasty flavors so there are many possibilities of donuts to choose from. Raised/old-fashioned/cake donuts are 80 cents. Twists and bars are 90 cents. Fancies, including bear claws, fritters, and cinnamon rolls, are $1.40. There are several kinds of coffee drinks, starting at $1.25. The donuts are made using soy shortening and vegetable oil so they seem light and not greasy. The buttermilk donut is amazing, with just the right amount of sugar frosting and gooey deliciousness to make it a wonderful treat.

In the ice cream section, there are a staggering 56 flavors of Cascade Glacier ice cream, plus seasonal flavors. Single cones are $2.25 and double cones are $3.50. Regular shakes are $4.25 and large shakes are $4.95. A one-scoop sundae is $3.15.

The restaurant was started by Victoria Gomez and Jorge Martin Del Campo. Jorge has been in the donut business for 23 years, and his experience shows in his finished product. The couple moved to Oregon from southern California where they operated a donut shop in Southgate. The Martin Del Campos have owned their Portland store for 5 years. Ice cream was added to their menu to help generate business during the summer slack time for donuts. No matter whether it is snowing, sunny, or somewhere in between, if you are hungry for donuts or ice cream, you will have many options at Tonalli's in N.E. Portland.

Address: 2805 NE Alberta, Portland, OR 97211
Phone: 503-284-4510
Hours: 6:30 a.m.-midnight every day
Restrooms: ADA accessible

Two Tarts Artisan Sweets for the Soul

What do you get when you make dozens and dozens of macaroons? The answer is no joke; it is a lot of yolks. If you're the clever folks at Two Tarts Artisan Sweets, you then come up with the brilliant idea of making your own homemade ice cream with those leftovers. Not only is the ice cream creamy and delicious by itself, it also makes a wonderful filling for little ice cream sandwiches.

Ice cream is available at Two Tarts only during the summer. Don't let that stop you from visiting the heavenly little shop in Northwest Portland. You will fall in love with the many varieties of bite-sized cookies, brownies, and bars that make this a must-stop spot for dessert.

I admit I was a little skeptical when I first saw the size of the treats. Most are about the size of a 50-cent piece. My uncertainty melted away with my first bite of baked bliss. I found the explosion of taste and texture in one or two of these mini-masterpieces completely satisfying my craving for sweets. I also ordered the best cup of cinnamon hot chocolate I have ever tasted.

Each dessert costs 80 cents. You can buy a baker's dozen (13) for $8. There are lots of tasty choices. Among them is the Lil' Mama, a cookie sandwich with two rich chocolatey wafers and a vanilla bean butter cream frosting in the middle. Earl Grey brownies are moist brownies with a frosting of Earl Grey-infused chocolate ganache. If your heart yearns for the tropics, order a Coconut Passion Macaroon. This tiny islet of tropical paradise consists of two toasted coconut macaroons with a tropical passionfruit butter cream filling.

I was lucky enough to stop by on a day when there were two flavors of ice cream. The coffee ice cream has a nice coffee punch. The spice ice cream was also nice. Ice cream sells for $1.25 for a small bowl.

Address: 2309 NW Kearney, Portland, OR 97210
Phone: 503-312-9522
Web: www.tartnation.wordpress.com/about/
Hours: Tuesday-Saturday 10:30 a.m.-6 p.m.
Sunday noon-5 p.m.
Restrooms: ADA accessible

Portland
Things to See and Do

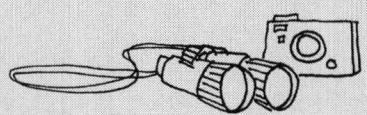

Eastbank Esplanade

On the east side of the Willamette River, across from downtown Portland, the city has designed a beautiful, well-maintained, and mostly flat scenic 1.5-mile biking/walking/strolling trail called the Eastbank Esplanade. The Esplanade starts below the Hawthorne Bridge near OMSI and continues north to the Steele Bridge. There are several easy access points from the Esplanade to downtown Portland. You can cross the river using the Hawthorne, Morrison, Burnside, or Steele Bridges. Bikers and walkers, some with their dogs or strollers, share the trail with few mishaps, a testament to Portland friendliness.

For a leisurely 3-mile walking and biking loop, start at the Hawthorne Bridge and continue north to the Steele Bridge. Cross the river, and continue south along Waterfront Park until you get to the Hawthorne Bridge. Follow the trail under the bridge and then take the loop that gets you to the top of the bridge. Cross the Hawthorne Bridge and you are back to your starting place. Along the way are wonderful views of the City and life along the river. Stop to rest at one of the conveniently located benches and enjoy people-watching.

At the south end of the Eastbank Esplanade, the trail merges with the Springwater Corridor, a well-paved biking and walking trail that runs south along the river, past OMSI, Oaks Amusement Park, and Sellwood Park, before turning east to extend itself to the city of Boring, 21 miles away.

The Hat Museum

I love hats, so I was delighted when I discovered the Hat Museum in southeast Portland. Located in the historic 1910 Ladd-Reingold house, I felt a little like I was going to visit Alice from Alice in Wonderland. Talk about a feast for the eyes! Besides hats all around the room, there was a couch made from a 1966 Cadillac, a British phone booth, and so much more. There to greet us in the middle of it all was Alyce Cornyn-Selby, dressed in a black vintage outfit to match the age of the house, and of course, in a hat. She is the keeper of the hats, and for the next hour she took us on a delightful tour of the house that contains more than 700 hats. Alyce is a walking encyclopedia of all things hat-related, and her tour touched on the history of the hat, especially from the 18th through 20th century, trends in the evolution of the hat, and a look at present-day hats. The museum has vintage hats, men's hats, women's hats, costume hats, hats that have appeared in movies, novelty hats, and hats of all colors, materials, and shapes.

Make time to visit this quirky museum. They say clothes make the man (or woman) but I am not so sure. I think maybe it is the hat. After your visit, you will want to pull out your hats and start wearing them again! Now, I wonder where I put my French foreign legion hat...

Address:	1928 SE Ladd Ave, Portland, OR 97214
Phone:	503-232-0433
Web/email:	**www.hatmuseum.com or justalyce@usa.net**
Hours:	All days. Reservations required. Hours are 10 a.m.-6 p.m.
Admission:	$15/person. Cash and checks only.
Additional information:	Limited accessibility. There are stairs with handrails. There is a small gift store.

International Rose Test Garden in Washington Park

Portland is known as the City of Roses for a very good reason: its exquisite roses. To view more than 500 varieties, visit the Washington Park Rose Garden during the months of late May through early September when the roses are in bloom. The garden has five areas: the Royal Rosarian Rose Garden, the Gold Medal Rose Garden, the Miniature Rose Garden, the Shakespearean Garden, and Portland's International Rose Test Garden. The Test Garden was established in 1917 and it is the oldest public rose test garden in the United States.

Visitors are treated to a feast for the senses as they walk through rows of flowers bursting with color. The garden is located in SW Portland and has a spectacular, postcard-perfect view of the city below with Mt. Hood in the background. Remember to take the time to stop and smell the roses. The aromas are intoxicating.

When you are finished admiring the gardens, stop by the Rose Garden Store where you will find lots of rose-themed merchandise to remember your trip. Books, vases, gardening supplies, and more are there for you to browse. The International Rose Test Garden is one of Portland's finest tourist attractions.

....

Address:	Rose Garden Store, 850 SW Rose Garden Way, Portland, OR 97205
Phone:	503-227-7033
Web:	**www.rosegardenstore.org**
Hours:	The gardens are open 7:30 a.m.-9 p.m. every day
	The Rose Garden Store is open:
	Spring: 10 a.m.-4 p.m.
	Summer: 9 a.m.-7 p.m.
	Fall: 10 a.m.-4 p.m.
	Winter: Closed December 23rd-March 12
Admission:	FREE
Restrooms:	ADA accessible
Additional information:	The International Rose Test Garden is operated by Portland Parks and Recreation. For more info, call 503-823-2223.

Kidd Toy Museum

Discovering the Kidd Toy Museum is like finding buried treasure. From the outside of this plain, windowless building, you would never expect what awaits you inside. In fact, locating the correct address is THE clue to finding the museum because the only outside hint is a paper note attached to the front door that tells the name of the museum and the hours it is open to the public.

Once inside, you will feel like you have discovered gold. F. E. Kidd created this fabulous collection of toys and other memorabilia, mostly dating from 1869-1939, over a lifetime. Starting with an impressive collection of toy vehicles over 35 years ago, Mr. Kidd expanded his interests and began to collect other toys and objects. Both youngsters and the young-at-heart will ooh and aah over old-fashioned metal circus wagons, fire engines, trains, planes, and other mechanical toys. Many are cleverly designed. Just looking at the toys in their displays, it may be difficult to figure out how they work or move. Don't by shy. Ask the lady who works at the museum. She is very knowledgeable and is happy to answer your questions.

There is a little something for everyone in the three jam-packed rooms of this eclectic museum. Included are a wonderful display case of railroad locks, as well as lanterns and other railroad artifacts. There is an extensive display of both mechanical and non-mechanical banks that were once very popular. Dolls and famous cartoon characters are scattered among the displays. Older adults from their 60s to 90s will probably remember some of these toys from childhood and will love reminiscing and explaining how they work to their grandchildren and others.

The toys on display reflect the culture of their time. Today we might call some of those toys politically incorrect, but at the time they reflected white American values and culture. Today we can see how far American culture and our worldview have changed by looking back to an earlier time in America through the toys of its children. You may find yourself wondering, "What will future generations say about OUR toys?"

Address:	1301 SE Grand Ave, Portland, OR
Mailing Address:	PO Box 22367, Milwaukie, OR 97269
Phone:	503-233-7807
Web:	**www.kiddstoymuseum.com**
Hours:	Monday-Thursday 12 noon-6 p.m., Friday 1-6 p.m. For groups of 10 or more, please call ahead. Off-hour tours may be available through special arrangement.
Admission:	FREE
Additional information:	Time needed to visit the museum: ½ hour to 1 hour, depending on your interests.

Lloyd Center Ice Rink

Lloyd Center Ice Rink is an eye-catching showpiece in the Lloyd Center, Portland's first open-air mall, which opened in 1961 to great fanfare. With retail stores huddled together around the outdoor ice rink, Lloyd Center was an instant hit with shoppers. The ice rink provided a unique way to entertain the kids while the grown-ups went shopping. It was once the rink where Tonya Harding, the both famous and infamous Olympic ice-skater, occasionally skated.

As other, enclosed, warm-in-winter malls started popping up in the Portland area, Lloyd Center got a facelift to remain competitive. The entire mall was enclosed. The remodel was a bonus to the skating rink because now skaters are much warmer than they would be in other ice skating facilities where the indoor temperature is frigid. At Lloyd Center, Grandma doesn't need to be pried off the bench and ice chiseled off after watching a skating lesson. She can relax and enjoy watching in warm comfort.

There are lots of activities at Lloyd Center Ice Rink. Public sessions are available each day for general ice- skating. Group and private ice-skating lessons are offered for both kids and adults. A camp for kids called Kool Kamp is held during summer vacation. Lloyd Center Ice Rink hosts an event called the Ice Crystal Classic in November. It attracts skating clubs from as far away as Canada and Northern California. The Olympic sport of curling, a sport that does not require the ability to ice skate, is quite popular now. The curling club meets at the rink seasonally, usually between October and

March. The club offers novices the chance to try out this unusual sport. Call their website for more information about this opportunity. Even if you do not skate or curl, it is fun to watch the activities from the rail around the rink, from the bridge above the rink, or from the second-floor balcony. If you happen to be at Lloyd Center at 1:15 p.m., you might see two regular skaters who put on a skating exhibition Tuesdays-Fridays at 1:15 p.m.

For gawkers, after the skaters have left the ice, there is the zamboni, a machine that shuffles around and around the rink several times a day to add a fresh coat of ice to the surface after ice-skating sessions. According to Ken Paul, one of Lloyd Center Ice Rink's shift supervisors, people will take the time to stop and stare at three things: the ocean as the waves go in and out, the flames in a fireplace, and the zamboni as it travels around the rink. He gave me a tour of the room where the zamboni is stored. It has an electric motor with a top speed of 9 miles per hour. Mr. Paul pointed out that the zamboni only makes right turns easily, so that affects the pattern that the zamboni makes as it refreshes the ice. Keep that in mind as you are mesmerized by the icy pattern left by the zamboni.

Address:	953 Lloyd Center, Portland, OR 97232
Phone:	503-288-6073
Web:	**www.lloydcenterice.com**
Hours:	Call for current times for skate sessions.
Admission:	For public skating, admission is $6.50 and skate rental is $3.50.
	Friday night Rock n' Skate admission/skate rental is $8 from 7:30 p.m.-10:00 p.m.
	Saturday night admission/skate rental is $8 from 7:30 p.m.-10 p.m.
Restrooms:	ADA accessible
Additional information:	For information about skating lessons, call 503-288-6073. For information about curling, contact Evergreen Curling Club P.O. Box 12162, Portland, OR 97212 or **www.evergreencurling.org** The club sometimes has open houses so people can try curling to see if they like the sport.

Oaks Amusement Park

Summertime means Oaks Amusement Park is up and running, drawing hundreds of kids and their parents to the historic park on the east bank of the Willamette River in Portland, just north of the Sellwood Bridge. Oaks Park is the oldest continually running amusement park in the U.S., having opened its doors in 1905. The original goal of the park was to get people to use the trolley on weekends. Nowadays, many businesses entice families to join the fun by offering special deals for ride tickets at the amusement park. Check before you go to see if you can get in on one of the many ride specials. Entrance to the park is free.

Not to be missed is the 1912 Herschell-Spillman Carrousel, a masterpiece of craftsmanship. Giraffes, horses, lions, and other animals gracefully leap up and down as the carrousel spins around with riders, both old and young, perched on their backs.

There are thrill rides for every age and adventurer. The old-fashioned Ferris wheel takes riders high in the sky for a bird's eye view. A miniature train loops around the park. For younger kids, there are kiddy cars that go around in a circle, a twirling tugboat, a fairly tame roller coaster, a long slide, and other rides to delight without a lot of fright. For older thrill-seekers, bumper cars crash into each other with abandon at one end of the park while other wild, stomach-churning rides are waiting at the other end of the park. The park also has go-carts.

Overlooking the Willamette River, 25 picnic areas are available for companies or groups to reserve throughout the park. It is possible to have an event catered by the park, or you can arrange your own food. Oaks Park also has an indoor pavilion that can be rented for weddings, dances, and special events.

On-site concessions sell hamburgers, cotton candy, soft drinks, soft-serve ice cream cones, and more. The ice cream sells for around $2 and comes in vanilla, chocolate, or swirled. The brand of ice cream varies. The cones are a wonderful treat on a hot day.

Address:	7805 SE Oaks Way, Portland, OR 97202
Phone:	503-233-5777
Web:	www.oakspark.com
Hours:	The rides are open Spring Break through the first week of October. Call for specific day and times.

Admission: FREE admission to the park and free parking. Fee for carnival rides and food. Call or visit website for current prices
Restrooms: ADA accessible

Oaks Roller Skating Rink

Oaks Roller Rink is in a beautiful setting. It is part of Oaks Amusement Park, located on the east bank of the Willamette River. The wooden floor skating rink was opened in 1905. After the original floor was ruined by a flood in 1948, a new floor made of Michigan maple was designed that rests atop about 500 sealed 50-gallon drums. When a flood hits, ropes are freed and the barrels float, lifting the floor above the water and saving it from ruin. This system has saved the floor during two floods.

The skating rink itself is huge. Besides the main section there is an area with gently rolling ups and downs and another area with bars for beginners to grab hold of when they are learning to skate. A snack bar and spectator area are on one side of the rink while lockers, restrooms, and a game room are on the other side. If you are lucky, you will be able to skate to the lively sounds of the Wurlitzer pipe organ, whose pipes are directly above the rink. There is a bank of signs that light up on a wall next to the organ player that indicates whether the skaters should skate in pairs, women only, men only, or all skate.

General public skating sessions are available year round. The rink is open every day except Mondays. Call for times and prices. In addition to public skating, lots of different kinds of lessons and activities are offered, including pre-school skating lessons, speed skating, roller derby, dance skating, and more.

Address: 7805 SE Oaks Way, Portland, OR 97202
Phone: 503-233-5777
Web: www.oakspark.com
Hours: Open every day except Mondays. Open during school holidays. Call for information, times, and prices
Admission: Call for current times and prices.
Restrooms: ADA accessible

Oregon Museum of Science and Industry (OMSI)

OMSI is a playground for the mind. The hands-on exhibits will exercise your knowledge, stretch your imagination, and keep you entertained for hours. The terrific, scientific concepts that are demonstrated are sure to pique the curiosity of both kids and adults. Whether you have always wondered about architectural design principles for creating buildings, bridges, and roller coasters, or you wonder how music can be explained by algebra, you are sure to have more than a few "aha" moments. Life sciences, physics, chemistry, and more are all presented to tickle the budding scientist in all of us. The fun of learning is at its best at OMSI.

The exhibits are designed to entertain and educate at the same time. For example, visitors can play a game called "four-in-a-row," a game similar to tic-tac-toe. Many kids and adults are familiar with the game. At OMSI, it is played with a new twist. Players move their balls into position using a robot's arm. This common game has just changed into something novel and challenging! How cool to be in control of a robot's arm and to see how it works! A whole new fascination with robots may evolve from just this one experience.

There are several special programs at OMSI that require an additional fee. OMSI has a planetarium with regularly scheduled shows. OMSI also houses a dome-shaped theater called OMNIMAX. Periodically, there are traveling exhibits that come to OMSI. Outside the main building is the USS Blueback, a retired submarine that is open for tours. Tickets for each of these special events can be purchased at the front box office.

OMSI has a small restaurant that serves a variety of lunch and snack items including Thai food and Mexican food as well as burgers and hotdogs. Snack foods such as yogurt parfaits and chips, and lots of drink choices are available. There is seating both indoors and outdoors. OMSI is located on the Eastbank Esplanade and has a beautiful view of downtown Portland and the Willamette River just outside its doors. It is a perfect lunch spot on a warm day.

The excitement about science does not have to end with your visit. OMSI's wonderful gift shop has lots of science-related kits, books, and toys to take home and enjoy. The merchandise is high quality at a reasonable price.

If your kids love OMSI, be sure to check out the science camps that are offered during the summer. Day camps and week-long camps lure campers back year after year. Just like at the main OMSI complex, they are fun, educational, and exciting. Contact OMSI for dates and times of summer offerings.

Address: 1945 SE Water Ave, Portland, OR 97214
Phone: 503-797-4000
Web: **www.omsi.edu**
Hours: Tuesday-Sunday 9:30 a.m.-5:30 p.m.
OMSI is open on Mondays when Portland Public Schools are closed.
Closed Christmas Day and Thanksgiving Day.
Cafe is open Tuesday-Friday 11 a.m-3 p.m.
(Open on Mondays when PPS are closed)
Admission: Go to web for current prices and packages
Restrooms: ADA accessible

Oregon Zoo

The 64 acres of the Oregon Zoo, located on the west side of Portland, are filled with a menagerie of animals that would make Noah proud. World famous for its Asian elephants, the zoo also houses animals from around the planet. Whether you love the big animals, like the rhino and giraffe, or you are fascinated by the smaller creatures, like the colorful lorikeets or Madagascar Hissing Cockroach, there is a lot to see in this Eden for animals.

There is always something happening at the zoo. During the summer, visitors flock to hear a series of evening musical concerts. Guests bring blankets and lawn chairs and relax on the lawn near the elephant enclosure. Before the concert, they can enjoy an evening picnic dinner brought from home or a meal purchased from the zoo's restaurant. From late November through December, the zoo is lit up at night for ZooLights. This is a time for visitors to see the animals at night after the sun goes down. Other special events are scheduled during the year.

Besides all the wonderful animals, there are two trains that start out from the zoo. One is a sleek, modern train called the Zooliner. The other is an old-fashioned steam locomotive that would fit right into the 1800s. Passengers can take one of two train trips. The summer route takes visitors up into Washington Park. Guests may get out and look around before catching another train back to the zoo. The winter route takes guests around the perimeter of the zoo. This route is especially popular during ZooLights, when the zoo is festively lit at night from late November-December.

There are lots of options for a snack or meal. Three restaurants have seating areas. Several kiosks offer light fare. Foodcarts are strategically sprinkled in the park for a quick pick-me-up. And yes, you can find Oregon ice cream! Cascade Glacier ice cream is for sale in a couple of locations. Single-scoop cups are $2.50 and double-scoop cups are $3.50.

Plan a trip to the zoo. It is always an adventure, no matter what time of year. By the way, there are several animal exhibits that will get you in out of the rain, so don't let a few Oregon raindrops keep you away!

Address:	4001 SW Canyon Rd., Portland, OR 97221
Phone:	503-226-1561
Web:	**www.oregonzoo.org**
Hours:	Open every day except Christmas.
	April 15-September 15, 9 a.m.-6 p.m.
	September 16-April 14, 9 a.m.-4 p.m.
Admission:	Adults (12-64) $9.75, Seniors (65+) $8.25,
	Children (3-13) $6.75, Infants (2 and under) FREE
Restrooms:	ADA accessible
Additional information:	You may choose to bring your own sack lunch or snack. Contact the zoo for summer concert dates and other special events.
	There is a 20% discount for groups of 20 or more.
Parking:	$2

Pier Park (Disc Golf)

Pier Park is one of Portland's magnificent public parks. During the summer it is popular because of its seasonal pool, open air tennis courts, playground, and picnic areas. Scattered among the ancient fir trees that tower above the park and shade much of the landscape, the city has installed a wonderful, FREE disc golf course.

Disc golf is a fairly new sport that was first played using frisbees. As the sport evolved, the equipment has become more sophisticated. It is played with round discs that look like the old-fashioned frisbees except they are a little smaller and are built with a variety of different flight capabilities. Several companies manufacture discs. Some discs are designed to fly straight, some curve to the left, and some curve to the right. Just as in traditional golf, there are drivers, mid-range discs, and even putters. The game uses much of traditional golf etiquette. The object of the game is to throw the disc in the least number of throws into a metal chain basket that sits above the ground. The biggest difference between traditional golf and frisbee golf is that the equipment for disc golf is much cheaper and many of the courses in Oregon are FREE.

Pier Park has an 18-hole/basket course. Each hole starts on a concrete pad that the player uses to start the throw. Disc players use a special step, called a cross-step, to hurl their frisbee toward the basket. At the beginning of each hole, there is a sign that indicates where the basket is located on the course, and the distance to the basket. The signs are helpful because the baskets are gray and they are sometimes hard to see from a distance. At Pier Park the baskets are periodically switched from one of two locations so there is a long course and a shorter course.

Whether you decide to play nine holes or eighteen, or some number in between, you will find disc golf a fun way to get in a walk and spend time with friends. At Pier Park you will have the bonus of being surrounded by a beautiful park setting.

Address:	Pier Park, 8660 N Columbia Blvd, Portland, OR 97203
Phone:	503-283-7747
Hours:	The park is open 5 a.m.-midnight
Admission:	FREE
Restrooms:	Rustic restrooms in park

Additional information:	Alcohol is prohibited in city parks and dogs require leashes.

To get started with equipment, visit:

Address:	Next Adventure "Portland's Alternative Outdoor Store" 426 SE Grand Ave, Portland, OR 97214
Phone:	503-223-0706
Web:	**www.nextadventure.net**
Hours:	Monday-Friday 10 a.m.-7 p.m. Saturday 10 a.m.-6 p.m. Sunday 11 a.m.-5 p.m.
Additional information:	For a list of Disc Golf Courses in Oregon: www.oregondiscgolf.com

Portland Aerial Tram

Look up into the hills on the west side of the Willamette River south of downtown Portland and you will discover a series of massive buildings clinging to the hills. Sometimes known as "pill hill," the area is home to the Oregon Health Sciences University (OHSU), Shriner's Hospital, the Veterans Administration, and Doernbecker Children's Hospital. Over the years there have been so many expansions to the site that there is no more room to expand up there. Trying to find parking can be a nightmare.

To allow for future expansion of the medical facilities and to relieve the parking congestion, land was purchased directly below the medical complex near the Willamette River, and an aerial tram now links the two campuses together. The tram whisks patients and passengers from convenient parking below up 3,300 linear feet to the medical facilities.

You don't have to be a patient to use the tram. The short trip up the hill provides a breath-taking view of the city and of Mt. Hood in the distance. Hold on to a pole as you pass the first tower. There is a little swaying action that can catch you off guard! After arriving at the top of the tram, take a walk into the building directly ahead of you. Find the walkway that goes between the hospital and the Veterans Administration building. The view from there is wonderful. Then head on back for the return trip.

Address:	3303 SW Bond Ave, Portland, OR 97239
Web:	**www.portlandtram.org**
Hours:	Monday-Friday 5:30 a.m.-9:30 p.m.
	Saturday 9 a.m.-5 p.m.
	Sunday 1 p.m.-5 p.m. (June-September only)
	Closed on most major holidays as well as the Friday after Thanksgiving, the 5th of July, Christmas Eve, and New Year's Eve.
Admission:	Roundtrip fare $4/person. Children 6 and under FREE. Riders only pay for the ride up the hill. Riding down does not require a ticket.
Restrooms:	ADA restrooms available in buildings at either end of the tram
Additional information:	Tickets for the tram are available at a kiosk near the lower station. The machine only accepts credit and debit cards. No cash. During high winds, the tram may not be running.

Portland Ukulele Association

It is hard not to smile when you think about ukuleles. From Tiny Tim's Tiptoe through the Tulips to Israel "Iz" Kamakawiwo'ole's version of Over the Rainbow and What a Wonderful World, ukulele chords resonate with joy. The ukulele is a versatile instrument. Pop songs, blues, camp songs, and western songs all sound good on the ukulele. Portland is now blossoming with budding uke players, thanks to Marianne Brogan. She has been teaching ukulele lessons in the Portland area for nine years. She is also the founder and director of the Portland Ukulele Association, Portland Ukulele Festival, and Ukulele Band Camp.

Thanks to Marianne's efforts, there are many opportunities to try out these amazing little four-stringed powerhouses. Once a month, at Artichoke Music, located in southeast Portland, visitors and residents can drop in for a guided lesson. Loaner ukuleles are available for those who do not own one of these little gems. This class is good for people who would like to have some structured practice. This class is also $10/participant.

For those who want more individual instruction, or to find out about other opportunities to get together and play with other uke players, check the Portland Ukulele website.

Looking around the room during one of the monthly lessons, I was struck by what a diverse group of people are attracted to this instrument. From teenagers to retired folks, they seem to come from all walks of life. Yet they sit side by side and share a morning filled with song as they strum away, trying to master a new strum pattern or way to play a chord. At the front of the class is Marianne, a wonderful, patient teacher. With her encouragement, each student walks away with a feeling of accomplishment and a new technique to work on until next month's lesson. They also walk away with a slightly lighter step and a smile.

Address:	Artichoke Music, 3130 SE Hawthorne Blvd., Portland, OR 97214
Phone:	503-232-8845
Web:	**www.artichokemusic.org**
Hours:	Tuesday-Thursday 11 a.m.-6 p.m., Friday-Saturday 11 a.m.-5 p.m., Sunday 1 p.m.-5 p.m., closed Monday
Restrooms:	Not ADA accessible
Additional information:	For Portland Ukulele Association, contact www.pdxuke.org or pua@teleport.com or call Marianne Brogan at 503-679-0391.

Powell's Bookstore

If you are the kind of person who loves to get lost in a good book, then Powell's Bookstore in downtown Portland is definitely the place for you. In fact, it is easy to get lost in a stack of books in this literature lover's paradise without even cracking one open because Powell's is so amazingly large. Powell's downtown Portland location is four stories tall and takes up a whole city block. There are elevators as well as stairs to each level. To help patrons navigate through the labyrinth of books, the store is divided into nine rooms color-coded according to a major category of book. Despite the amazing volume of books, the store is brightly lit and feels light and airy.

Walking through the rooms is like walking through a book lover's candy store. It is easy to spend an hour or two just wandering through the rooms browsing at the titles and subjects that catch your eye.

To help patrons find a particular book, Powell's has computer kiosks conveniently located throughout the store to aid your search, as well as a knowledgeable staff who will happily assist you. Powell's sells used copies as well as new editions side by side, so sometimes you can save a little money if a used copy is available. Powell's also buys used books from the public during specific hours. However, they do not necessarily buy every book that is brought to them. To be eligible for buy back, Powell's buyers check to see if there is a need for a particular title. If Powell's accepts the book, it offers store credit that can be used for purchases at Powell's or cash. The store-credit amount is larger, which is an enticement for many.

If your brain or feet need a break during your visit, there is a coffee/tearoom on the main floor where drinks and snacks are available for purchase. It is also a great place to people-watch.

Powell's claims to be the world's largest independent new and used bookseller in the world. Besides the main downtown Portland location, there are three small Powell's bookstore at PDX, two in the Hawthorne neighborhood, and one at Cedar Hills Crossing. Powell's also boasts a huge online business. However, if you have the time, definitely go to the main store on Burnside in Portland.

Address: 1005 W Burnside, Portland, OR 97209
Phone: 503-228-4651
Web: www.powells.com
Hours: 9 a.m.-11 p.m. daily
Restrooms: ADA accessible

Rose City Classic Dog Show

Portland is nationally known as a dog-friendly town. Nowhere is this more evident than at the Rose City Classic Dog Show, one of the biggest dog shows in the country. It is held in January each year at the Portland Expo Center in North Portland. Over 160 different breeds enter the competition.

Dog owners bring their pooches from all parts of Oregon and beyond. The dogs spend four days strutting their stuff to find the dog that best exemplifies their breed. The winners of each breed then advance to a second competition, where the dogs compete in one of seven categories, assigned by their breed. The seven groups are called the sporting group, hound group, working group, terrier group, toy group, non-sporting group, and herding group. Winners from each of these categories then compete to determine which dog is "Best of Show."

Other kinds of events also occur during the dog show. Some dogs compete in events that demonstrate their obedience skills. Other dogs, those fleet of feet, show their agility as they run an obstacle course, much to the delight of the appreciative audience. It is a fun, almost addictive, sport to watch.

Besides the competition there are lots of folks available to answer any questions for prospective dog owners. They are happy to discuss types of breeds, temperaments, and special needs. It is also fun to walk into the preparation area when dogs are being gussied up for their star appearance.

Lots of vendors set up shop at the dog show. Whether your dog needs a new bowl, leash, treats, toys, or a soft place to lie down, you will find a doggie paradise to explore.

While you are at the dog show, check this out for yourself. Do dogs and their owners really look alike?

....

Mailing address:	Expo Center
	2060 N Marine Drive, Portland, OR 97217
Phone:	503-736-5200
Web:	**www.rosecityclassic.org or www.expocenter.org**
Hours:	Call for specific dates and times.
	Event takes place yearly in January.
Admission:	Call for current ticket prices.
Restrooms:	ADA accessible
Additional information:	Parking at Expo $8/car. To avoid parking hassles at this busy event, consider taking TriMet's MAX. www.trimet.org or 503-238-RIDE 7:30 a.m.-5:30 p.m. weekdays.

Rose Festival Grand Floral Parade

Portland celebrates the coming of summer each year with the Rose Festival, a tradition since 1907. One of the annual highlights of the festival is the Grand Floral parade. Bands, horses, beauty queens, floats covered in fresh flowers, civic leaders, clowns, and others wind their way from the Memorial Coliseum, down Martin Luther King Blvd., across the Burnside Bridge, and then through the streets of downtown Portland. The parade ends on the west side of the river at Lincoln High School. The parade is seen live by 500,000 people. (Many more watch the parade on television.) Parade-goers line the street, cheer from balconies of hotel rooms, and wave from the windows of office buildings. Others buy tickets to sit inside the Coliseum, at the beginning of the parade, so they can see the parade in comfortable chairs indoors. Still others buy seats for bleachers that are set up outside the Coliseum and at other locations along the route.

Many Portlanders attend the Grand Floral Parade as a family tradition. Everyone wants to get a good spot to view the parade. At some points along the route the crowd can be ten or more people thick. In 2008, the rules for saving space along the parade route changed. People cannot now mark off spots with duct tape, chalk, paint, etc.; however, 24 hours before the parade, you CAN lay down a sleeping bag, tent, or unfolded chair. Someone from your group must stay at the site, and groups and individuals can spend the night. People in wheelchairs or mobility-limiting conditions can go to a designated site in Pioneer Square to see the parade. Hopefully, the experience will now be more enjoyable for people who simply want to see the parade without having to stake out a place days in advance.

The parade starts at 10 a.m. at the Memorial Coliseum. It may take 30 minutes or more for the beginning of the parade to reach the Burnside Bridge, and even longer to arrive downtown. Take a lawn chair, blanket, or just plan to stand and enjoy the parade. Bring snacks. It is worth the wait to see this classy Portland event.

For parade or other Rose Festival info:
Address: Portland Rose Festival Association
Rose Building, 1020 SW Naito Parkway, Portland, OR 97204
Phone: 503-227-2681
Web: **www.rosefestival.org**
Date: Saturday in June. Contact Portland Rose Festival Association for exact date.

Saturday Market (and Sunday too)

Portland's Saturday Market started in 1974. The Portland Saturday Market brochure boasts with pride that it is the largest continually operating outdoor handcrafted arts and crafts market in the nation. Originally, the market was located at N.W. 1st and Davis. After two years it moved under the Burnside Bridge, shielding many vendors—and customers—from the unpredictable Oregon weather. In 2009 the market moved across N.W. Front Avenue to a new location in Waterfront Park.

From the first weekend in March until Christmas Eve, artisans, craftsmen, musicians, and purveyors of lots of good things to eat settle in to sell their original, handcrafted goods to a public that enthusiastically flocks to the market. The quality of the work displayed is top notch and the artisans happily talk to customers about their work. There is always an air of excitement at the market. Creative energy bubbles through the area creating its own micro-climate. Whether you are looking for a gift for yourself or someone else, whether you just want to take a stroll and see what is new at the market, or whether you are in the mood for some good food, people-watching, and perhaps a little music, Saturday Market has something for everyone.

Address: 108 W Burnside, Portland, OR 97209-4091
Phone: 503-222-6072
Web: www.portlandsaturdaymarket.com
Hours: Saturdays 10 a.m.-5 p.m.
Sundays 11 a.m.-4:30 p.m.
*During the week leading up to Christmas, the market becomes the "Festival of the Last Minute." It is open daily 11 a.m.-6 p.m., Christmas Eve 11 a.m.-3:30 p.m.
Restrooms: Port-a-potties

Stark's Vacuum Cleaner Museum

Stark's Vacuum Cleaner Sales and Service has been selling vacuum cleaners since 1932. Tucked away at the back of their retail store, the folks at Stark's Vacuum Cleaners have collected an impressive collection of over 200 old, and I mean REALLY OLD, vacuums, dust sweepers, and floor polishers. The oldest electric vacuum is a Regina Pneumatic Cleaner Model B built in 1908. Older still is an 1890s "non-electric push-type rotary fan suction cleaner" complete with clutch. These machines and many more show the ingenuity of inventors determined to help us keep our houses clean with the least muss, fuss, and dust. When you get home, you may feel like kissing your vacuum!

Address:	107 NE Grand Ave, Portland, OR 97232
Phone:	503-232-4101
Hours:	Monday-Friday 8 a.m.-7 p.m., Saturday 9 a.m.-5 p.m., Sunday 11 a.m.-4 p.m.
Admission:	FREE
Additional information:	Time needed to visit the museum: Allow 15 minutes.

3-D Center of Art and Photography

It looks like 3-D movies are here to stay. The 2009 hit, Avatar, brought a vividly colored new world to the screen. The 3-D movie added more than one dimension. It added a richness and depth to the flora and fauna that made the new environment all the more amazing, exciting, and believable. Audiences flocked to the theater to experience the new world of Pandora. More 3-D movies have followed. Soon 3-D television may be common in American households.

3-D may seem like a new technology, but it has been evolving since the Civil War, when some of the first 3-D photos were attempted. If you are curious about how 3-D photos are created, visit the 3-D Center of Art and Photography. Take a look at different ways 3-D can be rendered in photographs. Examine some of the antique and newer cameras used to create 3-D images. Learn about vision and the brain, and how 3-D technology actually tricks the brain into seeing two 2-dimensional pictures simultaneously as being in 3-D. View the art gallery of 3-D photography while looking through a special viewing apparatus. Sit back and enjoy a variety of experimental 3-D films that are sent to the Center for screening. Browse through the small gift shop. 3-D books, 3-D viewers, cards, t-shirts, and art supplies to make 3-D designs are all for sale.

If your curiosity is piqued by the Center, ask about upcoming classes that are open to the public. You may learn how to make your own 3-D photos and other 3-D techniques for the amateur photographer. Your visit to the Center may be the beginning of a new hobby!

Address: 1928 NW Lovejoy, Portland, OR 97209
Phone: 503-227-6667
Web: www.3dcenter.us
Email: info@3dcenter.us
Hours: Thursday-Saturday 11 a.m.-5 p.m.
Sunday 1 p.m.-5 p.m.
First Thursday 6 p.m.-9 p.m. (FREE)
Admission: Adults (15 years old and up) $5/person, Kids 14 and younger, FREE
Restrooms: ADA accessible

Additional information: The exhibits and movies rotate often so it is worthwhile to visit the center more than once.

Vaux's Swifts at Chapman Elementary School

"Birds of a feather flock together" doesn't come close to describing the event that takes place each night during September at Chapman Elementary School in NW Portland. The nightly "how many birds can you stuff into a chimney?" event makes "how many college students can you stuff into a phone booth?" look like child's play.

According to the Audubon Society of Portland, the Chapman site is one of the largest roosting sites for the birds in the world. They estimate that up to 40,000 Vaux's Swifts dive into the chimney at sundown on a single evening to rely on the safety of numbers and the warmth of other birds to help them get through the cooling nights of fall before they start migrating to Central and South America.

Each evening in September, starting at around 6, a crowd of spectators gathers on the hill behind Chapman School, where there is a great view of the chimney, to watch the nightly display. The small birds, described as "cigars with wings" gather in groups and circle the chimney, sometimes diving toward the opening before pulling up at the last moment to continue circling the area. As the sun sets, thousands and thousands of birds begin to spiral around and around the chimney in mass like a small tornado until they funnel down into the vortex like they are being sucked up by a vacuum. Then, several more thousand birds appear in formation, swoop down, around, and rocket in.

When I was there, I heard a gasp in the crowd as a hawk suddenly appeared and attempted to pick off one of the birds. The hawk soared back up into the air empty-handed and was followed by an angry flock of Vaux's Swifts, mad as hornets that the hawk would invade their space. Suddenly the tables were turned and it was the Swifts chasing the hawk. I guess there really is safety in numbers!

At about 8 all the Swifts are safely tucked in for the night and the show ends as abruptly as it starts. The audience claps enthusiastically and then gathers up assorted children, blankets, and picnic baskets before heading off into the night, some promising that they will be back soon to watch this amazing natural wonder. Both kids and adults seem to love the experience.

The Vaux's Swifts will be able to use this site for a long time. In 2000 the Audubon Society and Portland Public Schools worked with several local businesses and foundations to help preserve the chimney and raise $60,000 to install a gas heating system so the school would not have to rely on the chimney for heat. The chimney could then be dedicated to the Vaux's Swifts. (For several years before that time, the kids at Chapman School, whose mascot is the Vaux's Swift, wore sweaters and coats to school so the furnace would not need to be fired up until the birds left on their migration south.) Now the birds stay warm, and so do the students at Chapman Elementary School.

Address: Chapman School, 1445 NW 26th, Portland, OR 97210
Phone: School: 503-916-6295
Portland Audubon Society: 503-292-6855
Web: www.audubonportland.org
Hours: Nightly 6 p.m.-8 p.m. during September
Admission: FREE
Restrooms: Primitive restroom available at Wallace Park, adjacent to Chapman School.

Additional information: This is a community event, and just like the birds, we are all in this together. Please respect the neighborhood. Some neighbors are a tad touchy about people parking illegally and loitering after the event. Park in legal spaces and do not block driveways or double-park. There is free parking five blocks north of the school at Montgomery Park, located at NW 27th and Vaughn. Please pick up your litter and trash and take it with you. Leash your dog and pick up after your dog. Remember that it is illegal to consume alcoholic beverages on school property.

Westmoreland Milk Carton Races

For a wacky day watching almost-sea-worthy boats made out of milk cartons and milk jugs, stop by Westmoreland Park for the annual event, held in conjunction with the Portland Rose Festival in June. Starting in 1973, the boat races were held annually for 30 years until the casting pond was closed for repairs. Then there were problems with who would pay for the water to fill the pond. Happily, all that was resolved and the races started up again in 2009.

Sponsored by the Oregon Dairy Association, the boats are built by families or individuals using recycled plastic milk jugs and milk cartons and a lot of duct tape. Contestants attempt to race across the casting pond in Westmoreland Park. Some make it, and some don't, and that is what makes it fun to watch. There is a party-like atmosphere, and the crowd cheers for winners and sinkers alike. Consider entering this event yourself! It doesn't cost much to build the boat, and you will have a great time entertaining your family and friends.

Address:	Westmoreland Park, SE McLaughlin and Bybee Blvd., Portland
Website:	www.dairyfarmersor.com/milkcartonrace
When:	One day in June in conjunction with the Portland Rose Festival
Admission:	FREE
Restrooms:	Rustic city park restrooms ADA accessible

World Forestry Center

During Portland's 1905 Lewis and Clark Centennial Exposition, one of the most impressive buildings was the Forestry Center. It was a gigantic and beautifully crafted structure. Some of the logs used in the construction were 5 feet in diameter and more than 50 feet tall. The Center was billed as the world's biggest log cabin. It was also called Oregon's Parthenon, the Timber Temple, and the Gallery of Trees, according Mark Reed's book, which is available at the center. The building contained educational exhibits related to Oregon's important timber industry. After the Exposition, it remained a prominent tourist site, visited by over 10 million people. That all changed on Monday, August 17, 1964 when the building caught fire and was completely destroyed within three hours.

A new forestry center was built near Washington Park in 1971. The building has undergone several transformations over the years, including name changes. It is now called the World Forestry Center to acknowledge the importance of forests worldwide. The most recent remodel was done in 2005. The result is a well thought-out, fun, interactive experience for both kids and adults.

For a complete tour of the Center, start with the six-minute film, What Is a Forest? It describes the four kinds of forests on our planet. Then have fun on a simulated white water adventure. Next, experience the feeling of a smoke jumper as they try to land their parachute at an exact location. Then, get the feel of harvesting timber by climbing aboard a Timberjack Harvester. Try your hand at felling three marked trees on a video simulator.

Upstairs, exhibits about forests in other parts of the world are clustered in one part of the space. Go high in the trees in the rainforest. Visit the forests of South Africa. Experience the forests in Russia. Walk to the other side of the upper floor to see one of several traveling exhibits that change during the year. Between the two areas, notice the displays of petrified wood. The oldest slice is between 180-225 million years old.

Before you leave, don't forget to check out the gift store on the main floor. If you are a Smokey Bear fan, you'll be impressed by the variety of Smokey patches for your hat or backpack. Also, take time to admire the art and beautiful architecture throughout the Center.

Address:	4033 SW Canyon Rd., Portland, OR 97221
Phone:	503-228-1367
Web:	**www.worldforestry.org**
Hours:	Daily 10 a.m.-5 p.m., Closed Thanksgiving, Christmas Eve, Christmas Day
Admission:	See website for current prices
Restrooms:	ADA accessible
Additional information:	Allow 1-1 1/2 hours to see and experience all the fun this center has to offer.

Section 2
Near Portland

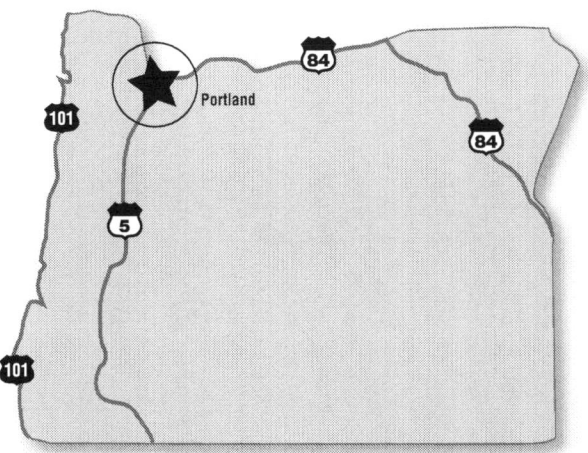

Oregon Minature Aircraft Squadron Annual Show, Near Banks

near Portland
Ice Cream

near Carver

Lavender Festival

The Beatles sing about strawberry fields forever, but there is something both relaxing and regal about seeing acres of purple Buena Vista lavender. With bees buzzing and humming peacefully in the fields, a trip to the Clackamas County Lavender Festival is a great way to celebrate the beginning of summer. The festival is in its fifth year and takes place on the last weekend in June when the lavender is in full bloom.

I went to sample the lavender ice cream made by Shane Reaney, the company that operates the Oregon Lavender Farm, where the festival is held. Using dried lavender, vanilla, and honey, the ice cream is all natural and tastes like... lavender. How is it possible to immediately recognize the flavor as lavender if you have never tasted lavender before? To me, it tasted how lavender smells. Is that bizarre or what! The ice cream is delicious and has a mild fresh flavor.

Being a young festival, the place is not overrun with vendors. There are several reasonably priced food carts at the festival as well as beautifully displayed fresh produce stands with fruits and vegetables. Lavender can be picked directly from the fields and purchased. A variety of plants are available for sale. Music fills the air. Horses from Dream Ridge Stables can be rented to take riders, with a handler walking the horse, around the lavender, for $10. This festival is perfect for a mellow day of hanging out with friends.

Address:	20949 S Harris Rd., Oregon City, OR 97045
Phone:	800-289-8427
Web:	**www.libertynatural.com/olf**
When to visit:	The festival is held on the last weekend in June.
Admission:	FREE
Restrooms:	Restrooms are available. The parking is in mown fields and most of the walking area is uneven and would be difficult to maneuver wheelchairs. However, there are some concreted areas and a disabled restroom is located in one of the buildings.
Additional information:	The site can be rented for weddings and other events.
Getting there:	Drive 5 miles past Carver on Springwater Road and watch for signs.
Warning:	If you are allergic to bees, take your Epipen! I forgot mine but I was happy to see both an ambulance and fire engine at the event.

Lake Oswego

Lake Oswego Ice Creamery and Restaurant

Located just off State Street, the Lake Oswego Ice Creamery and Restaurant serves 26 flavors of Tillamook ice cream and 6 flavors of Cascade Glacier ice cream. This is a very kid-friendly store. To help little kids get a better view of the ice cream selections, a short, movable stool is provided. Kids can then peek into the colorful tubs of ice cream before they decide on their favorite flavor. The staff encourages youngsters to take their time, knowing it is an important decision.

I go back to this creamery again and again because I LOVE their hot fudge sundae with Tillamook white licorice ice cream. They put a little hot fudge in the bottom of the glass before the ice cream is added. The hot sauce melts the ice cream just enough to bring out the wonderful licorice flavor. Together, the licorice and hot fudge are heavenly. The whipped cream and cherry on top only add to the bliss.

A single-scoop cone is $2.75, a double scoop-cone is $4.50, and a kid's scoop is $2.25. For waffle cones, add $1. Ice cream floats are $4, ice cream sodas are $4.25, and milkshakes are $4.50. A mini-banana split is $2.75, a regular sundae is $4, and a large sundae is $5.25. Sundaes come with a topping of your choice, whipped cream, nuts, and a cherry. A banana split is $5.50. Extra toppings cost 95 cents each. Customers may choose from hot fudge, candy "worms," pineapple, cookie pieces, and marshmallow cream.

Besides ice cream, this restaurant offers a full range of menu items. Breakfast is served from 7 a.m.-11:30 a.m. Monday-Saturday and 7 a.m.-noon on Sundays.

....

Address:	37 SW "A" Avenue, Lake Oswego, OR 97034
Phone:	503-636-4933
Hours:	Monday-Thursday, and Sunday 7 a.m.-9 p.m., Friday-Saturday 7 a.m.-10 p.m.
Restrooms:	Not ADA accessible
Additional information:	Orders can be called in ahead of time for quick pick-up.

near Lake Oswego

Mt. Hood Ice Cream Company

Resurrecting the name of an Oregon ice cream company that was in business from 1904 to 1921, the Mt. Hood Ice Cream Company is one of the new kids on the block. Started in 2008 by Pasha and Justin Luber, Mt. Hood Ice Cream Company offers three flavors of ice cream: Vanilla Glacier, Mountain Mint Chip, and Chocolate Avalanche. The ice cream is sold in pint containers only, usually for about $4.59. You will only find this brand in a select number of stores in the Willamette valley area. Look for Mt. Hood Ice Cream in the following grocery stores: Market of Choice, Lamb's, Wizer's, Roth's.

Part of the profit from the sale of Mt. Hood Ice Cream goes to The Mountain Rescue Association, a non-profit group that offers rescue services and mountain safety education.

....

Web: www.mthoodicecream.com

To find locations for Mt. Hood Ice Cream:

Market of Choice	www.marketofchoice.com
Lamb's Markets	www.lambsmarkets.net
Wizer's	www.wizers.com
Roth's	www.roths.com

McMinnville

Alf's Ice Cream & Burgers

Who says Elvis is dead? Near the Linfield College campus in McMinnville is Alf's Ice Cream & Burgers. There you can see Elvis, a capuchin monkey dressed in tiny jeans. He is the trademark of this long established restaurant. Elvis is in a glass enclosure adjacent to the inside seating area. He also has windows facing the outside so guests dining at the outdoor picnic tables can get a glimpse of him. He in turn has a window to the world.

At the restaurant, you can choose from a variety of burgers, fries, and other reasonably priced lunch and dinner items. You will also discover 20 flavors of homemade ice cream. Kid's cones are $1.80 and are scooped with an old-fashioned implement that extracts the ice cream into a cylinder that perfectly fits on the cone. Regular cones are $2.59, a pint is $4.19, and a quart is $6.19. For a waffle cone, add 75 cents. For a sugar cone, add 15 cents. Sundaes are $3.59 for a small and $4.59 for a large.

Milkshakes are made with Alpenrose soft serve ice cream and flavoring. You can get a regular shake in 21 flavors. Kid's size (12 oz.) is $2.49. The 16-oz. is $3.19, the 21-oz. is $3.89, and the extra large (32 oz.) is $5.69. Specialty shakes including Oreo, Butterfinger, peanut butter, walnut, hazelnut, and cheesecake range in price from $3.09-$6.19.

I tried two flavors of homemade ice cream in a sundae. I selected cherry cheesecake, which is an adult favorite at the store, and licorice, because it can vary a lot in taste based on the brand. The cherry cheesecake was great, with a nice rich flavor. The licorice ice cream was neither white nor black. It was an interesting purplish color. It had the most intense licorice flavor of any ice cream I have eaten in the state. I wished that I had skipped the sundae part. The ice cream was so good it didn't need embellishment.

Between the ice cream and Elvis, Alf's is an interesting stop for a bite to eat.

Address:	1250 SW Baker St., McMinnville, OR 97128
Phone:	503-472-7314
Hours:	Winter: Sunday-Thursday 11 a.m.-8 p.m., Friday-Saturday 11 a.m.-9 p.m. Summer: Sunday-Thursday 11 a.m.-9 p.m., Friday-Saturday 11 a.m.-10 p.m.
Restrooms:	Not ADA accessible

Serendipity

Good, old-fashioned service, generous portions, and great atmosphere await you at Serendipity Ice Cream in McMinnville. Remodeled to capture the feel of an old-time ice cream parlor, this cute store features an antique player piano that cranks out delightful tunes. On display is a beautiful cash register that was probably used at the turn of the century. Behind the counter are jars of hard candy. Twenty-four flavors of Cascade Glacier ice cream are available for purchase. Regular cones are $3.25, large cones are $4.25, and hand-rolled waffle cones are 70 cents extra. Sundaes are $4.25 and $5.25. Milkshakes are $3.75 and $4.75.

I had my mind set on ice cream but even before I got through the front door, someone on the street said, "I hear they have great homemade soups." I discovered they also have a wonderful special: soup, warm bread, AND a scoop of ice cream for $5.95 (cup of soup) or $6.95 (bowl of soup.) Intrigued, I asked Wendi, the restaurant's manager, which soup was their best-seller. "We have different soups every day but we always have white bean chicken chile soup because it is the most popular." With that recommendation I was on my way to savoring the best cup of soup I have ever eaten. The white bean soup was spicy, like chili, with chunks of chicken, and the warm homemade corn bread was moist and delicious. As I was finishing up, Wendi came up to the table and said, "You know, this special comes with either a scoop of ice cream or a cookie. All of our cookies are made fresh daily from scratch right here in our kitchen." So on a whim I tried the oatmeal white-chocolate craisin cookie and it was definitely a winner.

Serendipity has been in business for ten years. It is a division of Midvalley Rehabilitation, Inc., a non-profit organization that provides training for adults with developmental or other disabilities. This business is a great example of inclusion at its finest.

Address:	502 NE 3rd St., McMinnville, OR 97128
Phone:	503-474-9189
Hours:	Summer: Monday-Thursday 11:30 a.m.-9 p.m., Friday-Saturday 11:30 a.m.-10 p.m., Sunday noon-9 p.m. Winter: Monday-Thursday 11:30 a.m.-7:30 p.m., Friday-Saturday 11:30 a.m.-10 p.m., S unday noon-7:30 p.m.
Restrooms:	ADA accessible

Additional information: Monday is 20% senior discount day.
There is a 20% discount for Linfield students.

Getting there: McMinnville is about 35 miles west of Portland.
From Portland, take Hwy 18 west toward the coast and take the McMinnville exit into town. Follow SE 3 Mile Lane. which becomes 3rd Street.

From Lincoln City, take Hwy 18 east. Exit toward Hwy 99W toward McMinnville (sign for Hwy 99W/Linfield College/City Center. Continue straight onto SW Baker Street. Turn right at NE 3rd Street.

Newberg

Jem 100 Ice Cream Saloon

It's noon on a rainy Sunday morning and the place is jumpin' at Jem 100 Ice Cream Saloon in Newberg. I enter to the sounds of "Bali Hai" from the Broadway show South Pacific as they waft through the restaurant from speakers somewhere within. All the large 50s-era red and white vinyl booths are already occupied by families and couples from the after-church crowd so I opt for a seat at the counter. It is surprising how many people are here at this time of day. The town looked a little sleepy as I drove through.

Jem 100 is the perfect place to go for lunch and an ice cream treat. They have a menu of hamburgers, sandwiches, soups, salads, and hot dogs, all at reasonable prices. The waitresses are very friendly and efficient. They seem happy to see each new customer as they arrive. The saloon offers 32 flavors of Alpenrose, Umpqua, and Cascade Glacier ice creams. (There are actually more than 32 flavors but they are rotated during the year.) Single cones are $1.95, double cones are $2.95, and kid's cones are $1.55. The waffle cones are made on site and sell for an extra 50 cents. Small sundaes are $2.85 and large sundaes are $3.40.

Address:	208 N Main St., Newberg, OR 97132
Phone:	503-538-6191
Web:	www.jem100.com
Hours:	Sunday-Thursday 11 a.m.-10 p.m., Friday-Saturday 11 a.m.-11 p.m.
Restrooms:	ADA accessible
Getting there:	Hwy 99W is the major highway between Portland and Newberg. It is also on one of the main routes between Portland and Lincoln City and the Oregon coast. When you get into Newberg, look for Main Street or follow the sign toward Hwy 240. Jem 100 is just north of Hwy 99W on Hwy 240.

North Plains

Elephant Garlic Festival

I had serious doubts about eating garlic ice cream, probably because most of my friends either said, "Yuck!" when I mentioned where I was going, or else their faces suddenly morphed into ones I almost didn't recognize, for their crinkled noses, squinty eyes, and pursed lips said, in no uncertain terms, "No garlic ice cream will pass through these lips!" So I ventured out to North Plains by myself on a Sunday afternoon trying to keep an open mind.

The three-day garlic festival has a variety of activities to keep families busy. There is a parade on Saturday plus a fun-run, music, and much more. Daily kids' activities include a jumping house, crawl tube, and face painting. Free information about garlic abounds, and a variety of garlic products are for sale. There was a big sale of used books. This year's attendance was about 30,000 people.

The garlic ice cream booth was nestled among the food vendors who sold an assortment of food both with and without garlic. The garlic mashed potatoes booth had a line of people waiting patiently for their whipped delight. A fireman told me that they were delicious. I was on a mission, though, so I stepped right up to the ice cream booth and met Dan Fox, owner of Active Culture, a frozen yogurt store in Portland. He told me that he had contacted the festival four years before to see if they would like a frozen yogurt booth at the event. He was told that what they really needed was someone to make garlic ice cream.

Mr. Fox called around to several ice cream makers, and no one would make garlic ice cream for him because the garlic would smell up their machines and they'd have a hard time cleaning their equipment so their next flavors would not taste like garlic. Finally, Fox bought Cascade Glacier vanilla ice cream and took it back to his shop to transform it into garlic ice cream.

"Making garlic ice cream is not a fun process. It is smelly and sticky and gets on your hands and arms," he said matter of factly. The first year he made 30 gallons and sold out on Friday, with none left for either Saturday or Sunday. Last year he made 78 gallons and this year he will sell over 90 gallons of garlic ice cream.

So who buys the garlic ice cream? It turns out that a very friendly group of people line up to try the treat. Two men that I spoke with were coming back for seconds. One said he was going to get a larger size this time so he did not have to keep coming back. Mr. Fox told me that one man came back four times on Saturday and three times on Friday. A 75-year-old lady buys three gallons each year that she puts into pint containers so she can enjoy garlic ice cream all year long.

How did I like the garlic ice cream? It had a surprisingly mellow, mild flavor that was quite tasty. I liked it. If I ever need to ward off vampires or mosquitoes, garlic ice cream is the way to go!

Address:	Jessie Mays Community Center
	30955 NW Hillcrest, North Plains, OR 97133
Phone:	503-647-2619
Web:	www.funstinks.com
Hours:	Second weekend in August
Admission:	FREE
Restrooms:	ADA accessible
Additional information:	No pets allowed. Parking within two blocks of festival for $4/vehicle. Free open- air shuttle available from parking lot to entrance of festival.
Getting there:	Take Hwy 26 west from Portland about 14 miles. Get off at exit 57 and follow the signs to the Elephant Garlic Festival.

FUN FACT

Oregon Dairy Farms

Oregon has approximately 280 dairy families. They collectively have about 120,000 cows. The average farm is 300 acres and has 450 dairy cows.

Woodburn

Paleteria El Paisanito

What a joy to discover Mexican ice cream and their popular cousins, fruit bars called paletas, right here in Oregon! Practically a Mexican staple, paletas are sold on many Mexican street corners by vendors with little carts filled with the sweet treats. They are popular because they are all naturally made, using both common and exotic fruit to tickle the taste buds. When the fruit is used to make ice cream, it is equally flavorful and comes in scoops rather than bars.

Paleteria El Paisanito is one of the only Mexican ice cream stores in Oregon and is located in Woodburn. The 14%-butterfat, mostly naturally sweetened ice cream is a real taste sensation. It takes ten minutes to make a three-gallon bucket of ice cream, and then the mixture has to freeze overnight before it is the right consistency to serve. Some flavors still contain small seeds to retain their authenticity. Owner Bertha Gomez's favorite flavor is from a tropical papaya-like fruit called mamey. Many customers clamor for coconut strawberry cream and maple walnut. Besides ice cream, there are a variety of water-based sorbets in flavors such as pineapple and prickly pear. Altogether, there are over 27 flavors from which to choose a delicious treat. Single scoops are $2.25, a double scoop is $3.25, and triple scoops are $4. Large cones to hold the ice cream are $.25 extra.

The shop owners, Daniel and Bertha Gomez, got their start peddling other peoples' brands of ice cream and popsicles on the streets of Gervais, Woodburn, and Hubbard. Five years ago they took a risk and moved from her pushcart into an indoor location in Hubbard. They bought a paleta machine, and began experimenting with flavors and textures until they developed their own unique Mexican-style popsicles. They added ice cream to their line of products. Bertha's dream of owning her own business finally came true! Now they have moved into a new location in Woodburn.

Since the beginning, running the store has been a family affair, with Bertha, her husband Daniel, and their five children all pitching in to manufacture the products and mind the store. Since then, an aunt and a cousin have joined in the operation. Nowadays, Mrs. Gomez multi-tasks and oversees the entire operation, supervising family in the back room as they wrap paletas in individual cellophane wrappers. At the same time she cooks a batch of freezing paletas, watching as they hang suspended in a tray surrounded by a circulating liquid to help them freeze. Her older daughter, Erica, helps out at the front counter where the finished paletas and tubs of ice cream are waiting for customers to enjoy.

If you have ever wanted to try your hand at selling paletas, cute little pushcarts, complete with distinctive bells to announce your arrival, are available for rent. Daniel Gomez makes each cart with freezer boxes from Mexico. You can buy paletas at a discount from the store to sell for your own profit or as a fundraiser. Paleteria El Paisanito is well worth the trip.

Address: 429 N Front St., Woodburn, OR 97071
Phone: 503-981-9087
Hours: 11 a.m.-8:30 p.m. daily
Seasonal operation. Call for dates.
Restrooms: No

near Portland
Things to See and Do

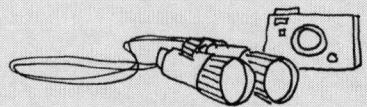

near BANKS

Oregon Miniature Aircraft Squadron (OMAS) Annual Show

I don't know if pigs fly but I did see a flying lawn mower at the OMAS model aircraft air show. There were also two 6-foot-tall "super-heroes" who rocketed across the sky, diving, and swooping, surely looking for evil to stamp out. These were just two of the many flying aircraft that filled the sky at the club's 29th air show. The annual event is about an hour's drive west of Portland. Planes zip, turn, and do stunts with names like double jammers, hammerheads, knife edge t-passes, and fountains. Combat planes, trailing 30-foot streamers of crepe paper, twist and turn to outmaneuver each other as they attempt to cut the ribbons from each other's planes.

The drive itself is worth the trip. Motoring through the lush farmland and rural roads make the trip a relaxing get-away from the city. The miniature airstrip is leased to OMAS from Lewis Farm, a big outfit that grows cherries, filberts, prunes, and corn. During the few lulls in the air show, spectators can look past the airstrip to a pasture where hay is being baled. The land used by OMAS also includes a small pond where miniature floatplanes take off and land. Once in a while, a plane will crash and splash into the pond. Then a rescue kayak paddles out to retrieve the wreckage.

Chairs are set up for spectators at the event, or you can bring your own lawn chairs. Sitting under one of the shade trees makes for a mellow day. Hotdogs, sodas, and other snacks are for sale at a little out-building. A couple of outhouses are located behind some tall trees. The people running the event are nice and the crowd is appreciative. You might see raptors lazily circling the event from high above. Imagine what must be going on in their minds!

Address:	Lewis Farm, 46035 NW Strohmayer Rd. near Banks, OR
Web:	**www.omas-rc.org**
Hours:	Two days in August. Check website for exact dates. Open 9:30-4 p.m. on the days of the event.
Admission:	$5/car for parking. Admission to the event is free.
Restrooms:	Port-a-potties
Additional information:	Snacks are available for sale on site. You may bring your own picnic lunch and lawn chairs.

near GASTON

Tree to Tree Adventure Park

Have you ever dreamed of thumping your chest and yelling "Me Tarzan," or tapping your chest and exclaiming "Me Jane," or scratching your chest and screeching "Me Cheeta," just before taking off from your perch, swinging through the air on a jungle vine high in the treetops? Well that experience, or a reasonable facsimile, is now yours to enjoy. Tree to Tree is a new "aerial adventure course" just outside of Gaston, Oregon, on a beautiful wooded property. Open since Memorial Day 2010, it is the creation of Harry Beres.

The inspiration for the course came after Harry discovered the popularity of aerial courses in France and England. He purchased 26 beautiful acres in rural Oregon to begin his enterprise. The current course is strung through four to five acres of majestic trees. It includes 48 "elements," 12 of the elements are ziplines. There are plans to expand and add more ziplines.

The adventure begins with a stop at the information booth. Participants are outfitted with a hardhat and harness. They watch a short video about safety and using the equipment. Then the group gathers outside and meets their trained group leader who gives directions and guides the group through the course. The course starts out close to the ground to give visitors confidence and experience with the equipment. As the course progresses, the elements slowly gain elevation. Some branches of the course are higher than others. Safety is stressed throughout the course, and from what I saw, most participants err on the side of caution. Even so, 3-4 rescues are performed each day as participants end up in, shall we say, awkward positions.

The course itself is a series of innovative challenges that lead the participant from tree to tree. One element is a series of swinging platforms that are hung with spaces in between that the guest must cross. Another element is a wall with handholds and footholds that the participant uses to cross the space. Still another element, a giant spiderweb, is at the end of a zipline, awaiting guests as they careen into its web. There are several points where would-be Tarzans or Janes can decide they have had enough fun and they want off the course.

The park is often used by corporations for teambuilding, as well as by schools, youth groups, and civic organizations. It is a great place to enjoy with your friends or family. Reservations are required. There is no age limit, but participants must be able to reach 5 feet up with their arm extended. It is also important to wear shoes that have a closed toe. No open shoes are allowed.

Address: 2975 SW Nelson Road, Gaston, OR 97119
Phone: 503-357-0109
Web: **www.treetotreeadventurepark.com**
Email: info@treetotreeadventurepark.com
Hours: Seasonal operation, Memorial Day-Thanksgiving
Admission: See website for current prices
Restrooms: ADA accessible

Additional information: Reservations are required. Call for specials.

Getting there: From Portland, take US Hwy 26 west. Take exit 57 for Glencoe Rd. toward North Plains. Turn left at 1st Street/NW Glencoe Road. Turn right at NW Zion Church Road. Continue onto NW Cornelius Schefflin Road. Slight right at NW Verboort Road. At the traffic circle, take the second exit onto NW Martin Road. Turn left at OR- 47 South/Quince Street/State Hwy 47 S. Turn right at SW Scoggins Valley Road. Turn right at SW Nelson Rd.

GLADSTONE

The Children's Course

Tucked away between two apartment complexes and just off busy McLoughlin Blvd. in Gladstone is The Children's Course. It is also home to a program for at-risk youth called The First Tee. The golf course property was purchased in 1996 by an Oregon philanthropist, Duncan Campbell, who believed that youngsters could develop life-long values and life skills through golf. The Children's Course is operated as a non-profit. Each year The First Tee teaches golf to thousands of youth between the ages of 7 and 17. Discovery Golf introduces 4-6-year-olds to the game.

In the fall and spring, The First Tee works with schools in the Portland Metro area to identify students who might benefit from learning the core values of golf. Counselors and school administrators select students for the program. From there, The First Tee has been able to shatter barriers that often leave at-risk youth out of sports programs. One of the biggest barriers to participation is transportation. The First Tee picks up and delivers students to and from their home schools to lessons. Students pay for the classes, but no student is turned away because their family cannot afford the program. Students in the program can earn golf clubs, golf shoes, and golf shirts by their continued participation.

During the summer, The First Tee program offers golf lessons for all local youth. Summer day camps, weekly lessons, group lessons, and individual instruction are all scheduled. There are also programs for children with special needs. Golf classes are taught on the main golf course. There is also a separate five-hole short course nestled within the main golf course that is used for instruction.

The Children's Course is open to the general public. It is a 9-hole, par 3 course. Adults as well as children are welcome to play on the links. The green fees are some of the lowest in the area. If you do not have your own set of golf clubs, you can rent them for a nominal fee at the clubhouse. If you are brand new to the game and would like to try it out, check in at the clubhouse and ask about golf etiquette. It will keep the grounds looking good for all players. Whether you are a beginning or an experienced golfer, The Children's Course is a fun short course for golf.

Address:	19825 River Rd., Gladstone, OR 97027
Phone:	503-722-1530
Web:	www.thechildrenscourse.org
Hours:	Daily 7:30 a.m.-sunset. Closed Christmas Day
Admission:	Juniors (17 and under) $5/9 holes, $8/18 holes, Adults $10/9 holes, $15/18 holes, Seniors (60 and older) $7/9 holes, $12/18 holes
Restrooms:	Not-ADA accessible
Additional information:	Pull cart rental $2, rental golf clubs (Adult & Jr.) $3/set Call or go to the website for more information about summer golf lessons for students.

near HILLSBORO

Rice N.W. Museum of Rocks and Minerals

When you play the guessing game "Twenty Questions," each game starts with the question, "Is it animal, mineral, or vegetable?" If you are curious about what falls into the "mineral" category, visit the Rice N.W. Museum of Rocks and Minerals. In one building, you will find an extensive display of rocks, minerals, and crystals that are all found in the Pacific Northwest. You will see many beautiful examples of thunder eggs, Oregon's state rock. Thunder eggs are a popular Oregon rock-hound treasure. In nature, they have a distinctive round or egg-shape. When they are split open, there is a surprising beauty within. The display at the Rice Museum is incredible. It includes the largest "opal filled" thunder egg in the world! You will also see fine examples of Oregon's state gem, the sunstone.

The main building of the museum, which was once the home of Helen and Richard Rice, is a ranch-style home. The house was awarded a place in the National Registry of Historical Places in 2006. Downstairs, you can see the Dennis and Mary Murphy collection of petrified wood with over 400 specimens on display. You can also get a close-up look at thousands of crystals and gems from around the world. On the main floor there is a display of meteorites. Another display shows examples of gold ore. In a separate, dark room on the main floor, you can see fluorescent minerals that glow when seen with a black light.

On the main floor don't miss the video about the discovery of the "Alma Rose" rhodochrosite from Colorado. (The Alma Rose itself is found downstairs.) The video is a good introduction to the tenacity of miners who spend hundreds of hours mining in the hope of finding something interesting to show for their work. The rose color of the rhodochrosite is breathtaking. Also on the main floor are a saber-tooth tiger's skull, the skull of a cave bear, fossils, and more. Don't miss the dinosaur eggs!

To complete your stay, visit the gift store. You will find rocks, minerals, and gems that you can take home. After your visit to the museum, you will come away with a new appreciation for minerals, crystals, rocks, and rock hounds.

Address: 26385 NW Groveland Drive, Hillsboro, OR 97124
Phone: 503-647-2418
Web: **www.ricenorthwestmuseum.org**
Email: info@ricenorthwestmuseum.org
Hours: Open 1 p.m.-5 p.m. Wednesday-Sunday
Closed major holidays
Admission: Adult admission $7, Seniors (60+) $6,
Students (5-17) $5,
Kids four and under are FREE.
Restrooms: ADA accessible. There is also an elevator at the museum.

McMINNVILLE

Evergreen Aviation & Space Museum

During World War II, Henry Kaiser, a major U.S. shipbuilding magnate, teamed up with the eccentric movie producer, aviator, and engineer Howard Hughes to design and build a flying boat that could transport up to 750 military troops. With an $18 million government contract, they set out to build three prototypes. There were two important stipulations in the deal. They were not supposed to use any materials (i.e., metals) that were crucial to the war effort and they were not to use any skilled personnel already employed in aviation design or construction. With these two caveats, a flying boat was designed made from choice birch wood. Hughes trained young engineers and mechanics on the job. Together, they built a 320-foot wingspan airboat, a huge airplane by anyone's standards.

Eventually, Kaiser backed out of the project, leaving Hughes with the burden of completing the contract. The project was not without its detractors. A congressional committee hauled Hughes into its chambers to demand how the money had been spent, accusing him of misappropriation. One plane had been constructed, not three. The plane had never lifted off the ground. Some thought the plane was so large that it could not fly. The plane became known as the Spruce Goose. The whole episode incensed Howard Hughes.

In 1947, the plane was transported in pieces to the Long Beach California dry-dock where it was assembled. With Howard Hughes at the controls, the plane briefly lifted off the harbor in Long Beach, proving that it could fly. After this one and only flight, it then went into storage, where it remained for 33 years, with Hughes paying the annual storage costs of $1,000,000 a year.

When Hughes died, the plane was rescued from demolition. It was separated into 38 pieces and shipped to Oregon, no easy feat, where it became the first plane, and the centerpiece, of the Evergreen Aviation & Space Museum.

Today, the museum consists of three gargantuan buildings. One building houses the Spruce Goose and over 150 planes, helicopters, and flying machines. Lots of interesting displays and short videos are interspersed throughout the museum, with airline seats cleverly used for seating. Kids of all ages will love the hands-on exhibits. Upstairs there is a fascinating display of guns from the time of Lewis and Clark to the present. Also, there is a gift shop and dining area that serves luncheon items. There, you will find 12 flavors of Cascade Glacier ice cream. A single cup or cone is $2, a double scoop is $4. A waffle cone is $3. Milkshakes are $4.50. The second building shows I-MAX movies. The third building is dedicated to the space program.

The many volunteers at the museum will help you get the most out of your visit. Regular group tours happen daily at no extra charge. See the admission desk for the day's schedule. In the space museum, I met Earl Scott, a retired aeronautical space engineer and commercial aviation engineer, who is a wonderful storyteller and expert on man's journey into space. He gave me a wealth of fascinating information that truly enriched my experience in the museum.

A new lodge and water park is opening Summer 2011.

Address:	500 NE Captain Michael King Smith Way, McMinnville, OR 97128
Phone:	503-434-4180
Web:	**www.EvergreenMuseum.org**
Hours:	Daily 9 a.m.-5 p.m.
	Closed Thanksgiving, Christmas, and Easter Sunday
	Close at 2 p.m. on Christmas Eve
Admission:	Go to web for current prices.
Restrooms:	ADA accessible
Other information:	AAA cardholder discount of $4.
	If you want to see the cockpit of the Spruce Goose or have your picture taken in the cockpit, there is an additional fee. You can walk up the stairs and see the inside of the plane at no additional charge.

NORTH PLAINS

Horning's Fishing and Picnic Hideout

I can't help it. I hear "Hernando's Hideaway" playing in my head when I visit Horning's Fishing and Picnic Hideout. It must be the similarity of titles, but it is a catchy tune and adds a little intrigue. Horning's is in a beautiful, tranquil spot just west of Portland off Hwy 26. There is a general entrance fee of $3/person ages 6 and up. This fee goes toward the purchase of fish, paddleboats, and frisbee golf. The grounds provide a picturesque setting for picnicking. Camping is available for tents ($15/night for up to 4 people), group camping ($5/person/night) and RVs ($20/night.) Horning's also has space to rent for company picnics, weddings, and family reunions.

Horning's is a perfect place to take kids who want to experience the joys of fishing or for adults who are hungry for some fresh fish. Horning's has poles and bait available as well as a crochet-needle-type tool to get the hooks out of the fish that are caught. Horning's has two good-sized ponds where folks can fish from the banks with a remarkably good chance of catching a fish. When I was there, one family caught a 3-lb. trout that was a beauty to look at, while another family caught a string of several smaller trout. There is no need for a fishing license here since the ponds are on private property. However, there is a charge for fish that are caught. Fish under 2 lbs cost $5/pound and fish over 2 lbs. cost $6/lb. Catch-and-release fly fishermen can try their luck for $7/hour. Paddleboats can be rented to cruise around the ponds for $10/hour, $5/half-hour, or $30/all day.

Horning's also has three 18-hole disc golf courses. The shortest course glows at night. The longest course is called "The Beast." Golfers can pay to play by the day or they can purchase season passes. January-April passes are $60, May-August passes are $40, and September-December passes are $20.

Horning's Hideout is a family-run business that has been a private park since 1983. Before that it was a cattle ranch run by Richard and Jane Horning. Jane Horning originally moved to the area at the age of 19 with her husband. They settled on the land to work a cattle ranch. Her husband said, "Someday we are going to have a lake right there," and he pointed down to an area below their family home. In their home, Mrs. Horning raised four children, churning butter, making bread, and living a simple old-fashioned life. In 1972 the pond was built just like her husband promised, and in 1973 the first fish were introduced into the pond. The cattle ranching business ended when Mr. Horning died. Fortunately, before he died, Mr. Horning saw the beginning of his vision for a park.

Horning's Hideout is now operated by Jane Horning and her son, Bob Horning. The pond is still well stocked with delicious trout. When you come fishing, Jane Horning is still there to help you with poles and bait so your family can catch tasty, fresh fish. Fishing is open year round to visitors. The fishing starts at 8 a.m. and stops at 8 p.m. or dusk.

Address: 21277 NW Brunswick Cyn Rd., North Plains, OR 97133
Phone: 503-647-2920
Web: **www.horningshideout.com**
Hours: 8 a.m.-8 p.m. Daily.
Restrooms: ADA restroom is available. Outhouses are also on site.

Additional information: For large groups, call for reservations.

Getting there: Take Hwy 26 west from Portland to Exit 57. Drive 1.5 miles on Glencoe Road and then turn left onto Pumpkin Ridge Road. Drive 5 miles. Turn right on Brunswick Cyn Road and continue 1 mile.

Warning: If you are allergic to bees, be sure to take an EpiPen. Bees and yellow jackets love to hang around fish.

Section 3
The Columbia River Gorge and I-84

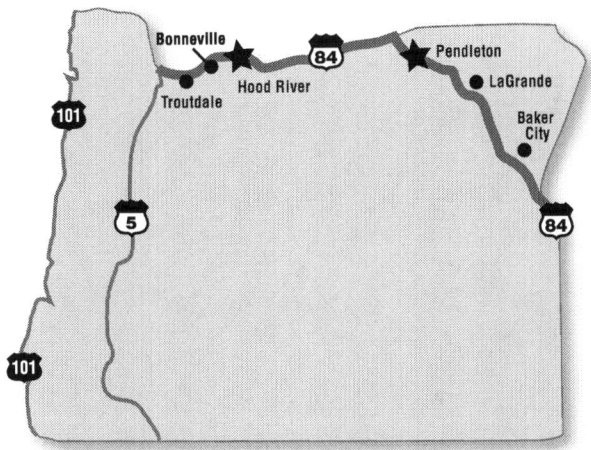

Multnomah Falls

The Columbia River Gorge and I-84

Ice Cream

Boardman

C & D Drive-In and Bakery and Poppy's Pizza

On long road trips it is nice to have some favorite places where you can just get off the freeway easily, grab a bite to eat, use the restroom, and then get back in your car and be on your way. C & D Drive-In could become that kind of place for your family. The place itself is a little odd, but it seems to work.

There are two walk-up counters adjacent to each other. There are also two small dining areas on opposite sides of the restaurant. Each counter has the same menu. Each counter delivers their orders to the dining area on their side of the restaurant. Soooooo....if you arrive, say, and you aren't speaking to your traveling companion(s), you can give yourselves a little time out while you go to opposite corners and cool off with something to eat and drink. If you have squabblers in your car that can't decide between burgers and pizza, you are also in luck! Attached to the drive-in is Poppy's Pizza. In fact, it is owned by the same folks who own the drive-in. It has the same cooks as the drive-in, and its own seating area, but hey, if you wanted to take your pizza next door, or bring your burgers in from the other side, no one would blink an eye at you.

Home of the Bozo burger, they are not clowning around when they cook up this ¼ -pound burger with bacon and cheese ($5.60) for those who are extra-hungry. Their regular burger is $3.35 or $3.85 with cheese. Besides burgers and sandwiches, there is an assortment of breakfast and dinner items. Homemade brownies and cookies will test your willpower. On the other side of things, pizzas sell for $12-$16.

Oh, and about their ice cream. They sell a variety of Umpqua hard ice creams. Try a huckleberry cheesecake milkshake ($4/small, $5/medium, $7/large.) It will make your tastebuds sing with joy! They also have homemade waffle cones (from $2.25-$3 for a single scoop), sundaes, and banana splits.

Then, after a bite to eat, you can be on your way with easy access back onto the freeway. You'll be fuller, and hopefully just a little bit happier, because of your stop. Don't forget to let your passengers get back into the car.

....

Address:	103 N Main St., Boardman, OR 97818
Phone:	541-481-4981 or 541-3399
Hours:	6 a.m.-9 p.m. daily. In the summer, they stay open until 10 p.m.
Restrooms:	ADA accessible only for women.
Getting there:	Just off exit #164 on Hwy 84, 164 miles east of Portland.

Hood River

Apple Valley Country Store and Bakery

For a delicious seasonal milkshake while traveling the Fruit Loop, stop at the Apple Valley Country Store. Huckleberry and marionberry shakes are both made with Sunshine vanilla ice cream. The huckleberry shake has lots of berries. It is the most popular flavor until late fall when pumpkin shakes become the rage. The seasonal shakes are $4.50. If you would prefer an ice cream cone or cup, Tillamook ice cream is offered for $3/single scoop and $4 for a double scoop.

Besides ice cream the country store has a mouth-watering variety of homemade jams, pepper jellies, syrups, and pie-fillings. Pies, with crusts homemade from scratch, are for sale, either by the slice, by the whole pie baked and ready to eat, or as a u-bake pie that you can take home, heat, and enjoy.

On select weekends during the summer and early fall, visitors can purchase special delicacies. Apple or pear dumplings and different kinds of fruit crisps are popular. Barbeques are also fired up on special weekends. Visitors can enjoy an old-fashioned lunch in a beautiful country setting.

Address: 2363 Tucker Rd., Hood River, OR 97031
Phone: 541-386-1971
Web: www.applevalleystore.com
Email: info@applevalleystore.com
Hours: March: Saturday-Sunday 10 a.m.-5 p.m.
April-May: Wednesday-Sunday 10 a.m.-5 p.m.
June-October: 10 a.m.-6 p.m. daily
November-December: Wednesday-Sunday 10 a.m.-5 p.m.
Restrooms: ADA outhouse in front of store
Getting there: Hood River is about 1 hour east of Portland on I 84. Take Exit 62 in Hood River. Turn right onto Cascade Avenue and immediately turn right again on Country Club Road. Travel to first stop sign and turn left on Barrett Drive. Turn right at second stop sign (at the 76 Station), which is Tucker Road. The store is about two miles farther on the left.

Mike's Ice Cream

2011 marks the 25th anniversary of Mike's Ice Cream in downtown Hood River. This seasonal ice cream store opens each year on April 1 and closes each year on Halloween. Mike's is one of the few places in the state outside of Eugene that serves hard-to-find Prince Puckler ice cream. On hot summer days, visitors line up to enjoy a luscious ice cream treat at this cute and quirky ice cream shop. A single scoop cone is $3 and a double cone is $4. Mike's also offers a senior cone (for people 65 years and older) for $2. For customers with small appetites, ask for the baby-baby scoop ($1) or the baby scoop ($2).

Mike's also has a variety of sundaes, including a hot fudge sundae ($4.50) a banana split ($6), a screaming brownie sundae ($5), and a huckleberry hot fudge sundae ($5). If you want to experience a real Northwest treat, order one of Mike's specialty fresh huckleberry or strawberry milkshakes ($5.50 small/$6 large.) For coffee lovers, try the espresso shake made with beans from the Hood River Coffee Company.

Mike's Ice Cream originated when Tassie Mack and Mike Kitts moved to Hood River to pursue their love of windsurfing. Mike said he could not live in a place that did not have an ice cream store, and so he and Tassie started their own scoop shop. They first bought a building that was had been a tack shop. Mike and Tassie remodeled it into a business they called the Ruddy Duck. At the Ruddy Duck you'll find clothing for men, women, and children, as well as a variety of other dry goods. Next, they moved the horse trailers out of the vacant lot next door to the Ruddy Duck. They built a very simple, but cute, ice cream shop. Out in front of the ice cream shop there is a small grassy area with benches and tables for customers to enjoy their ice cream treats.

Until two years ago, many of the kids who got ice cream at Mike's enjoyed their treats while sitting in the branches of the dogwood tree that spreads its branches into Mike's front yard from next door. Then, without notice, the owner next door trimmed the tree so kids could not get up into the tree. The community was aghast. After all, the tree was part of the collective memory of Hood River kids for two generations. Mike and Tassie decided to build a climbing structure so that kids could once again eat their cones in a world of their own, high up in the ancient pink dogwood tree. Below, parents still stand in the shade of the marvelous tree as they chat with other parents and friends and enjoy their own ice cream treat. You might even see them sipping one of the special shakes that Mike's whips up: Huckleberry, Strawberry, or Espresso.

Take a good look at the kids working behind the counter at Mike's. Each one is a 4.0 student. Twenty students are hired each season, and everyone in town knows that if a student gets good grades, he or she may apply for a chance to work at this very fun, happening kind of place. What an incentive!

Have you ever wondered what happens to leftover ice cream at the end of the summer season? At Mike's it is given out on Halloween to lucky trick-or-treaters. There must be a bunch of happy kids in Hood River on October 31!

No matter when you go through Hood River during the summer season, make sure a stop at Mike's becomes a tradition. You will love the ice cream and the casual atmosphere. Just looking at this colorful little shop will make you smile.

Address: 504 Oak St., Hood River OR 97031-2183
Phone: 541-386-6260
Hours: 11 a.m.-11 p.m. daily, April 1-October 31
Restrooms: ADA accessible
Driving: Hood River is about 1 hour east of Portland on I-84. Take Exit 63.

La Grande

Hought's 24 Flavors

I was sitting at the counter enjoying a leisurely hot fudge sundae when two middle-school aged boys burst into Hought's ice cream store in La Grande. It was just about 3:15 and the two kids were wound up after a day sitting in class. They bounced around the store and laughed and talked like they were best friends. One of the boys laid a quarter on the counter and the server offered up a kid-sized ice cream cone. It was then I realized I had stumbled into maybe the only ice cream store in the state with a happy hour for kids! Looking at the energetic, carefree faces of the two amigos, I caught a glimpse of one of the favorite childhood memories they would be recounting in just a few years.

From 3 p.m. to 5 p.m., Carla Sorweide, the owner of Hought's 24 Flavors, offers snacks at piggy bank prices for students on their way home from the nearby school. Corn dogs are 50 cents, a small regular fries is 75 cents, and a kid-sized cone is a quarter. There is also the occasional special. On this day it was a free ice cream bar with the purchase of a small fries.

Hought's is located on a corner of town that borders both the commercial district and the old residential area of La Grande. It is a friendly, inviting building that seems to have a steady stream of people stopping by for lunch or a quick snack. From moms with their baby strollers to boomers in their, well, boomer years, the staff serves up to 40 flavors of Cascade Glacier ice cream with a smile and good cheer. Their sundaes are made with homemade hot fudge. One scoop in a cake cone is $2 and small sundaes cost $2.50. Milkshakes start at $3.95. Besides ice cream, Hought's offers a variety of homemade burgers, hot dogs, and homemade fries. Hought's is not a fast food restaurant so relax and enjoy the wait. You will be rewarded with good home-cooked food.

Sorweide seemed genuinely surprised when I told her that her store was famous in Eastern Oregon. "Yes," I said, "when I asked people from Pendleton to Joseph to Baker City, from gas station attendants to people in Chambers of Commerce where to go in La Grande for ice cream, they all said, 'Have you been to Hought's?'" After visiting Hought's, I can see why it has earned such high praise in this part of the state. It is a relaxing, homey kind of place with good people and good food.

Address: 602 Adams St., La Grande, OR 97850
Phone: 541-962-7856
Facebook: www.facebook.com/pages/Houghts-24-Flavors/291787912770
Hours: Winter: 11 a.m.-9 p.m., closed Sundays
Summer: 11 a.m.-10:30 p.m. 7 days a week
Restrooms: Not ADA accessible

Getting there: Coming from the west, take exit 259 to merge onto US30 East LaGrande. Keep left at the fork.

Coming from the south, take exit 265 for US Hwy 30/Or-203 toward La Grande/Union. Turn left at OR-203 N/US Hwy 30 West/Adams Avenue.
Turn right at Adams Avenue.

Pendleton

Mission Market

Apparently cowboys in Pendleton are not ice cream connoisseurs. Local restaurants and ice cream shops seem to get their ice cream from the local Cash and Carry Store. None of the restaurant workers I talked to in the downtown area thought they were serving an Oregon brand. I finally had to go out to the Umatilla Indian Reservation and seek out the Mission Market to get my hands on some delicious Umpqua ice cream. A junior cone is just $1 and a single scoop cone is $2. A single waffle cone is $3. The Mission Market is a convenience store located at "four corners," at the intersection of Mission Road and Highway 331, just a couple of miles east of Pendleton's old town district.

Address: 46493 Mission Rd., Pendleton, OR 97801
Phone: 541-276-9137
Hours: Summer: Monday-Saturday 7 a.m.-9 p.m.,
Sunday 8 a.m.-8 p.m
Winter: Monday-Saturday 7 a.m.-8 p.m.,
Sunday 8 a.m.-7 p.m.
Restrooms: ADA accessible

Getting there: Coming from Highway I-84, take Exit 216 toward Milton-Freewater. Mission Market is at the intersection of Mission Road and Highway 331, just a couple of miles east of Pendleton's old town district.

FUN FACT

Oregon Cows

About 75% of Oregon cows are Holsteins and about 20% are Jersey cows. The average milk production per cow is 19000 pounds annually. Most cows are milked twice a day. I am sure they find it a great relief.

Troutdale

Troutdale General Store, Ice Cream Parlor & Confectionary

Passing through the town of Troutdale, a gateway to the old Columbia Gorge Highway, be sure to stop at the Troutdale General Store. The owners, Terry and Jodi Smoke, have created a perfect store for tourists looking for just the right souvenir or for a quick bite to eat. It is festively decorated for the seasons year-round. The main floor is dressed out for whatever current holiday is coming up. But, if you are in the mood for something a little Halloweenish in the middle of July, you will find it downstairs, where out-of-season decorations and ornaments are always on display. They may inspire you to get an early start on your own holiday decorating.

Besides holiday fare, there is a feast for the eyes as you wander around the store. You may have to walk more than one loop because you are sure to miss something unique and delightful on your first go-around of this jam-packed store. Toys, gadgets, home decorations, and more are artfully displayed throughout three floors. On the main floor, one section has a wonderful assortment of unusual candies that will make your sweet tooth sing with joy.

Then there is the ice cream parlor. It is a wonderful reproduction of a traditional parlor. It has an enormous late 1800s antique oak mirrored back bar and stools that belly up to a beautiful wooden bar. The bar was originally used as a counter in the old Troutdale Bank so it is an historical part of the decor. Tables and chairs are available in the dining area for customers to relax and enjoy their visit.

Cascade ice cream is served in the parlor. A single scoop on a regular or sugar cone is $2 and a double scoop is $4. For a waffle cone add 75 cents. Try a hot fudge sundae for $3.95 (single scoop) or $5.95 (double scoop.) Also on the menu are sundaes with names such as "The Columbia Gorge Sundae" ($6.95), and "The Mount Hood Sundae" ($6.95). Old-fashioned milkshakes are $3.95.

Breakfast and lunch items are also on the menu. Already-made breakfast casseroles with intriguing names like Sausage Swiss Brunch and Baked Oatmeal with Peaches line a display case. Raspberry (or marionberry) cream cheese Danishes ($3.95) and assorted containers of yogurt (1.50) might just hit the spot. Any entree would taste great with one of the General Store's many coffee or hot chocolate drinks. During weekends, smoked salmon chowder is a lunchtime specialty of the store. It keeps customers coming back for more.

Whether you stop at the beginning of your trip to the Columbia Gorge, or drop in after a day of fun in the Gorge, check out the Troutdale General Store. It will put the perfect exclamation point on your day.

Address: 289 E Historic Columbia River Hwy., Troutdale, OR 97060
Phone: 503-492-7912
Hours: Monday-Friday 7:30 a.m.-5 p.m.,
Saturday-Sunday 9 a.m.-5 p.m.
Restrooms: ADA accessible

The Columbia River Gorge and I-84
Things to See and Do

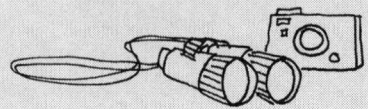

near BAKER CITY

Oregon Trail Interpretive Center

I always suspected I would have made a lousy pioneer crossing the country to reach Oregon. I hate dust. I have asthma. My sister says no matter how long I train, I will never be able to walk the Portland Marathon fast enough to finish, even if I am given ten hours. My plantar fasciitis would have me limping within the first ten miles. I know I would whine constantly. Let's not even talk about lack of indoor plumbing, regular showers with soap and shampoo, and no gummie bears and water stations at regular intervals.

My misgivings were confirmed beyond a doubt when I visited the Oregon Trail Interpretive Center just outside of Baker City. The detailed, lifelike dioramas of scenes from the Oregon Trail helped me relate to the plight of these people who looked a lot like any of us. I took the time to stop and hear their stories and learn about the hardships they endured. Some of the settlers walked the entire distance without shoes! If you consider that a marathon is a little over 26 miles, the 2000-mile Oregon Trail is the equivalent of about 77 marathons!

The stories of the pioneers at the museum are stories of perseverance, hope, hardship, and desperation. It is the story of people who banded together with the common goal of making it to Oregon. It was a difficult trek. The Oregon Trail is lined with the graves of those too old, too weak, or too sick to finish the journey. Kids and adults died in accidents and from diseases they picked up along the way. Heartache seems to have been a constant shadow.

Surprisingly, the story of the Oregon Trail is not a very old story. The start of the migration west in the 1850s is not all that long ago from present day in the grand scheme of things. My family is only four generations away from the pioneers. Oregon is a young state.

Outside the museum are replicas of covered wagons that might have been used on the journey west. There are periodic re-enactments of pioneer life during the year. Volunteers demonstrate skills that would have been typical of folks on the trail. Visitors can also enjoy a walk outdoors to the mine exhibit.

Take time to hop off the freeway and visit the Oregon Trail Interpretive Center. It will give you insight into the life of the pioneers who settled the West.

Address:	Bureau of Land Management National Historic Oregon Trail Interpretive Center P.O. Box 987, Baker City, OR 97814
Phone:	541-523-1843
Website:	**oregontrail.blm.gov or www.blm.gov/or/oregontrail**
Hours:	Open daily except Christmas, Thanksgiving, New Year's Day April-October 9 a.m.-6 p.m., November-March 9 a.m.-4 p.m.
Admission:	Call for current entrance fees.
Restrooms:	ADA accessible
Getting there:	The Center is five miles east of Baker City on Highway 86. Take Exit 302 from I-84.

near BONNEVILLE

Bonneville Fish Hatchery

Bonneville Fish Hatchery is the perfect place to get a great look at two of Oregon's native fish species, rainbow trout and white sturgeon. Relax and enjoy viewing magnificent rainbow trout in outdoor ponds during your self-guided tour. For a quarter, you can buy specially formulated pellets to feed the trout. In another pool, you can observe white sturgeon that are more than ten feet long and weigh over 450 pounds. If the white sturgeon look prehistoric, it is because the species is known to be between 144 and 206 million years old (Jurassic period). An individual sturgeon may grow up to be 20 feet long and live to be 100 years old.

The gift store is operated by the Oregon Wildlife Heritage Foundation. It is open at the hatchery from March 1 through November 30. You will find many featured items by local artists at this shop.

Visitors in October and November have the opportunity to observe the spawning of adult Coho and Chinook salmon. An indoor viewing area and video will help visitors understand how this fascinating process, with support from the hatchery, help salmon survive.

Address: 70543 NE Herman Loop, Cascade Locks, OR 97014
Phone: 541-374-8393 or 541-374-8820
Web: http://www.dfw.state.or.us/resources/visitors/bonneville_hatchery_more.asp
Hours: Hatchery is open daily at 7:30 a.m.-6 p.m. Pacific Standard Time, 7:30 a.m.-8 p.m. Pacific Daylight Time Visitor center open 9 a.m.-5 p.m. daily. Closed Thanksgiving, Christmas, New Year's Day
Admission: FREE
Restrooms: ADA accessible

Eagle Creek Hike

My favorite hike in Oregon is along the Eagle Creek trail in the Columbia Gorge. It is best to go on a dry day because sections of the trail can get slick. Periodically, I read in the newspaper about someone who has slid off the cliff, leading to their untimely death, so be careful and stay on the trail. In the past I have led several groups of elementary-aged children on this hike and we always had a wonderful time with no problems. I think the best times to hike this trail are between June and September.

The trailhead starts at the end of a parking lot and winds its way along the east side of Eagle Creek, gradually gaining in elevation until the creek can be seen far below. I like the sounds I hear on this hike: the creek, the falls, and if I am lucky, the rustling trees. In the spring the wildflowers add a touch of color to the landscape. The trail gently rises and falls. There are places where the trail narrows and there is a steep drop-off down to the water. From these vantage points, there are some spectacular views of the hills and trees across the creek on the other side. At one point along the trail, there is a cable handrail that I always use, just to be safe, because the ground is uneven and sometimes slick. I guess I am basically a chicken at heart. The trail then meanders away from the creek, past a small waterfall where you step across a little stream. Then shortly the trail crosses a small bridge. At about 2 miles, you will see Punchbowl Falls. This is a great place to stop for a rest or maybe a snack or lunch while you enjoy looking at the falls.

Some people like to turn around here and head back to the trailhead, but if you are still eager to explore, a 1.3 mile hike farther will take you to High Bridge. The view of the creek and the steep carved walls of the canyon from the bridge is picture perfect. From High Bridge, turn around and head back to your car. On a hot day when you reach the trailhead, you might want to take off your shoes and soak your weary feet in the creek before getting back in your car. The total distance for this hike is 6.6 miles, a perfect walk and a hike you will always remember.

Restrooms: There is a large restroom building on the left just after you have exited the freeway and then turned right to enter the park. You will see a large parking lot. There is also a small restroom near the trailhead. There are no facilities on the trail.

Additional information: Parking requires a U.S. Forest Service Day pass. They are available at Multnomah Falls for $5. Take your valuables with you. There are numerous car break-ins.
Plan to go early in the day before the trail gets crowded. In the fall, it is worth parking at the main restroom and then walking back toward the exit to look in the calm water at the bottom of the creek for salmon that are resting before continuing their journey to spawn.

Getting there: From Portland, take I-84 east past Multnomah Falls and then take the Eagle Creek exit. Follow the road until you get to a stop sign and turn right. Proceed as far as possible until you get to the trailhead or until you run out of parking places. When exiting the park, you can only turn east on I-84. Go to Cascade Locks and then turn around to head back to Portland.

Coming from the east, go past Eagle Creek and exit at Bonneville Dam. Then turn around and head east on I-84 until you reach the Eagle Creek exit.

near **Bridal Veil**

Multnomah Falls

Oregon has many spectacular waterfalls. One of the most visited is Multnomah Falls, situated in the beautiful Columbia River Gorge. Multnomah Falls is the tallest waterfall in Oregon and the second highest year-round waterfall in the United States. Visitors travel to the falls all year to admire the dramatic, plummeting water. The volume of water at the falls changes with the seasons. Water surges off the top of the falls during the spring run-off and occasionally freezes during icy winter blasts. Whatever the season, the view is dramatic, romantic, and just plain fun to see.

Multnomah Falls is one of the most accessible waterfalls in the state. Visitors do not need to hike miles and miles for a glimpse of the falls. In fact, the falls can be seen from I-84. For people traveling on I-84, there is a parking lot between the northbound and southbound lanes of the freeway. After parking, visitors walk a short distance under the freeway. They then carefully cross the old Columbia Gorge Highway. At this point, visitors have several choices. They may walk a short distance to see the falls. If they want a closer view, walking a short one-quarter mile path leads to the historic Benson arch bridge. At the bridge there is a great view of the falls and the pool at the base of the falls, where the water from above crashes down, sometimes creating a spray of water.

Multnomah Falls can also be the starting point for some wonderful hikes. From the Benson bridge, if you are willing to take the one-mile, fairly steep switchback trail to the top of the falls, you will be rewarded with an unforgettable view. Standing at the top of the falls, you will see the water as it plunges from its creek bed over the edge to the waiting pool far below. From this height, the people and cars below look like miniature ants and toys. Hear the rushing water as it cascades down the cliff and spend some alone time at the top of the falls, sitting by the creek, just relaxing or reading.

If you are even more adventurous, there are several trails that continue from the top of the falls. I especially like the trail that goes from the top of Multnomah Falls through the woods over to Wahkeena Falls. The walk is wonderful in itself. As a bonus, you will be able to experience Wahkeena Falls on your way back to the base of the cliffs. From the bottom of

Wahkeena Falls, it is a short walk back to Multnomah Falls.
There are lots of things to see and do at Multnomah Fall's historic day use lodge. It houses a visitor center with lots of information about the area. You will find detailed maps to help you plan out a hike. There is a gift store with souvenirs. The restaurant at the lodge serves breakfast, lunch, and dinner. Outside, there is a concession booth that sells snacks, including Alpenrose soft-serve ice cream for $3.25. Enjoying an ice cream cone while admiring the falls will be a memory you remember long after your trip.

Address:	50000 Historic Columbia River Hwy, Bridal Veil, OR 97010
Phone:	503-695-2376
Web:	**www.multnomahfallslodge.com**
Hours:	Winter: Monday-Thursday 10 a.m.-6 p.m., Friday 10 a.m.-8 p.m., Saturday 8 a.m.-8 p.m., Sunday 8 a.m.-6 p.m. Summer: May 1-November 1, 8 a.m.-9 p.m., seven days a week
Ice Cream Concession:	Summer: 8 a.m.-9 p.m. Winter: 10 a.m.-4 p.m.
Restrooms:	ADA accessible
Additional information:	A lovely alternate route to Multnomah Falls is to take the Historic Columbia River Highway. Coming from Portland on I-84, take Exit 17 toward Troutdale or Exit 22 at Corbett and follow the signs. You will drive by Crown Point. From this spot you will have wonderful photo opportunities for dramatic views of the Gorge. Then you will pass eight waterfalls, including Multnomah Falls, before getting back on I-84 at Exit 35 for a speedier trip home.

near **Hood River**

Hood River Fruit Loop

When the fall air is as crisp as a newly picked apple, it's time to head out to the Columbia River Gorge and Hood River. Plan to make a day of it. Take a leisurely drive around the 35-mile Hood River Fruit Loop. The road winds through orchards of pears, apples, peaches, and cherries with many stands along the way where you can buy fresh produce. Fruit wines are available for tasting. Scenic spots for picnicking are numerous. Fields of colorful dahlias, lavender, and other fresh flowers are a delight for the eyes. Mt. Hood and Mt. Adams stand in the background, making the scene picture perfect for snapshots.

Since 1992, over 30 of the growers in the Hood River area have banded together to promote the area as a scenic destination. A map of the loop is available at many of the sites. Take your time and stop and explore. Whether you are just out for a drive or you want the freshest pickings right out of the orchard, the Fruit Loop has something for everyone. Look for special events that take place often during the summer and early fall.

Address: PO Box 168, Odell, OR 97044
Phone: 541-386-7697
Email: info@hoodriverfruitloop.com
Hours: Times vary by season.
Restrooms: Restrooms vary by site.
Getting there: Hood River is about 1 hour east of Portland on I-84. Take Exit 63 or 64 and follow signs to Hwy 35. Look for Fruit Loop signs along the way.

Windsurfing and Kiteboarding

Windsurfers and kiteboarders from around the world travel to Hood River each year to experience the thrilling water sport opportunities here on the Columbia River. The Columbia Gorge winds provide some of the best and most consistent wind conditions for Pacific Northwest windsurfing and kiteboarding enthusiasts.

From spring through early fall, and especially on sunny afternoons when the wind picks up speed, it is not unusual to see several hundred kites and sails flying back and forth across the river.

Whether you are an experienced sailor or you want to watch some exciting turns and launches into mid-air, take a few minutes to enjoy this spectator sport. Drive to the parking lot on the north side of the freeway at Exit 63. Park and walk to the beach where the windsurfers and kiteboarders lay out their equipment on the lawn. Try to pick a place where you won't get bonked on the head by a board or sail. Then, sit back, relax, and enjoy the action. This is a great place to take action photo shots. It is also perfect for a summer picnic.

Restrooms: ADA accessible
Getting there: Hood River is about 1 hour east of Portland on I-84. Take Exit 63.

La Grande

Eastern Oregon Fire Museum & Learning Center

Spend just 30 minutes strolling through the part of a converted firehouse that now houses the Eastern Oregon Fire Museum and you'll appreciate how far fire fighting has advanced since the late 1800s when destructive out-of-control fires regularly caused significant property damage in western towns like La Grande. Check out the vintage fire trucks that are being restored at the museum. Look at exhibits that mark the evolution in fire fighting equipment as it has changed over the years. When you get home, you will be motivated to check your smoke alarms!

Besides fire memorabilia, a section of the museum is dedicated to La Grande's law enforcement officers. An old-time sign shows fines for such infractions as public spitting, disorderly conduct, and more. Talk about getting tough on crime!

Address: 102 Elm St., La Grande, OR 97850
Web: www.oregonmuseums.org
Hours: By appointment only. Call 541-963-8588 to schedule a tour.
Admission: FREE
Restrooms: ADA accessible

Pendleton

Charmin' Pendleton

What a great idea! Stop by one of two "trailheads" in Pendleton, either the Chamber of Commerce or Shari's Restaurant. Purchase an inexpensive starter charm bracelet for $1 or buy one that comes with a signature charm for $5. While you are at a trailhead, also pick up a free charm map. Then follow the map to any or all of 40+ participating businesses in Pendleton. The map shows pictures of the charms you will find at each stop. At each marked location, you can buy that store's pewter charm(s) to add to your bracelet for $1.50. Most stores have chosen a charm that is somehow associated with their business.

Even without the map, participating businesses can be spotted by the bright yellow placards near their doors. Each placard has a number that indicates that particular store's number on the charm trail. Visit as many or few of the stores as suits your fancy. Dress up your bracelet, and leave town with a cute, inexpensive souvenir to remind yourself of all the fun places and attractions you saw on your trip to charmin' Pendleton.

Trailheads: Pendleton Chamber of Commerce
501 S Main St., Pendleton, OR 97801-2261
541-276-7411 or 1-800-547-8911
Open Monday-Thursday 8:30 a.m.-5 p.m.,
Friday, 10 a.m.-5 p.m., and summer Saturdays,
10 a.m.-5 p.m.

Shari's Restaurant (at Exit 210)
319 SE Nye Ave, Pendleton, OR 97801
541-966-9009
Open 24 hours a day

Correction Connection

The image of prisoners hammering out license plate numbers as a way of vocational training always seemed a little weird to me. I mean how transferable is that skill? How can you add it to your resume without being obvious that you were in the slammer? Can you really write under work experience, "Pounded out matching pairs of one of a kind works of arts for car bumpers, no two sets alike" without potential employers saying, "Hey, I think this guy (or gal) has done a little time."

In 1994, Oregon voters passed a law that all inmates must be employed or in a training program while they are behind bars. The idea was to change the public's image of prisoners lazing around all day watching television, playing cards, and eating three meals at the taxpayer's expense. The public wanted prisoners to do work that would help offset the cost of their time in jail. At the same time voters wanted to provide meaningful work or training that prisoners could use once they were released from prison.

From this thread of thought Prison Blues came to life. Inmates at the Eastern Oregon Correctional Institution in Pendleton learn to make tough, rugged blue jeans that will last a long time. They also screen-print t-shirts with novel designs. The Correction Connection in Pendleton is a stylish shop on Main Street where you can buy Prison Blues merchandise and support the program. Besides the jeans and t-shirts, there are well-made jean jackets and other attire that are all reasonably priced. Most have the motto "Made on the inside to be worn on the outside" somewhere on the product. The Correction Connection is also the place to go to learn about early Pendleton law enforcement. Notice the posters and framed news articles on the walls. You will find a picture of Til Taylor, the first sheriff of Pendleton. Read about his murder and the hangings that followed.

What do the inmates get out of this? Besides learning a trade, they are paid "prevailing industry wages"; then, 80% of their earnings are deducted and go to pay for restitution, incarceration costs, taxes, and child support. The other 20% is given to the inmate for personal expenses at the prison canteen, to help pay family expenses, or to put in a trust fund that prisoners can draw from when they are released from prison.

So this is a win-win opportunity. You can buy some great jeans that may last longer than a life sentence, and the inmates can get some of their life back before the end of their sentence.

Address: 363 S Main St., Pendleton, OR 97801
Phone: 541-276-1169
Web: www.correctionconnectionprisonblues.com
Hours: Monday-Saturday 10 a.m.-5:30 p.m.
Getting there: Correction Connection is located in old town Pendleton on Main Street. Driving from Portland on I-84, take Exit 207 and head toward downtown.

Coming from LaGrande on I-84, take Exit 213 and head to downtown.

Hamley and Company

For cowboy duds, check out Hamley in Pendleton. Stylish fashions fit for rodeo queens and bronc riders are all nicely displayed in this high-end store. Whether you need a hat for the Pendleton Round-Up, a nice new pair of boots to kick around in, a beautifully tooled leather belt, a flashy belt buckle, or you just want to admire fine Western craftsmanship, Hamley is the place to go. Besides clothing, Hamley also carries a variety of jewelry, leather goods, and gifts that are unique and would make wonderful souvenirs of your trip.

One room in Hamley is filled with saddles and horse gear that will impress the horseman and tenderfoot alike. Hamley is famous for their handmade saddles. They show superb craftsmanship and are works of art. So whether you are in the mood to browse or buy, a trip to Hamley and Company is definitely worth a stop on your trip to Pendleton.

Address: 30 SE Court, Pendleton, OR 97801
Phone: 541-278-1100
Web: www.hamleyco.com
Hours: Monday-Thursday 9 a.m.-6 p.m.,
Friday-Saturday 9 a.m.-8 p.m.,
Sunday noon-6 p.m.

Pendleton Woolen Mill

Pendleton Woolen Mill is a sixth-generation, family-owned Oregon company famous for beautiful woolen blankets and apparel that are sold around the world. The Pendleton Woolen brand is especially known for its warm wool shirts for men, woolen outfits for women, and unique Indian trading blankets. The looms at the Pendleton location make high-quality, intricately patterned jacquard blankets. The blankets are so durable they often become family heirlooms. I love both the colorful Indian blankets and the more muted original designs created for some of the United State's national parks.

Stop by the mill in Pendleton. See the full line of Pendleton Woolen goods for sale in the showroom. Also browse for discounts in the blanket outlet. Visit the Pendleton Private Collection of Indian artifacts. Take the 20-minute tour of the factory. Tours start at 9 a.m., 11 a.m., 1:30 p.m., and 3 p.m. Reservations are not required, but the tours fill up on a first-come basis.

Address:	1307 SE Court Place, Pendleton, OR 97801
Phone:	541-276-6911
Hours:	Monday-Saturday 8 a.m.-6 p.m., Sunday 9 a.m.-5 p.m.
Restrooms:	ADA restroom

Pendleton Underground Tour

Take a walk to the wild side of Pendleton's colorful, not that distant, past on the 90-minute Pendleton Underground Tour. The guides are great storytellers who will regale you with tales of cowboys, ladies of the night, and the Chinese baths that cowboys took before they visited the ladies. As you stroll along the tour, you'll hear stories of the illegal moonshine, mayhem, and gambling that were all part of the underworld world in Pendleton until the 1930s. See where Chinese laborers lived and worked underground. Visit Hop Sing's Chinese laundry. See an opium den and secret passages that were used during raids. Visit a meat market (the kind where they actually sold meat.). Believe it or not, there was even an underground ice cream parlor. Talk about decadent!

Then you will visit the "Cozy Room" bordello, a second-story establishment in downtown Pendleton that was open for business until 1953. Visit Miss Stella's private living quarters and the rooms where her girls worked and lived. There is even a chapel.

When you get back to the beginning of the tour, go to the room that adjoins the gift shop and watch the video of Duff Severe, one of the finest saddlemakers in the country, who lived and worked in Pendleton. Listen to him tell his life story. On display near the video is a darling set of miniature saddles that Severe made. The workmanship is exquisite.

The Pendleton Underground Tour will be one of the highlights of your trip to Pendleton. It is a glimpse of history that your history book left out.

....

Address: 37 SW Emigrant, Pendleton, OR 97801
Phone: 541-276-0730 or 1-800-226-6398
Hours: Open all year. Call for current times and reservations.
Admission: $15-20/person

Additional information: Because of the stairs and the few places of uneven ground, the tour is not suitable for people in wheelchairs. Once a year, the mannequins in the underground tour are replaced by over 75 actors who bring the place to life. What a wild tour that must be! The regular tour is for all ages over 6. The once-a-year tour is for ages 16 and up.

Section 4
Off the Beaten I-84 Track

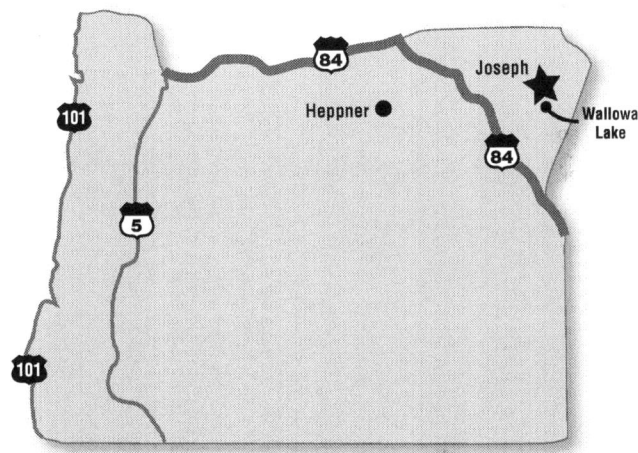

Wallowa Lake Tram

Off the Beaten I-84 Track

Ice Cream

Heppner

Sweet Productions Ice Cream Parlor & Diner

Heppner is off the beaten track, about a 45-minute drive from the Heppner exit on I-84. Its biggest claim to fame is that it was almost wiped off the map by a flood in May 1903 that killed about 200 people who were taken by complete surprise by a wall of water that surged through town. Heppner is also the county seat for Morrow County. The county courthouse is the most photographed courthouse in the state. On St. Patrick's Day, the town of Heppner, population 1200, swells with between 3000 and 5000 participants who come for the annual festivities celebrated in this Irish stronghold. Heppner is also home to the Morrow County Agricultural Museum.

On Main Street you will find Sweet Productions Ice Cream Parlor & Diner. The diner is tucked in a corner of an antique and gift store and is decorated in a retro style that will take you back to the '50s. Black, red, and white checked floor, decor, and jukebox all add to the nostalgia.

Jodi Chapa, the owner of Sweet Productions, is also the best cake maker in town. She loves to bake cakes for special occasions. Customers come to the diner for the fresh, moderately priced food and ice cream treats. Tillamook ice cream cones are $1.50. Waffle cones are $3.25. Sundaes start at $3. For something different, try the $4 Pink Elephant, which actually looks like a pink elephant! It is made with a blend of strawberry soda over Tillamook strawberry ice cream, a pink wafer cookie, a cherry eye, and a whipped cream face and trunk. For the sporting crowd, take the challenge and see how fast your group of 1-10 people can eat the Brain-Freeze, priced at $21.25. It comes with 15 scoops of ice cream, banana slices, cookies, four different toppings, sprinkles, Hershey kisses, and cherries. The record time so far, as indicated on the wall of fame, is 9 kids who polished one off in 3 minutes and 7 seconds.

Whether you stop at Sweet Productions for lunch or an ice cream treat, you will be impressed by this ice cream oasis surrounded by a sea of farm country. Oh, and by the way, a cup of black coffee here costs 50 cents. Where can you beat that?

....

Address: 233 N. Main St., Heppner, OR 97836
Mailing Address: P.O. Box 1104, Heppner, OR 97836
Phone: 541-676-8022
Web: www.sweetproductions.homestead.com
Hours: Monday-Friday 8:30 a.m.-5:30 p.m.,
Saturday 9:30 a.m.-3 p.m.,
Closed Sunday and most holidays
Restrooms: ADA accessible

FUN FACT

What percentage of American households purchase ice cream?

90% of American households purchase ice cream. Americans are the largest per capita ice cream eaters in the world.

Joseph

Mad Mary's Soda Shop

"You must be crazy to do this," said Mary Burn's family. She had just announced she was going to open a gift store/soda fountain in a large building on Main Street in Joseph. From that comment, the store got its name, Mad Mary and Company.

The ice cream parlor is a wonderful find. It looks the part, bright and cheery in red, white, black, and chrome. Sparkling clear glass ice cream dishes are lined up behind the long counter. In front of the counter is a row of red stools, just waiting for ice cream lovers to come and place their orders. Several tables for two to four people complete the seating arrangements.

The menu has a variety of breakfast and lunch items, from omelets and waffles, to Crabby Mary's crab salad and turkey-lurkey sandwiches. Mary's also serves old-fashioned flavored colas, in either cherry, chocolate, or vanilla flavor for $2.50. Mary's serves 5 flavors of Cascade Glacier ice cream. One scoop in a cone or dish is $1.95. The Mad Mary is just one of several specialty sundaes. It comes with eight BIG scoops of ice cream, hot fudge, caramel, Oreos, cookies, whipped cream, and a cherry, all for $9.95.

Mad Mary's has the distinction of being the ice cream shop that opens the earliest in the state for ice cream! So whether you just need a break from window-shopping, a pick-me-up from hiking, or just a plain old ice cream fix, Mad Mary's is the place to go in Joseph.

Address:	5 S. Main St., P.O. Box 199, Joseph, OR 97846
Phone:	541-432-0547
Web:	www.madmaryandcompany.com
Hours:	7 a.m.-6 p.m. daily except four winter holidays. January and February the soda shop closes at 5 p.m.
Restrooms:	ADA accessible
Additional information:	The gift shop opens at 9 a.m.

Off the Beaten I-84 Track
Things to See and Do

Joseph

Valley Bronze of Oregon

Have you ever wondered who makes those huge bronze monuments that honor fallen heroes, mark important historical events, and guide us to the entrances of museums and other important landmarks? Have you ever wondered how people build such amazing works of art that endure and inspire us long after the artists are gone? Believe it or not, Joseph, Oregon, a small rural town smack dab in the middle of cowboy country in northeastern Oregon, a place that could be voted "most unlikely place to find a bronze foundry," in fact has two foundries. The original foundry, started in 1982, is called Valley Bronze of Oregon. They have an art gallery in Joseph that includes an eclectic assortment of small bronze sculptures for homes and businesses to suit a variety of tastes.

For a real treat, sign up for the 90-minute foundry tour. It starts at the gallery in Joseph. Come early so you can browse the gallery at your leisure. The tour starts with a short video describing the process of casting, from the artist's original sculpture, often done in clay or wax, to the final product. Visitors then take their cars and travel about a half mile away to see the foundry itself. Guests are led from room to room where they have a first-hand look at how each step of the process works. Visitors will see a variety of art pieces in different stages of completion. Finally, the tour stops for a visit to the monument room where the HUGE monuments are made, just like the smaller ones, but on a gargantuan scale. They are magnificent. Your appreciation for bronze sculptures will skyrocket. Your tour will become an unforgettable part of your vacation!

Address: 018 S Main St., P.O. Box 669, Joseph, OR 97846
Phone: 541-432-7445
Web: www.valleybronze.com
Hours: Gallery hours Monday-Saturday 10 a.m.-5 p.m. For tours, call for exact dates and times.
Admission: FREE gallery. The foundry tour is $15/person.
Restrooms: ADA accessible in the gallery. Difficult access on the foundry tour.
Getting there: The gallery is in the heart of downtown Joseph on Main Street.

Your Country Store

I like tin signs. I don't know why. Maybe it is the nostalgia. Maybe it is the art. Whatever it is, I was delighted when I discovered Your Country Store in downtown Joseph. It is filled with over 700 tin signs, thanks to the owner, John Dundas. John and his wife opened this store in 2004 as a way to fill in some of their retirement time. When they were first finding stock for the store, John's wife told him to go out and find some "guy gifts" for the new gift store. He settled on tin signs. Six years later they are busier than they want to be, but people love the tin signs and other interesting gift ideas in the store. They also carry some "BLT," bath, linens, and towels, the previous owner's specialty. John is now adding books to the store's inventory, a sure way to attract more customers. It is the tin signs that will keep me going back though. From Western signs to commercial signs and Saturday Evening Post replicas, they are all fun to see. As for me, I bought the one with an ice cream sundae that says "Hot Fudge."

Address: 017 S. Main St., Joseph, OR 97846
Phone: 541-432-2031
Email: highland80@juno.com
Hours: Monday-Saturday 10 a.m.-5 p.m.

at Wallowa Lake

Wallowa Lake

Wallowa Lake, nestled in northeastern Oregon at the foot of the rugged Eagle Cap Wilderness area, is a great spot for a summer family get-away. There are plenty of activities to keep both kids and adults entertained for days. The lake itself is a boater's playground. Paddle boats, canoes, kayaks, rowboats, and motorized boats can all be rented at the marina adjacent to the state park during the summer. Swimming in the lake is delightful on a hot day. The lake is also a fisherman's paradise, being the home of Kokanee salmon, a landlocked salmon that never goes to the ocean but instead lives its life in the lake. The fish eventually migrate up a small creek that feeds into the lake to spawn. In the summer of 2010, a world record 9.67-pound Kokanee was caught in Wallowa Lake.

At the east end of the lake, lodging is available for all kinds of travelers. For the budget-minded, the state park has room for RVs, trailers, and tents. There are even a couple of yurts for rent. (Reservations should be made in advance for summer travel because the state park and other lodging can fill up fast.) Outside the state park are commercially owned cottages, inns, and cabins for rent at a range of prices.

Near the lodging are a variety of commercial, crowd-pleasing activities. Go-karts, bumper boats, miniature golf, horseback riding, a tram ride to the top Mt. Howard, and parasailing on Wallowa Lake are all offered during the summer months. Of course, there are also snack shops, souvenir stores, and restaurants, shuffled in amongst the other shops to lure in the tourist.

The top of Mt. Howard is the launch site for paragliders, who take the tram to the top of the mountain and then glide to the bottom, landing near the state park.

Wallowa State Park:	www.oregonstateparks.org/park_27.php or call 503-986-0707.
Wallowa Lake Marina:	www.wallowalakemarina.com or call 541-432-9115
Wallowa Lake Tramway:	www.wallowalaketramway.com/summer.htm or call 541-432-5331

Eagle Cap Parasailing: www.wallowalakeparasailing.com or call 541-432-1214

Eagle Cap Wilderness Pack Station: www.eaglecapwildernesspackstation.com or call 541-432-4145 or emailgorbett4@msn.com

Watch Kokanee Salmon Spawn

After Labor Day, most of the summer tourists have packed their bags and gone home. The kids have started a new year of school. Many of the seasonal tourist attractions at Wallowa Lake have tidied up and latched their doors, marking the end of the summer season. The air now has a cool nip in the morning and the light filters through the trees at just a slightly different angle than during summer. The vegetation begins to turn the colors of Fall. It is getting quieter.

Then, magically almost, the landlocked Kokanee salmon begin to leave Wallowa Lake and swim upstream into the small, almost empty river that flows toward the Eagle Cap Wilderness Area. Not all the Kokanee, of course, but hundreds of those who have heard the call of nature. It is not an easy paddle upstream for these single-focused creatures. Once they get the urge, they struggle over rocks and boulders, straining against the river's current. They rest in quiet pools before summoning the strength to continue their journey. Sometimes the fish, who turn bright orange with a gray head for this final trip, seem to shimmy their way up the stream with buddies, silently cheering each other on as they are compelled to continue up, up, up the river. When they can no longer fight their way upstream, exhausted, they make peace with the river, lay their eggs, and then die, leaving their worldly body to rot and become food for their unborn young. Their eggs will soon hatch and, nourished by their parents, continue the lifecycle by swimming back into the lake to enjoy their short life of freedom.

Even if you have the good fortune to be at the lake at the right time of year it is easy to miss this marvel of nature. I almost missed it. The fish are driven, but the process is quiet. Incredibly quiet. I saw a few people standing on a small bridge just before the entrance to the state park. I thought they were just taking pictures of the Fall stream. I overheard two people talking about seeing the Kokanee, and that is the only reason I knew to walk to the bridge. Peering down, I was amazed to discover that they were orange, as bright as goldfish. During their life in the lake they are normally a more subdued fresh water "fish" color.

I decided I wanted to get an even closer look so I walked through the state park day use area and began climbing over rocks and across sandbars that had once been part of the stream during the surging spring waters. Now the water was just a trickle. I found a place where there was a quiet pool of water with Kokanee barely moving, resting for the next part of their one-way journey. Some of the fish were little, not much bigger than six inches, while many were around a foot long. I understood the bigger fish spawning. A world record Kokanee had been caught earlier this summer that weighed in at 9.67 pounds. Why would the little ones spawn when they were so small? As they struggled right along with their bigger brethren I wanted to tell them, "Go back! Go back! It isn't time for you yet. You are too small." Still they continued upstream. For these little guys there was no turning back.

In another pool I found a dead Kokanee, lying on the bottom, being rocked by the current, looking gray and utterly spent. At the surface of the pool there was a six-inch fish, much browner than the rest, circling and taking little nips of air. Was he deciding whether to join the others or not? He wasn't like the others. He had not changed colors. I watched for a long time. It almost looked like he was turning orange in front of my eyes, but maybe it was just the sunlight flashing across his back. Around and around he went. Deciding, deciding. Did he really have a choice? Had he accidentally followed other fish up the stream? Was he curious? What happened to him, you may ask. I don't know, because I turned away. I felt like an intruder. I continued my walk on up the river. I watched others Kokanee swim. I cheered a few on. I felt bad for the ones who perished. Mostly I was awed by the power of nature I had witnessed. It makes you feel small, seeing a phenomena this big, a species silently fighting for its survival. I came away with a new reverence for nature.

When: After Labor Day
Where: The stream that flows out of Wallowa Lake near the State Park.
What time of day: This event seems to continue throughout the day.

Wallowa Lake Tramway

Gliding to the top of Mt. Howard from the base of Wallowa Lake, I wondered if this is how if felt to float to heaven. The gondola slowly ascended on the 15-minute ride to the top, and the scenery just kept getting better and better. Peeking down through the trees below, I hoped I would spot a deer or other wildlife. No luck on this trip.

At the summit of Mt. Howard, the tram ends. Visitors can get off and take their time roaming around on several short trails that each end in a spectacular view. Whether you stop to admire the acres and acres of multi-colored quilted farmland below, or the rough and rugged Eagle Cap Wilderness Area, the sights are well worth the journey to the top. In fact, standing on any of the overlooks, you feel like you're on top of the world. The air is thinner and the light seems brighter. The alpine plants and vegetation are worth getting down on your hands and knees for an even closer look. It is a wonder of nature they can survive such harsh conditions. The chipmunks along the trails will entertain you as they pester you for chipmunk treats you can buy in the restaurant at the summit.

Then after hiking, oohing and aahing, stop for a bite to eat at the summit restaurant before riding the tram back down to the bottom of the mountain. You will come to realize why Wallowa Lake Tramway was voted "Best Views in Oregon" by Oregon magazine.

Address:	59919 Wallowa Lake Hwy, Joseph, OR 97846
Phone:	541-432-5331 (summer)
	503-781-4321 (winter)
Web:	**www.wallowalaketramway.com**
Email:	info@wallowalaketramway.com
Hours:	Open mid-May-September 10 a.m.-last ride down at 4:30 p.m. Call for specific times early and late in season.
Admission:	Go to Web for current prices
Restrooms:	ADA accessible port-a-potties
Getting there:	Wallowa Lake Tramway is about one-half mile past the entrance to Wallowa State Park.

Section 5
I-5 Freeway

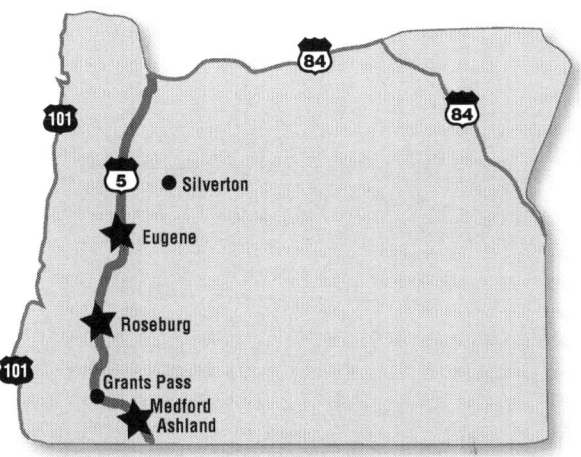

Ashland 4th of July

I-5 Freeway
Ice Cream

Ashland

Zoey's Cafe

Located on the main street in Ashland, Zoey's Cafe features 40 flavors of B.J.'s all natural homemade Oregon ice cream. The cafe is in a perfect location for a restful break after window-shopping, a walk through Lithia Park, or before (or after) seeing a play at one of three nearby Shakespeare Festival theaters.

Ice cream cones and cups are sold by the ounce. The smallest serving size is a junior scoop (4 oz.), costing $2.29 and the largest scoop is called a triple (16 oz.) and costs $4.99. For a waffle cone, add 50 cents. Milkshakes are $4.99, malts are $5.50, and floats are $3.50. If you are in the mood for a sundae, Zoey's offers six different toppings. A small sundae costs $4.50 while the largest sundae on the menu, a large banana split, costs $7.99.

Also on the menu are breakfast and lunch items. Breakfast croissants, tropical fruit oatmeal, and a selection of bagels are all reasonably priced from $2.50-$5.00. Lunch is served until 3 p.m. and menu items include homemade calzones, croissant sandwiches, foccacia sandwiches, wraps, and more from $5.00-$7.00. Soups and salads help round out the menu. Not included in the price of menu items is Ashland's 5% sales tax.

Address:	199 E. Main St., Ashland, OR 97520
Phone:	541-482-4794
Hours:	(On all days, lunch is served until 3 p.m. During the summer, ice cream is available until midnight.) Monday-Thursday 8 a.m.-4 p.m., Friday-Saturday 8 a.m.-10 p.m., Sunday 8 a.m.-5 p.m.
Restrooms:	ADA accessible
Other Information:	Zoey's does NOT accept checks, American Express, or Discover cards. There is a $3 minimum on credit cards.

Eugene

Prince Pückler's Ice Cream

No book about Oregon ice cream would be complete without including Eugene's regal Prince Pückler's Ice Cream. A Eugene icon since 1975, the brand was introduced to Oregon by Jim Robertson. Robertson learned to make ice cream after a two-week internship in San Francisco at Bud's Ice Cream Shop. He paid Bud for the right to use the recipes and then opened up a scoop shop with 30+ flavors in the Atrium building in Eugene. In 1976 Prince Pückler's loaded up their tubs of ice cream and moved across the street from their current location. In the mid-1980s, they moved into the corner shop on 19th Street they have called home ever since. All the ice cream is made a short distance away in a Eugene warehouse.

Prince Pückler's now serves 40 flavors fit for royalty, using an ice cream base especially made for them by Lochmead Dairy. Prince Pückler's is a chocolate-lover's paradise. Their Bittersweet Nugget contains a dark chocolate with chocolate chips. One of my favorites, Galaxy, is a combination of chocolate malt ice cream with white and semi-sweet chocolate chips. It really is out of this world! Robertson suggests that if customers want to try one flavor that best shows off the Prince Pückler's brand, choose Chocolate Lover's Chocolate.

Prince Pückler's also serves lots of non-chocolate ice cream flavors. Oregon Chai ice cream and Green Tea ice cream are two of the more unusual flavors. Try Fresh Banana or White Licorice ice cream. Eight, that's right, eight flavors of coffee ice cream are available daily. There are also many sorbets and frozen yogurt flavors available at the shop.

A single cone or dish of this fabulous ice cream is $2.85. For a waffle cone, add 40 cents. A single scoop sundae is $3.65 and includes bananas, almonds, whipped cream, and a topping. Single scoop milkshakes are $3. A banana split is $5.75. Prince Pückler's offers weekly specials. Hot fudge sundaes are $2.95 on Tuesdays. Sundaes with delicious Euphoria chocolate are $3.25 on Fridays.

It isn't every ice cream store that can boast that the President of the United States stopped by for ice cream, but that is exactly what happened at Prince Pückler's. President and Mrs. Obama stopped at Prince Pückler's when they were campaigning for the presidency in Oregon. The President's choice? Mint Chocolate Chip. It is now the #1 seller at the store. Pictures from the President's stop are proudly displayed on the walls of Prince Pückler's.

The wonderful, medieval-looking fellow that proudly serves as the Prince Pückler logo was drawn by Tom Kelly, a Eugene artist. Prince Pückler's is named in honor of Prince Hermann Ludwig Heinrich von Pückler-Muskau, a German nobleman who lived from 1785-1871. A German dessert called Furst-Pückler-Eis (Prince Pückler ice cream) was named after him. The dessert is similar to Neapolitan ice cream, which consists of three distinct layers of ice cream: vanilla, strawberry, and chocolate.

Address: 1605 E 19th St., Eugene, OR 97403
Phone: 541-344-4418
Web: **www.princepucklers.com**
Hours: Daily noon-11 p.m. (except some holidays)
Restrooms: Not ADA accessible

History of Oregon Ice Cream Company

Tom and Julie Gleason purchased a small ice creamery called Dutch Girl Ice Cream in 1996. Located in Eugene, the Dutch Girl brand had been in business since 1938, making Super Creamed Ice Cream. The Gleasons changed the name of the company to Oregon Ice Cream.

But Tom kept finding another brand of ice cream in their home freezer. When he asked Julie why they were not eating their own brand, she said the family favorite was another national brand. Tom decided they needed to change their product. So, Tom, Julie and their team set out to create a whole new kind of ice cream. Well before organic products became popular, the Gleasons and their team created Julie's Organic Ice Cream, and Julie's has been churning out 14 flavors of organic ice cream since 1999. Today the Julie's Organic label can be found on a variety of sorbets, yogurts, and ice cream sandwiches. New gluten-free ice cream flavors will be added to their expanding line of gluten-free products.

Then the Gleasons noticed that their youngest son Alden LOVED milkshakes. The pint-sized containers really did not have enough ice cream to make several milkshakes. They asked Alden to pick his four favorite flavors and Alden's brand ice cream was born. Alden picked Chocolate Chocolate Chip, Vanilla, Strawberry, and Cookies and Cream. The Alden's Natural and Organic ice cream brand now includes 10 flavors. Alden's ice cream is a little softer than other brands so it is more easily scooped. The consistency is perfect for making milkshakes. It also has fewer calories than Julie's ice cream, a good thing for weight-conscious teenagers. Since 2006, Alden's Natural and Organic ice cream comes in a 48-oz family-friendly container called a "scround." The unique shape allows for easier scooping without getting messy hands in the process. The carton is rectangular with rounded vertical corners.

Like many Oregon ice creameries, the Oregon Ice Cream Company has become a family affair. Alden has been the resident Internet expert at Oregon Ice Cream since he was a youngster. Marilyn Lasseigne, the company's PR director, remembers picking Alden up from school when he was in grade school so he could come fix a problem with one of the company computers. Today, Alden manages the IT department. He is also responsible for security procedures, and he manages communications for the company, using the latest technology. The Gleason's oldest son, Jerrad, also works for the company.

You can find both Julie's Organic Ice Cream and Alden's Natural and Organic ice cream in many retail outlets in Oregon. Julie's Organic Ice Cream products are now sold nationwide and in several foreign countries.

Oregon Ice Cream also makes the Cascade Glacier brand. It is only available at scoop shops. It comes in 88 different flavors and is sold to scoop shops in three-gallon containers. Cascade Glacier has some unique flavors. One of the new flavors is called Beachcomber and has "pop rocks" in it for a mouthful of popping energy. Some of Cascade Glacier ice creams come in vivid, wild colors that especially appeal to kids.

The Oregon Ice Cream Company also works with private labels, making the private stock on their equipment to the private label's specifications. Well-known Ciao Bella and Jamba Juice products are made at the Oregon Ice Cream Company. Happily, I found out that Oregon Ice Cream makes the ice cream bars for Costco. At $1.50 for a humongous ice cream bar dipped in chocolate and then smothered in almonds, it is the best deal for an ice cream bar anywhere.

What is the future of Oregon Ice Cream? With Cascade Glacier in scoop shops, Julie's Organic and Alden's in retail stores, and a creative staff that is always looking for the next niche in the ice cream market, Oregon Ice Cream is destined to remain a major player in the ice cream market. Their products can already be found in many parts of the United States. They employ over 200 people. They strive to use local ingredients, grown right here in Oregon. We should all thank our lucky scoops that Tom and Julie Gleason chose to get into the ice cream business.

FUN FACT

Quality

Oregon ranks nationally in the top 5 states for milk quality.

Grants Pass

Grants Pass Pharmacy

Coffee for 10 cents and old-fashioned phosphates for a quarter? Yes, it is still true today at the Grants Pass Pharmacy, going strong since 1933. It continues to serve great food at reasonable prices. With 16 flavors of Umpqua ice cream, and featuring the pharmacy's original bar and fridge, the soda fountain is the centerpiece of this working pharmacy and gift store. Regulars stop by for their prescriptions and a little something from the affordable list of food and ice cream treats. The price to eat at the counter is slightly cheaper than if food or drink is ordered "to go." If you are in the mood for lunch, ten sandwiches are on the menu, from peanut butter and jelly ($2.95) to egg salad ($3.50) to tuna deluxe ($4.95) and beyond. Hot dogs are $1.25. The soup of the day is $2.50. Hot cocoa, tea, and milk are available for $.75. One-scoop sundaes, covered with one of six different toppings is $2.50, while a two-scoop sundae is $3. Ask for "the works" and for 25 cents extra, whipped cream, nuts, and a cherry can be added to the sundae. Banana splits are $4.50. Do you just want an ice cream cone or dish? One scoop is $1.25 and two scoops are $2. Ice cream floats and ice cream sodas are each $2.25. Try a milk shake for $3.25. Add malt for 25 cents. With these prices and locals raving about the food, the Grants Pass Pharmacy will surely continue to attract customers for a long time to come.

....

Address:	414 SW 6th St., Grants Pass, OR 97526
Phone:	541-476-4262
Hours of soda fountain:	11 a.m.-3 p.m. daily
Restrooms:	ADA accessible

Jacksonville

Bella Union Restaurant and Saloon

Mama mia, this restaurant has some great pizzas, but better yet, my oh my, it has WONDERFUL mud pie, that heavenly combination of Oreo cookie crust, Umpqua Espresso Madness ice cream, hot fudge, and whipped cream. Friends and family will want to share with you. In fact, they may think they are doing you a favor by helping you eat it, so never let them know that as you smile across the table, you are secretly thinking of stabbing them with your fork so you can have it all to yourself. Yes, it really is that good, and worth the $5.95 per slice. There is lots of good food here at Bella Union and there are other desserts available, but I stick by their mud pie!

The Bella Union is located in Jacksonville, a town that is listed as a National Historic Landmark Community. With many original brick and wooden buildings preserved from the 1850s, it is a very cute town to explore and work off the calories of the mud pie. The architecture is impressive and the stores are great for browsing. Jacksonville is also home to the Britt Festival, a series of musical events that take place in an outdoor venue under the stars during the summer. Jacksonville is well worth a stop on any vacation to southern Oregon.

Address:	170 W. California St., Jacksonville, OR 97530
Phone:	541-899-1770
Web:	www.bellau.com
Hours:	Lunch Monday-Saturday 11:30 a.m.-4 p.m., dinner nightly 4 p.m.-10 p.m. Sunday Brunch 10 a.m.-2 p.m. Lounge open every night until midnight
Restrooms:	ADA accessible. There is a ramp that enters the restaurant. However, it opens into a banquet room that is sometimes in use so please call ahead to make sure it is usable.

Junction City

History of Lochmead Dairy

One of the new trends in food consumption today is to buy and eat locally grown products. Lochmead Dairy has been a leader of this movement even before it became the popular thing to do. Starting in 1941, Howard and Gladys Gibson purchased 120 acres of farmland near Junction City. Howard's father, H. H. Gibson, who was a vocational agricultural teacher at Oregon State University at the time, helped his son with financing for the new farm. Soon after purchasing the land, Howard and Gladys bought 100 Holstein milk cows and started a dairy. They raised five children on the farm. As they grew to adulthood, each was given the opportunity to join the family business. Four of the children accepted the invitation.

Today, the Lochmead Dairy is a fourth-generation, family-owned and family-operated farm. Mike Gibson takes care of the farm. Jock runs the bottling plant. Buzz Gibson oversees the dairy operation. Since the 1980s, Pat and her husband Gary have managed the company's 44 Dari-Mart Convenience stores that are scattered around the Junction City, Eugene, and Corvallis areas. At Dari-Mart stores, you will find many Lochmead dairy products. Today, seven of the four siblings' children also work for the family business.

Lochmead Dairy believes in maintaining sustainable and environmentally sound business practices. They work diligently to make sure their products are as fresh as possible. The 600 cows at today's dairy are all born and raised on the farm. They are never given growth hormones. Over 80% of the cow's feed is grown on the 3000 acres that now provide crops for the farm. Milk from the farm travels a mere four miles to the processing facility. You can't get milk much fresher than that!

The family saying is, "We make what we want to eat and sell the rest." They believe in the importance of knowing the origin of the ingredients they use in their products. The family grows many crops that are used in Lochmead ice cream. Scott Gibson grows peppermint and he distills the oil for the flavoring found in Lochmead's peppermint candy and oregon mint fudge ice creams. 2011 will mark the first year that Lochmead will use their own delicious, family-grown blueberries in their blueberry ice cream. Mike Gibson grows the hazelnuts on the farm that inspired the creation of Oregon hazelnut fudge ice cream.

Lochmead Dairy is sensitive to the carbon footprint created from dairy cows. Burping and pooping are the main sources of pollution. To help neutralize their impact on the environment, Buzz Gibson is working to create energy from manure and cow-produced methane. Today, Lochmead generates enough electricity to power 200 homes with the use of a methane digester.

Lochmead has been producing ice cream since about 1975. The family learned to make ice cream from Maurizio Paparo, the owner and chef of Excelsior Inn and Restaurant Italiano in Eugene. (You can still visit the Excelsior Inn and Restaurant today.) Lochmead ice cream comes in 22 delicious flavors. The ice cream is sold in half-gallon containers. Of the 44 Dari-Marts, 12 shops include scoop shops that feature Lochmead ice cream. You may also find Lochmead ice cream in natural food stores as far north as Portland and as far south as Ashland. If you are looking for some fantastic Oregon ice cream made with homegrown Oregon ingredients, enjoy delicious Lochmead ice cream.

....

Lochmead Dari-Marts with Scoop Shops (Call for their hours of operation or visit **www.darimart.com**):

325 S 3rd St., Harrisburg, 541-995-8375
875 Ivy St., Junction City, 541-998-3691
440 SW Western, Corvallis, 541-758-1422
1175 Cal Young Road, Eugene, 541-342-7325
835 W 28th St., Eugene, 541-344-1123
3425 Hilyard St., Eugene, 541-485-7915
6898 Main St., Springfield, 541-746-7198
93190 Long Tom Dr., Cheshire, 541-998-2822

Keizer

Thai Lotus

Sometimes you find wonderful ice cream is unexpected places. The Thai Lotus restaurant, which has been in business for eight years, is tucked away in a strip mall in Keiser. It has a wide variety of authentic, satisfying Thai dishes on the menu. It also has the most flavorful homemade coconut ice cream ($3.50/dish) in the state. The ice cream is served in a frosted glass ice cream dish. It is a perfectly white ice cream. The texture is smooth and it has a nice mouth feel. It has a rich coconut taste without being overbearing. In short, it is perfect. If you like the taste of coconut, this is the ice cream for you.

Address: 3858 River Rd., North, Keizer OR 97303-4866
Phone: 503-463-1985
Hours: Lunch Monday-Friday 11 a.m.-2:30 p.m.
Dinner Monday-Thursday 4:30 p.m.-9 p.m.,
Friday 4:30 p.m.-9:30 p.m.,
Saturday 4 p.m.-9:30 p.m., Sunday noon-8 p.m.
Restrooms: ADA accessible

Oakland

Tolly's Restaurant & Soda Fountain

Who would ever suspect that in the quiet little town of Oakland, Oregon, there would be an historic restaurant and ice cream fountain? Better yet, how many small towns can boast a chef who trained at the Culinary Institute of America (CIA) in New York? You will be in for a pleasant surprise when you stop off for lunch at Tolly's. Owned for the last three years by Myra Plant and her partner, Jeff Parker, the historic restaurant offers carefully prepared food to please patron's palettes. Besides an ice cream fountain, there is an adjacent fully stocked bar.

Parker, who is the resident chef, is determined to create the best burger on the planet, using ingredients that are fresh and local. He is passionate in his belief that people should know the "provenance," or source, of every ingredient in their food. Tolly's uses only grass-fed beef that has been specially ground for the restaurant. He was inspired by a trip to Hawaii and came up with the idea for a Maui Burger. The burger is made with a filling 6-ounce patty on a slightly smaller than average bun. The burger is covered with Maui onions. Customers can also order the burger with cheese, bacon, and/or mushrooms. You will pay more for these burgers than ones at fast food restaurants but it's worth it. The Maui Kurl is $8.95 and includes the burger with Maui onions. It also comes with your choice of long board fries, soup, or salad. Once you have eaten a Tolly's burger, you will know how a good burger is supposed to taste and you will be back for more.

Continuing with the Hawaiian theme, Parker has invented an unusual potato fry he calls "the long board." Local potatoes are cut lengthwise, baked, and then flash fried, with the peel still attached. The resulting fry resembles a long board surfboard that is crisp on the outside and wonderfully fluffy in the middle.

You will whoop for joy when you discover the old-fashion whoopie pie. It is basically a sandwich with cake on the outside and frosting on the inside. It comes in several flavors, including yellow cake with chocolate frosting, chocolate cake with chocolate frosting, and spice cake with a dreamy vanilla frosting. This summer the restaurant is going to introduce the whoopie pie ice cream sundae. It will feature a whoopie pie with a scoop of Umpqua ice cream on top. Customers will then add their own toppings, making each dessert a one-of-a-kind masterpiece. The whoopie pie ice cream sundae is expected to sell for $6.

Tolly's offers up to eight flavors of Umpqua ice cream, all served up the old-fashioned way from the soda fountain. Try a hand-dipped milkshake or order a delicious banana split or ice cream sundae. How about a float? Maybe you prefer a simple ice cream cone. The adults in your group can even order a special "adult shake" ($9.95) with alcohol added to give the shake an extra zip.

When you are finished eating, take time to wander up and down the streets and browse in some of the cute antique and specialty shops. Oakland is listed in the National Register of Historical Places. You will see some wonderful storefronts from the 1890s. Many have signs outside that tell what they originally housed. There is even an icehouse just down the street from Tolly's. Icehouses were important before modern refrigeration because that is how ice was stored before it was sold it to customers who wanted to buy ice for their iceboxes or to make their own ice cream.

Address: 115 Locust St., Oakland OR 97462
Phone: 541-459-3796
Web: www.tollys-restaurant.com
Hours: Sunday-Thursday 11 a.m.-3 p.m.,
Friday-Saturday, 11 a.m.-7 p.m.
Restrooms: ADA accessible

Rice Hill

K-R Drive-In

It seemed like a good idea at the time. The year was 1980-something. I had heard about this ice cream stop at Rice Hill, an easy exit off I-5 about halfway between Cottage Grove and Roseburg. It was supposed to have great ice cream cones. With the temperature stuck above the 90° mark, an ice cream cone stop sounded like it would hit the spot. My mother and I had been trapped together in an un-air-conditioned car for three hours, the hot wind from the open windows swirling around us like a tornado, our faces battered by our own hair as it whipped, blew, and slapped us from every direction. We had three more hours ahead of us until we reached my sister's house. It would be nice to at least get out of the car and stretch our legs and rest our faces for a few minutes.

The place didn't look like much. A prominent "No Public Restroom" sign stood out. A couple of old mobile homes were hooked up together. Several picnic tables sat under a makeshift cover. There was a walk-up window in one of the trailers that slid open so an order could be placed. After completing the order, the window slid shut abruptly with a slight click. "Humph. They must have air-conditioning inside," I thought. Customers then walked, or staggered, in the heat, about six steps to the left and lined up at a second window to wait for their food. It was obviously a popular place. When we arrived at the drive-in, there were at least ten people at each window. In the mind-numbing heat, I was getting hotter by the second, standing in line, shifting from foot to foot. All I could think about was getting an ice cream cone. I looked at the long list of Umpqua flavors posted on a board outside the trailer. I noticed the prices were very cheap. "Must be extremely small scoops," I remember thinking, "Maybe I had better order a large cone."

The next thing I remember is turning around to face the customers still in line with my "large" ice cream cone. I was sooooooo embarrassed. The cone was six HUGE scoops of ice cream tall, so tall in fact that I heard circus music in my head as I did a balancing act to keep the whole thing upright. Then, the sun's heat instantly began melting the ice cream at an alarming rate. I started licking that cone like my life depended on it. No matter where I licked, emergency licking was needed somewhere else. I could not hide my embarrassment by sneaking back into the car. My mother forbade me from getting into the car with the cone because it was fast becoming a dripping mess. (She, of course had ordered a small cone.) I couldn't even consider throwing perfectly wonderful ice cream away, so I just stood in the parking lot doing my best to look nonchalant as I tried to quickly eat the biggest ice cream cone of my life as if it was no big deal.

From that first sweltering day, the K-R Drive-In became a regular stop in all kinds of weather on trips to southern Oregon. Over the years some things have changed. Now I always order a "small" cone. The prices have gone up while the cone sizes have gone down slightly. The long lines don't seem as long anymore. Yet there are still an impressive number of Umpqua ice cream flavors to choose from, and Rice Hill continues to be a nice stop on a long drive between somewhere and nowhere else.

Besides ice cream, the restaurant has a variety of burgers, fries, and soft drinks for those ready for a lunch or dinner stop. The staff is friendly and the prices reasonable. For your four-legged friend, you can buy a "doggie dish." It consists of a scoop of ice milk with a dog bone. Baby cones are $2.50.

Address: 201 John Long Rd., Oakland, OR 97462
Phone: 541-849-2570
Web: www.krdriveinn.com
Hours: Spring: from May 1 and during Spring Break: 10:30 a.m.-8 p.m.
Summer from June 1: Monday-Thursday 10 a.m.-8 p.m., Friday-Sunday 10 a.m.-9 p.m.
Fall from Labor Day: 10:30 a.m.-8 p.m.
Winter from the third week of October: 11 a.m.-7 p.m.
Restrooms: No

Roseburg

History of Umpqua Ice Cream

Since 1931, Umpqua brand dairy products have been a familiar label for Oregonians wanting high-quality dairy products. The company's founders were Ormond Feldkamp and Herb Sullivan. They set up their business at the end of the railroad line in Roseburg, using a wooden icehouse to keep their products cold. They sold milk, butter, and perhaps ice cream to passengers at the railway station. Because they had an icehouse, it appears they might have overcome one of the biggest barriers to making ice cream, the need for ice. With modern refrigeration, we take ice for granted these days, but it was not too long ago that ice was a prized commodity. Ice was produced and then sold in blocks to families who would put it in insulated boxes, called iceboxes, to keep their perishable foods fresh. With an icehouse, perhaps Feldkamp and Sullivan had enough ice to make ice cream. If so, they would have been one of the first commercial ice cream producers in Oregon.

Besides selling dairy products to train passengers, Feldkamp and Sullivan began home delivery of their products to customers. The business continued to grow, and in 1936 a new brick building replaced the original building at their original location.

In the 1930s, an unnamed painter created the first logo for Umpqua. Using an already existing Indian head that was imprinted on a flour sack, he painted an Indian head that became the signature for Umpqua products. Over the years the logo has been simplified, but the tribute to Native Americans has continued.

In the 1940s, Umpqua introduced the half-gallon cylindrical-shaped container they call "the red round." They still use that container today.

In 1953, Herb Sullivan suffered a stroke. He sold his part of the company to Ormond Feldkamp. Today, after 80 years, Umpqua Dairy is still a family-owned and family-operated company with the third generation of Feldkamps leading the business toward even greater success.

In 1961, Umpqua introduced the "flavor of the month" program. Each month during the calendar year, one flavor is highlighted. Every August since 1961, Mountain Blackberry Revel has had that honored distinction, much to the delight of Oregon ice cream lovers everywhere.

Recently, Umpqua has added Beaver Tracks and Duck Tracks ice cream to support Oregon's two biggest state universities. Both ice creams are the same flavor. Chocolate-covered caramel footballs in a peanut butter ice cream with a fudge ribbon make this a fall favorite. What distinguishes the two ice creams is the colorful, school spirited packaging that contains the ice cream. Which one sells the most? It depends on who is having a winning season. Believe me, you won't find an Oregon Duck buying Beaver Tracks or vice versa! In 2010, Duck Tracks were a big seller because the Oregon Ducks played for the National Football title. OSU Beaver Track sales waned. So what happens during the Civil War game, when the state annually becomes divided between the OSU Beavers and the UO Ducks? Umpqua sells both Beaver Tracks and Duck Tracks in fairly equal amounts. They also diplomatically sell a neutral-looking three-gallon container of the ice cream simply called "Civil War." Smart move!

Umpqua makes 33 flavors of ice cream in 3-gallon tubs, and 22 flavors in half-gallons. Three types of vanilla ice cream are on the roster. Umpqua is always looking for new ideas for flavors, but their number one seller is still Vanilla. Steve Feldkamp, Chief Operating Officer, has two favorite flavors: Rocky Road, which is the number-one seller after Vanilla, and Mountain Blackberry Revel, a seasonal favorite. Umpqua Cookie Dough ice cream is another favorite in Oregon.

After 80 years in business, Umpqua has become a well-known Oregon brand. You can find Umpqua ice cream in many scoop shops in Oregon. It is also readily available in grocery stores throughout the state. Wherever you find Umpqua, you will appreciate the quality and flavors that customers in Oregon enjoy.

Silverton

The Silverton Coffee Station

Christy and Daryl Peters have owned the Silverton Coffee Station for almost three years. Christy, who is a native of Silverton, was working as a bookkeeper when she discovered that the space was for sale. Jumping at the chance to own her own business, she and her husband Daryl turned the former old-fashioned gas station into a unique coffee and ice cream shop. You will find a wide variety of coffee drinks, including house coffee, steamers, and espresso drinks. They also mix a variety of specialty drinks such as the Milky Way, Mud Slide, and Snickers. You can enjoy blended drinks like White Chocolate, Vanilla Bean, and Java Chip. Tea, hot chocolate, Italian sodas, and fruit smoothies are also for sale.

The Silverton Coffee Station serves 12 flavors of Cascade Glacier ice cream. Their best sellers are Espresso Explosion and Rainbow Sherbet. Baby cones or bowls are $1.50, single scoops are $1.95, and double scoops are $3.95. Vanilla or chocolate shakes are $3.75 for a 16-ounce shake and $6 for a 24-ounce shake. You can also order any other Cascade Glacier flavor of shake for $4 (16-ounce) or $6.25 (24-ounce). If you need a little caffeine hit, try the Espresso Shake ($4.25/$6.50) or the Java Trio ($4.50/$6.75).

Inside the scoop shop are several tables where customers can enjoy their coffee or ice cream treat. During the summer, tables fill the little patio outside so patrons can enjoy the summer weather. The Silverton Coffee Station is the perfect place to stop for a quick snack before going on to Silver Creek Falls State Park.

Address:	206 S Water St., Silverton, OR 97381
Phone:	503-873-0731
Hours:	Monday-Saturday 8 a.m.-5 p.m. year-round. Sunday 10 a.m.-2 p.m. (winter) and Sunday 10 a.m.-4 p.m. (summer)
Restrooms:	ADA accessible

I-5 Freeway
Things to See and Do

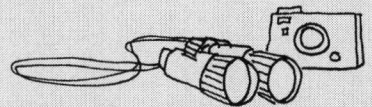

Albany

Albany Brass Ring Historic Carousel & Museum

A delightful surprise awaits you at the Albany Brass Ring Historic Carousel and Museum. Inside, you will find a wonderful assortment of carousel animals in various stages of construction. Each completed figure will be part of a new carousel that will surely be the capstone to Albany's downtown renovation. The finished carousel will be the result of the work of many volunteers who are lovingly carving, chiseling, puttying, and painting the collection of animals that will grace the revolving platform. The platform itself is made from old-growth Douglas fir cut to size with no knots. Visitors to the museum are welcome to walk among the carvings and talk with the craftsmen who spend their leisure time creating this beauty. There is also a small museum and gift store to browse.

The carousel and museum owe a debt of gratitude to the Dentzel family, who immigrated to the United States from Germany in the 1830s. They settled in Philadelphia in 1864 and began building some of the first carousels in the United States. In 1930, the family sold their business and moved to southern California. When Bill Dentzel III discovered that the Albany carousel was being built in the life-like Dentzel style, that is, with muscle definition and proper anatomy, the Dentzel family donated a 1909 mechanism to run the carousel.

When finished, the carousel will include 52 animals and 2 chariots. There will be 8 alternate animals so if an animal needs to be repaired, the carousel will not have an empty spot. Each animal has been sponsored and adopted by either an individual or group. Sponsorship costs $10,000 for an animal on the outer ring, $7,500 for a spot on the middle ring, and $5,000 to travel on the inner ring.

Sponsors become part of the creative process. They meet with the carousel's artist to design a unique creature. Each animal has a name and a back-story. Take Harriet the Frog, for instance. Harriet was sponsored by the human Harriet's children as a memorial to their mother. Because the real Harriet was born during the Depression, Harriet the Frog wears a flour sack. A love of gardening is remembered in her hat. The yellow rose adorning the hat was Harriet's favorite flower. Harriet bore twelve children, symbolized by the six polliwogs on each of her back legs. Harriet holds a jar of flies to remember her love of canning. What a wonderful gift to remember a parent and also provide smiles and fun for thousands of riders in years to come!

The carousel figures are carved from basswood that comes from the linden tree. Inside each figure is a time capsule containing the back-story and all the information about that animal's origins. The animals are hand-painted by a team of volunteers. Each animal requires more than 2000 hours to sand and paint.

Currently, the carousel is in the sixth year of its projected 10-year completion. When the carousel is finished, the building where it is now located will be torn down and a new carousel building constructed. It is not too late to get in on all the action. Volunteers are always needed to help with the carving and painting. Experienced carvers and painters are willing to teach the tricks of their trade to newbies. Volunteers can work flexible schedules. What a great skill to learn! If you would like to join in the process, call for more information.

Oh, and what will happen to all those master carvers and painters after the carousel animals are finished? It looks like they may stick around and start carving animals for private individuals. So round and round they go, when they stop carving, nobody knows!

Address:	503 First Avenue West, PO Box 965, Albany, OR 97321
Phone:	541-791-3340
Web:	**www.albanybrassring.com**
Email:	carouselproject@albanybrassring.com
Hours:	Monday-Saturday 10 a.m.-4 p.m., Wednesdays until 9 p.m.
Admission:	FREE
Restrooms:	ADA accessible

Ashland

4th of July in Ashland

Nobody salutes the 4th of July quite like Ashland, Oregon. Where else can you go to celebrate the big heart of America while watching a wonderful small-town parade that honors the American spirit and diversity at its finest. See hula dancers, belly dancers and Tai dancers, as well as Hispanics in colorful Folkloria costumes, all swaying, strutting, and stepping to their own beat as they dance up East Main Street. Politicians representing Ashland both locally and nationally drive, walk, bike, and even use Segways to transport themselves along the parade route, greeting their constituents and waving to the crowd as they pass by. There are several notable bands in the parade, including the Marching Macaronis from the Macaroni Restaurant who dress up as, you guessed it, macaronis, with just enough head and arm space so they can play their instruments. The Firehouse 5, who interestingly have six musicians, ride on a fire truck and actually go through the parade route twice. (You can never have too many bands in a parade.) A music teacher workshop in Ashland just happens to coincide with the 4th of July, and several HUGE flatbed trucks transport the music professionals along the parade route as they play foot-tapping, hand-clapping music to make you smile. Civic groups, neighborhood groups, and youth organizations in the parade are all welcomed by the throngs of people lining the street.

At the end of the parade, thousands of parade-goers follow the parade route to Lithia Park, where vendors are waiting to sell all kinds of foods and arts and crafts. Non-profit outfits, many of whom were just in the parade, also have booths to encourage people to get involved in their community in whatever way suits their sense of civic duty.

Soon after the parade, at the band shell within Lithia Park, the Ashland City Band, with roots dating back to 1876, sounds off with American songs to celebrate the 4th of July. The melodies of Sousa and other American classics drift through the air. There is nothing quite like hearing a concert band out-of-doors.

After the City Band disperses, other acts take to the stage. In 2010 a fantastic group called Brothers played. The two musicians, part of a larger group, played digeridoos, bagpipes, keyboards, and guitars to create an eerily haunting and beautiful kind of tribal music as different from the classical concert band as apple pie and vegemite. The musical diversity is a perfect example of the myriad ways people celebrate their freedom in this great American town. Although some of the musical acts may change from year to year, and changing political issues will continue to confound us, the true spirit of the 4th of July magically comes alive each year in Ashland. It will renew your hope in the American dream.

In the evening, as if to add an exclamation point to the day, there is a fireworks display that can be seen from anywhere in Ashland. Both the parade and fireworks display are made possible through the support and efforts of the Ashland Chamber of Commerce, community groups, and volunteers.

Address: Ashland Chamber of Commerce, P.O. Box 1360, 110 E. Main St., Ashland, OR 97520
Phone: 541-482-3486 ext.106
Web: www.ashlandchamber.com

Cave Junction

Oregon Caves National Monument
A tour of the Oregon Caves National Monument offers a glimpse into the dark, eerie world beneath us. The 90-minute tour walks visitors through one of Oregon's most amazing caves. You will feel like a real explorer as you tour this massive marble cave that was naturally carved out. Guides will explain the geology of the caves and the creatures that call it home. Learn how settlers discovered and explored the caves, as well as why the Oregon Caves earned the distinction of becoming a National Monument.

Address: 19000 Caves Highway, Cave Junction, OR 97523
Phone: 541-592-2100
Web: www.nps.gov/orca
Hours: Late March-Memorial Day weekend 10 a.m.-4 p.m., (During the last 2 weeks of April open Friday-Monday) Memorial Day weekend-Labor Day 9 a.m.-6 p.m.

	After Labor Day-Columbus Day 9 a.m.-5 p.m.
	After Columbus Day-Thanksgiving weekend
	10 a.m.-4 p.m., (in November Friday-Monday)
	December-late March CLOSED
Admission:	16 years old and under $6/person, 17 years and older $8.50/person
Restrooms:	ADA accessible
Additional information:	Wear warm clothing and hiking shoes. No backpacks are allowed in the cave. Flash cameras are allowed, but no tripods. The tour includes 500 stairs and uneven surfaces that might be wet. Passages can be narrow. Be prepared to squeeze through some tight spaces. Visitors must be at least 42 inches tall. Kids may not be carried through the cave.

Central Point

Crater Rock Museum

Rock hound enthusiasts will love the Crater Rock Museum in Central Point. Newly remodeled, it has ample room to display its many collections of rocks and minerals. You will also find other interesting artifacts and displays as well. For instance, scrimshaw used to be a popular, and often expensive, art form during the 1800s when whaling was a commercial business. Intricate pictures and designs were scratched into whale bone or tusks or elephant ivory. Black ink was applied so the design became visible. Scrimshaw was made into rings, pendants, cuff links, and other art pieces. With the end of the whaling industry and the banning of ivory imports, scrimshaw is rare today. The Crater Rock Museum has a nice selection of historic pieces that showcase this art form.

The museum has rare dinosaur eggs from China that are 100 million years old. You will also find petrified wood, lovely thunder eggs, and an extensive collection of arrowheads and Native American artifacts.

There is a lot to see at the Crater Rock Museum and a stop here is well worth your time.

Address: 2002 Scenic Ave #A, Central Point, OR 97502-2185
Phone: 541-664-6081
Web: www.craterrock.com
Hours: Tuesday-Saturday 10 a.m.-4 p.m.
Admission: $4/person, $2/seniors 55+ and students
Restrooms: ADA accessible

Eagle Point

Butte Creek Mill

"YOU made these?," my mother asked incredulously.

"Yes...," I answered somewhat defensively for the third time. A few minutes went by with Mom savoring another morsel of the scone I had just served her, using Butte Creek Mill Scone Mix and a few chopped dates.

"YOU made these?" she asked again.

"You know," I said, "if you keep asking me that question I'm going to get mad. YES, I made these scones. I used the Butte Creek Scone Mix we bought the last time we went to southern Oregon."

"Oh," she said, "Butte Creek Scone Mix. That explains it."

I just sighed.

We discovered Butte Creek Mill over 20 years ago, although the mill's history is much older, dating from its beginning in 1872. Over the years I regularly stop by when I am visiting family in southern Oregon. The mill is listed on the National Register of Historic Places. It is a fun place to visit, as much to explore the shelves for interesting pancake and waffle mixes, granola, and other goodies, as to watch the water-powered gristmill in action. The old-fashioned building with wooden floors has a real Old-West feel that somehow makes you feel like you have stepped back in time. Purchasing the flour products milled on location feels like a step in a healthy direction. Not only are the mixes healthy, they taste great!

As an added bonus, there is an antique store next door that has been converted from an old cheese factory. About a block away is a small park and one of the few remaining covered bridges in the state. A visit to Butte Creek Mill is well worth the trip!

Address: 402 N Royal Ave, Eagle Point, OR 97524
Phone: 541-826-3531
Web: **www.buttecreekmill.com**
Hours: Monday-Saturday 9 a.m.-5 p.m.
Sunday 11 a.m.-5 p.m.
Admission: FREE
Restrooms: There are men's and women's restrooms at the mill that are not ADA accessible. There is an ADA-accessible restroom at the museum next door.

near Gold Hill

House of Mystery at the Oregon Vortex

They say seeing is believing. You'll be rubbing your eyes more than once on this guided tour of one of Oregon's weirdest phenomena. The House of Mystery is situated on a half-acre of land that is reputed to be in a vortex, where the Earth's magnetic field is slightly askew. When you are within the vortex, odd things happen. People appear to change size when they change their physical positions. Golf balls appear to roll uphill. Brooms stand up on their own. Some visitors say they feel a slight dizziness or disequilibrium. Even blind visitors feel the pull of this force, discounting the theory that the effect is all an optical illusion. Experiencing these and other weird oddities will delight and entertain you and fellow travelers.

The area now known as the Oregon Vortex has a long history that your tour guide will be happy to relate in more detail. It was known as the "forbidden area" by Native Americans, whose horses did not want to enter the site. Early pioneers also felt the effects of this strange place. John Litster spent many years conducting thousands of experiments at the site in his attempt to understand this phenomenon. It is thought that he even corresponded with Albert Einstein. Litster eventually purchased the property and opened it to the public in 1930. Tourists have been flocking to the site ever since. The Oregon Vortex House of Mystery has been owned and operated by the Cooper family since 1960.

Okay, go ahead, and be a skeptic. In fact, you are invited to bring your own levels, balls, and measuring tape to assure that what you are seeing is not a trick. By the end of your tour, you will be scratching your head. It will make you wonder what else you need to rethink. Let's face it—life is a mystery.

Address:	4303 Sardine Creek Left Fork Rd., Gold Hill OR 97525
Phone:	(541)-855-1543
Web:	**www.oregonvortex.com**
Email:	mystery@oregonvortex.com
Hours:	Daily March-October
	March-Memorial Day 9 a.m.-4 p.m.
	Memorial Day-Labor Day, 9 a.m.-5 p.m.
	Labor Day-Halloween 9 a.m.-4 p.m.
Admission:	Ages 5 and under FREE, Children (6-11) $7,
	Adults (12-61) $9.75, Seniors (62+), $8.75
Restrooms:	Non ADA accessible, port-a-potties
Additional information:	Bring your camera. No video or audio recorders. Group discount for pre-arranged groups of 15 or more paid admissions. Parking O.K. for RVs, trailers, and buses Souvenir shop with limited snacks available at site.

Grants Pass

The Glass Forge

The Glass Forge is a wonderful place to watch glassblowing as three master craftsmen—Lee Wassink, Maurice Kreuzer, and Nathan Sheafor—create beautiful works of art. Together, they started their studio in 1998. They specialize in Venetian-style art glass, making bowls, bottles, vases, glasses, and artistic glass pieces. Using a pleasing combination of shapes, textures, and colors, their finished pieces stand out as one-of-a-kind treasures. Their studio has an impressive display of their work for sale. Their shop has an open-door policy for people who want to view the process of glassblowing.

Watching these three men as they are engaged in glassblowing is fascinating. First, it is hard to believe that anyone could reach into a white-hot oven and gather liquid glass on the end of a metal rod without dropping it or burning themselves in the process. Then, to be able to blow life into that blob of glass, color it with an assortment of colors, and mold it into a shape is impressive. To open the shape to form a bowl or glass seems magical. To add a handle or base seems impossible but these artists do it with little fanfare. Finally a little "clink" in the right place and the piece disengages from the rod and is put into an oven where it can cool uniformly. These three craftsmen make it look easy, but spectators will know they have seen something special.

Address:	501 S.W. G S., Grants Pass, OR 97526
Phone:	541-955-0815
Web:	www.glassforge.com
Hours:	Monday-Friday 8 a.m.-5 p.m., Saturday 10 a.m.-4 p.m.
Admission:	FREE
Restrooms:	ADA accessible

Medford

Harry and David Tour

Harry and David is a household name in Oregon. They are a hugely successful Oregon company famous for creating elegant fruit and gift baskets that make perfect presents for holidays or special occasions. The company sells their superior quality products in retail stores and through an extensive mail order business.

The company started from humble beginnings. In 1910, Samuel Rosenburg, father of Harry and David, moved from Seattle to the Rogue Valley in southern Oregon to start a pear orchard on 240 acres of land. Harry and David took over the business in 1914 after their father's death. The brothers' specialty crop was Comice pears, which they named "Royal Riviera." The business did well until the Great Depression. To boost their business opportunities, they went on trips to San Francisco and New York to convince successful businessmen to use their pears as business gifts. The strategy paid off and in 1934, Harry and David started their mail order business. In 1938 they started the "fruit of the month" club. It is still going strong today. Over the years products have been added to create an impressive line of mail-order gifts.

Today, there are 3200 acres of farmland in 22 locations in the valley devoted to raising fruit for Harry and David's. The company employs 1,200-1,300 full time workers and between 6500-7000 part-time workers during the busy packing season. Baskets sell from $30-$500. Besides pears, the baskets may include chocolates, Moose Munch, wine, and other treats. For fruit lovers in Harry and David's fruit of the month club, a different kind of fruit is mailed to members each month of the year.

The tour of Harry and Davis's is both fun and educational for kids and adults. Guests walk (or take an elevator) one flight up from the factory floor where they have a great view of the workers and conveyer belts below. Workers examine each pear, or fruit, for quality, then carefully wrap it, pack it in a special Harry and David box, and then send it down the line. As the box moves along down the line, other goodies may be inspected and then added. Every item has a special place in the box. The quality control is impressive.

After watching the packing process guests move on to view the making of one of Harry and Davis's most popular items, Moose Munch. A combination of popcorn covered in caramel, with chocolate and nuts, Moose Munch is a mouthful of sweet treat. Visitors also visit the candy kitchen where truffles are formed. Before leaving the tour, guests are given sample treats.

The tour starts at the Harry and David Store in Medford where guests are picked up by small buses and then driven to the factory, located several miles away. Cost for the one-hour tour is $5 per person. The $5 ticket can be redeemed on the day of the tour for $5 off any purchase of $40 or more at the Harry and David store.

Address:	Harry and David Country Village, 1314 Center Dr., Medford, OR 97501
Phone:	1-877-322-8000
Web:	**www.harryanddavid.com**
Hours:	Tours: Monday-Friday at 9:15 a.m., 10:30 a.m., 12:30 p.m., 1:45 p.m.
Admission:	$5/person
Restroom:	ADA Restroom at the store in Medford and at the factory.
Additional information:	Reservations are required. Call 1-877-322-8000. Best time of year for the tour is September-early December when packing of gift baskets is in full swing. During the summer, there is less to see on the tour.

near Merlin

Wildlife Images Rehabilitation & Education Center

Wildlife Images is an animal sanctuary in southern Oregon. Sick, injured, and orphaned animals are taken to this facility where they will have a good chance for survival. Over 1000 animals are checked by staff at the 26-acre sanctuary each year. They are evaluated, medically treated, nurtured, and then, if possible, they are re-released back into the wild. Some animals have physical injuries so severe they will never be able to survive in the wild. Other animals are those who have been raised by well-meaning humans who later discover that wild animals are just that, wild. When human-raised animals are brought to the sanctuary, they have lost their fear of humans. They have also lost the skills to live in the wild on their own. Many animals that cannot be returned to the wild find a new permanent home at Wildlife Images. They receive wonderful care and sometimes are able to live up to two times longer (or even more) than animals in the wild. In return, the animals serve as ambassadors to the sanctuary and help educate the public about wildlife.

The sanctuary was started by Dave Siddon, an animal lover par excellence. He became known as a person who could help stranded and injured animals. In the 1970s he began taking in animals to nurture them back to health. Even the state police brought him animals that had been injured on Oregon roads and highways. In 1981, Siddon started a non-profit to expand his project. In 1996, Dave Siddon died, but not before naming his son as the new director. The sanctuary is still flourishing. In fact, a new area is being added where raccoons and other water-loving creatures will be able to frolic in a natural environment of pools of water surrounded by natural vegetation.

Today, visitors can take a tour to visit the permanent residents who call Wildlife Images their home. Animals come from all over the world, but most of the animals are from Oregon. All of the animals have names and the guides greet each one like a long-lost friend. You will meet bald eagles, peregrine falcons, ravens, bobcats, bears, foxes, cougars, and a lot of waterfowl. Nubs, a badger, is a frisky resident that looks like he wants to play and will make you smile. He is often taken on walks by his caretaker, wearing a special harness. After seeing Ms. Jefferson, a majestic bald eagle, you will understand why bald eagles became our national symbol.

Visit Wildlife Images. It is a great spot to add to any trip to southern Oregon.

Address: 11845 Lower River Rd., Grants Pass, OR 97526
PO Box 36, Merlin, OR 97532
Phone: 541-476-0222
Web: **www.wildlifeimages.org**
Hours: Call for reservations. Tours are given seven days a week, rain, or shine.
Admission: Tours are by reservation only. Adults (18 years and older) $10/person, Youth (ages 4-17) $5/person, Children (3 and under) donation

Restrooms: ADA accessible

Additional information: Kids' wagon with cover for rain $5/hour
Golf cart rental (for up to 3 adults) $10/tour

near Silverton or Sublimity

Silver Falls State Park

Silver Falls Park is a fantastic place to go for a picturesque day-hike, picnic, or overnight camping. Visitors can hike on trails that connect to ten waterfalls. Choose your hike from a variety of trails that vary from less than a mile to 7.5 miles. A walk through the canyon of towering fir and western hemlocks, with waterfalls interspersed for added excitement, will be a trip you will always remember. Be sure to take your camera.

When you have finished your hike, you may want to take a cool dip in the swimming area at the south end of the South Falls Day Use Area. Check out the nature store, run by the Friends of Silver Falls State Park. Grab a quick lunch or snack at the South Falls Lodge, or bring a picnic lunch and enjoy watching the water in Silver Creek.

Hiking is not the only way to see the park. Although bikes are not permitted on the hiking trails in the canyon, Silver Falls State Park has miles of bike trails that allow visitors to explore other areas of this 9000-acre treasure. There are 14 miles of equestrian trails for riders and their horses to enjoy.

Overnight camping is available at Silver Falls State Park year round. Nightly rates are based on the time of year. October 1 to April 30 is called "Discovery Season" and the rates are slightly lower, while the prime season is May 1 to September 30.

There are 45 tent camping sites ($15/$19/night) and 52 sites with electrical outlets for trailers and RVs less than 60 feet long ($20/$24/night).

There are three group sites for tents ($51/$71/night) and two group sites for RVs ($101 plus $10/unit after 10 units). These group sites are open April 1 to October 31.

The park has 5 equestrian camping sites with corrals for horses ($15/$19/night) and one group equestrian site ($45/58/night). Horse camps are open April 1 to October 31.

Besides camping facilities, Silver Falls State Park has 14 rustic cabins; ten are 2-room cabins, and four are one-room cabins ($39/night).

For groups, Silver Creek Falls offers three reservable picnic shelters within the South Falls Day Use Area. In addition, a meeting hall can be rented for weddings, family reunions, and other events. Overnight sleeping facilities are available at the Old Ranch and the New Ranch. Reservations can be made at least two days prior to arrival and up to 9 months in advance of the arrival. Call for more details and prices.

The Silver Falls Conference Center offers both overnight accommodations and day use meeting halls for your group event. Contact the Conference Center at 503-873-8875 directly for their details and prices.

Address:	20024 Silver Falls Highway S.E., Sublimity, OR 97385
Phone *(for info)*:	503-873-8681 Ext. 31 or 800-551-6949
Phone *(for reservations)*:	800-452-5687
Email:	Park.Info@state.or.us
Admission:	There is a day use fee of $5/vehicle at this park. Annual day passes sell for $30 for one-year day passes and $50 for two-year day passes
Restrooms:	ADA accessible

Wilsonville

Family Fun Center and Bullwinkle's Restaurant

The Rocky and Bullwinkle Show was one of my favorite television shows growing up. The lovable characters had such an innocent, quirky take on life. These charming cartoon icons are the stars at Bullwinkle's Restaurant in Wilsonville. A part of the Family Fun Center, the restaurant features pizza and other light fare for kids and families who are visiting the complex. Rocky and Bullwinkle appear on posters, on television monitors, and on stage while diners eat. Unfortunately, the restaurant serves a non-Oregon ice cream. Don't let that stop you from spending time in the restaurant where the characters are still cute enough to make you laugh out loud. It will definitely make you smile.

Meanwhile, the sights and sounds of the fun center will beckon the whole family. Inside, the place is lit up like Las Vegas for kids. Kidopolis, a giant indoor climbing structure for kids 3 years old and up and who are less than five feet tall, will help active kids burn off some energy. There are video games galore. Coupon tickets are issued to game winners who can then trade their tickets for prizes at the end of their visit. Upstairs the games continue. There you will find Lazerextreme, where lazer tag is available for kids 44 inches and taller.

Outside the fun is more active. Batting cages, miniature golf, go-karts, bumper boats, and more will bring out the kid in all of us. The center is open year-round rain or shine. Some of the outdoor activities are not open during inclement weather, but even during the Martin Luther King weekend, kids were zooming around on the bumper boats, having a wonderful time during the brief sunshine. The clink of bats hitting balls and the roar of go-kart engines, together with voices filled with laughter and excitement, make this happy scene.

Bullwinkle's, as the whole complex is sometimes known, will keep kids and adults entertained for hours. It is a fun way to spend time with friends and family any time of year.

Address:	29111 SW Town Center Loop W., Wilsonville, OR 97070
Phone:	503-685-5000
Web:	www.fun-center.com
Hours:	Attraction hours: Monday-Thursday noon-8 p.m., Friday-Saturday 10 a.m.-11 p.m. Sunday 11 a.m.-9 p.m. Restaurant hours: Sunday-Thursday noon to 8 p.m. Friday-Saturday 11 a.m.-10 p.m.
Admission:	There are a variety of pricing options available. Guests may purchase tickets to single activities outside, or they may purchase value packages or all day unlimited passes. Check for special promotions. See website for current prices.
Restrooms:	ADA accessible
Additional information:	There is another Family Fun Center in Tukwila, WA.

Section 6
Off the Beaten I-5 Freeway

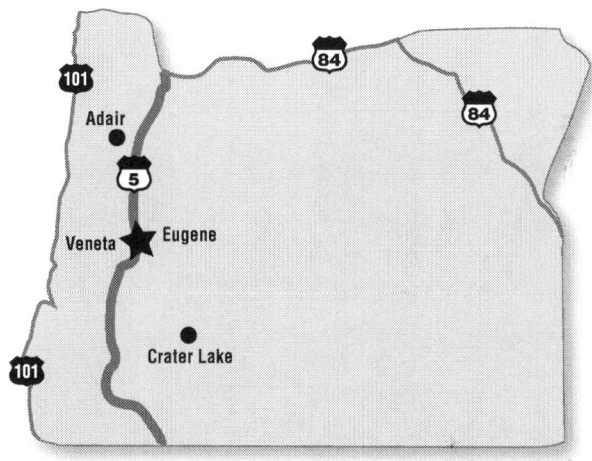

Crater Lake

Off the Beaten I-5 Freeway

Ice Cream

Adair

Jamocha Jo's Java and Ice Cream

In the blink of an eye, you can drive right past the former World War II military village of Adair. It once housed 45,000 personnel, but it is now a quiet village. If you are paying attention, though, the roadside sign pointing to Jamocha Jo's Java and Ice Cream drive-thru will probably catch your eye. Besides being a drive-thru, there is inside seating for about 20 people.

Nancy Higgins says she and her husband started the business to create a place where families and others can go to socialize and hang out, with a little something for everyone. Coffee is roasted on site (starting at $1.50). There are eight flavors of Cascade Glacier ice cream ($2.20/single scoop), plus cookies and other baked goods. In the summer Jamocha Jo's sponsors outdoor concerts to encourage families to get out and do something fun together. They also have created a "Hero of the Week" program. It recognizes someone in their community who is a "quiet" hero, giving of themselves selflessly to help make Adair Village a good place to live.

The real attraction of Jamocha Jo's is the friendliness of the owners and villagers who stop in for a cup of coffee or a little treat. You won't feel like a stranger for long as everyone is included into the conversation. It is surprising who might drop by. The fire chief or city administrator might duck in for a quick coffee to go. They will stop long enough to introduce themselves, answer your questions, and make you feel right at home in their village. Then they get their cup of coffee and head back to work. You may enter a stranger, but you won't forget the friendly folks in Adair. A leisurely stop at this spot will brighten your day.

Address:	6020 NE William R. Carr St., Adair, OR 97330
Phone:	541-745-2050
Web:	**www.jamochajos.com**
Hours:	Monday-Friday 6 a.m.-5:30 p.m., Saturday 8 a.m.-noon, closed Sunday
Restrooms:	ADA accessible
Additional information:	Across the highway is McDonald State Forest. There you will discover lots of hiking trails. **www.cof.orst.edu/cf/recreation/trails.php**
Getting there:	Jamocha Jo's is in Adair Village, located on Hwy 99W (Pacific Hwy) 5 miles north of Corvallis.

Off the Beaten I-5 Freeway
Things to See and Do

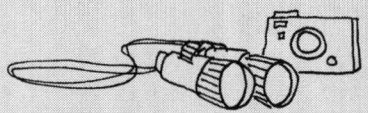

Crater Lake
Colors enrich our lives and yet sometimes we take them for granted. We all have our favorite colors that somehow resonate within our very being. Yet it is hard to explain why we prefer one color instead of another. I DO know that you have never truly seen the color blue until you have stared into the depths of Crater Lake on a clear day. Oh, you might think you know blue when you look at the sky or maybe you know blue from gazing at a stellar jay, but the intensity of the blue in Crater Lake can take your breath away. It is the kind of blue you want to drink in with your eyes so you will never forget it. In fact, if God has eyes, they must be the color of Crater Lake!

Crater Lake was designated a National Park in 1902 and is one of Oregon's most familiar icons. Its image even appears on the back of the Oregon state quarter that was minted in 2005 as part of a ten-year national state celebration. The lake was formed from a volcanic caldera thousands of years ago and is amazing, not only for its intense color, but because it is the deepest lake in the United States at 1943 feet. It is the seventh deepest lake in the world. There are no streams or outlets either into or out of the lake. The lake is fed solely from the yearly rain and massive snow that falls into it each year.

Tourists have several options when visiting the park, depending on the season. During the winter, with vehicles equipped for snow, hardy winter enthusiasts can enjoy snowshoeing and cross country skiing in the area. In the summer, when the park is more accessible by road, visitors can drive almost to the rim of the lake where they will find ample parking and a wonderful view. Hiking, camping, or just sitting around enjoying the views are all popular. Interpretive talks are regularly scheduled during summer hours. A lodge for overnighters is open seasonally. There is also a gift store, and several places to get a bite to eat. For those able to walk a challenging 2.2 mile trail down to a dock, boats take passengers on a ride out into the lake. For people curious about forest look-out stations, a short drive around part of the lake leads to a fairly easy trail that winds up to a working forest watch tower with beautiful views of Oregon as far away as the Klamath basin.

Whether you are an Oregonian, or a tourist, Crater Lake should be on your list of places to see in the state. You'll be glad you made the effort.

Address:	Crater Lake National Park, PO Box 7, Crater Lake, OR 97604
Phone:	541-594-3000
Web:	**www.nps.gov/crla**
Hours:	Hours and concessions vary by season.
Admission:	Admission to the National Park is $10/car for a 7-day pass.
Other information:	Reservations are needed for overnight lodging and for the boat.

near Veneta

Oregon Country Fair

I first heard about the Oregon Country Fair from my brother when we were in college together at the U of O in the early 1970s. He came back and reported that he had seen a 9-month-pregnant woman who had painted her stomach to look like a world globe. It made an impression.

In the 1980s I took my mother to the fair and asked her not to gawk. Soon we were both mesmerized, listening to the popeye-esque voice of Baby Gramps as he sang songs, including some made from palindromes. (A palindrome is a word, phrase, or sentence that is the same when spelled backwards and forwards, such as "A Toyota" in reverse is "A Toyota.") It made an impression.

In the 1990s I took my nephew Ross, who was about 5 at the time. Now, Ross was not the most talkative kid. As soon as he saw the tie-dyed shirts and the sign that proclaimed, "Oregon Country Fair," he clammed up and did not say a word for hours, although he did take a short break from silence when we went to the children's art space. He loved the jugglers and entertainers who performed at the fair. In fact, he was inspired to learn stilt walking and juggling from this early experience. The fair made an impression.

The Oregon Country Fair debuted in 1969. It is a fantastic three-day festival that, according to its website, "creates events and experiences that nourish the spirit, explore living artfully and authentically on earth, and transform culture in magical, joyous and healthy ways." You never know what magical thing you will come across as you tour the grounds. There is always wonderful, creative entertainment, fabulous healthy food, well-done arts and crafts for sale, and perhaps most importantly, a place to mellow out and celebrate the creative life. Go to the Country Fair. It will make an impression you will never forget.

Oh, and while you are there, be sure to try one of the delicious ice cream products available from the Springfield Creamery. Yum!

Address: The mailing address is 442 Lawrence St., Eugene, OR 97401, BUT the fair itself is actually located on property 12 miles west of Eugene on Hwy 126 near Veneta.

Phone: 541-343-4298

Web: **www.oregoncountryfair.org**

Hours: The fair is always on the Friday, Saturday, and Sunday AFTER the 4th of July weekend. The fairgrounds are open 11 a.m.-7 p.m.

Admission: No tickets are sold onsite. Tickets go on sale in May and are sold at Ticketwest. Ticketwest is in many Safeway stores or you can go to Ticketwest.com. Advance tickets are $20 for Friday or Sunday and $23 for Saturday. If you buy your tickets on the day of the event, the price is $23 for Friday or Sunday and $28 for Saturday. Three-day tickets are $51. Children 10 and under are admitted free with a paying adult. ADA tickets are $5 less, except for a 3-day ticket. None of these prices include handling fees.

Restrooms:	ADA accessible
ADA concerns:	The fair makes a concerted effort to be accessible and even has a group of people known as "4A," whose mission is to make sure everyone can enjoy the event. However, the fair is in an outdoor location with varying terrain. Call to make sure the area is accessible for your condition.
Additional information:	No alcoholic beverages are allowed.
Getting there:	**Bus:** Buses efficiently shuttle visitors from Eugene to the Country Fair. Buses leave every 10-15 minutes during the day. Go to www.oregoncountryfair.org for specific departure locations. **Driving:** The Fair is located 12 miles west of Eugene on Hwy 126. There is limited parking at the site. $7/vehicle if purchased in advance and $8/vehicle on the day of the event. You have to show a valid admission ticket to be able to park at the fair.

Section 7
North Coast Highway 101

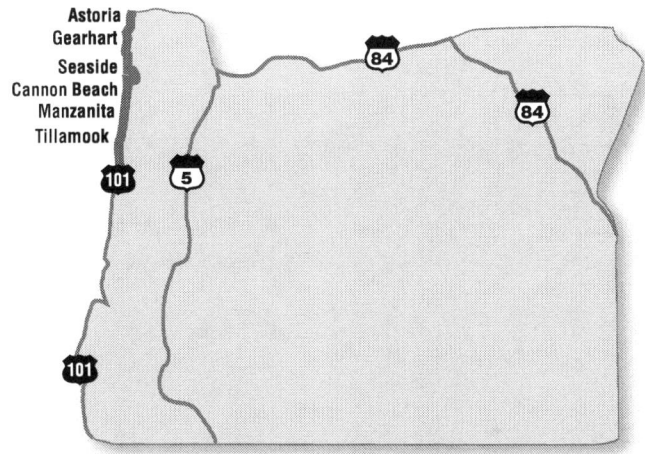

Sandcastle Building Contest, Cannon Beach

North Coast Highway 101
Ice Cream

Cannon Beach

Osburn's Ice Creamery

At Osburn's Ice Creamery in Cannon Beach, 24 flavors of Alpenrose, Cascade Glacier, and Tillamook ice cream are ready and waiting for you. The store is operated by Jim Osburn. He has been in the ice cream business in this coastal community since 1978. One of the specialties of the house is called "The Cone Dip" ($3.95). It consists of a cake cone with a scoop of hand-dipped ice cream that is then dipped in exquisite warm, dark, Guittard chocolate from San Francisco. This combo results in one of the best cones in the state, and that is saying a lot!

Osburn's considerable experience has helped him create some wonderful ice cream desserts. If the Cone Dip doesn't dazzle your taste buds, try one of the other delicious ice cream concoctions sure to satisfy the most adventurous ice cream eater. For example, try a Waffle Cone Sundae, a sundae made right in a waffle cone that costs $3.95. The "Cannon Ball" combines a tall hot expresso Americano in an ice cream float that coffee drinkers will love ($3.95). The most popular sundae is called "The Haystack" ($5.95). It consists of two scoops of ice cream with hot fudge, banana, nuts, whipped cream, and a cherry. Specialty milkshakes come in a variety of flavors and prices. The Chai milkshake costs $4.95, while the Espresso Shake is $5.25. Hard ice cream cones are $2.75/single scoop, $4.75/double scoop, and $6.75/triple scoop. Regular hard ice cream milkshakes cost $4.75.

For 25 years, Osburn's Ice Creamery has been serving a coffee lover's line of espresso drinks and fresh drip by-the-cup fresh-roasted coffee. They use 100% Estate Kona coffee that is shipped directly from Honolulu Coffee Roasters. So no matter whether you are sitting in a beach chair in Hawaii or lounging on Cannon Beach, you can sit and sip a cup of delicious, rich, Kona coffee. Osburn's also has numerous Italian sodas, smoothies, and organic teas.

Address: 240 N Hemlock St., Cannon Beach, OR 97110
Phone: 503-436-2578
Hours: Call for hours.

Additional information: Cash only

Gearhart

Gearhart Junction Café

The colorful neon sign for the Gearhart Junction Café caught my eye as I drove past Gearhart. I stopped and discovered a charming place for breakfast, lunch, or dinner. Inside, the cafe has the look and feel of a 50s diner, complete with counter service and comfortable booths. In actuality, the cafe has been in business for two years. It is stylishly decorated in blue, gray, and black. I wondered what I should call the color of blue. It isn't exactly a baby blue, and it isn't a steel blue. When I asked the owner, Pat Merrill, he laughed and said that a lot of customers ask about the color. He disappeared for a few minutes and came back with a color chart from Sherman-Williams. "Here it is," he said, "it's called Spa. I had a lady who came in the other day and asked about the color. She told me it was exactly the same color she wanted to paint her baby boy's bedroom." I had to agree. It is a very pleasing color and fits the décor of a café so close to the ocean.

The waitresses at the Gearhart Junction Café are very friendly. They bustle around and make sure everyone is served promptly. I ordered a hamburger. It was a great, old-fashioned burger ($5.75) piled high with lettuce, tomato, dill pickle, spread, and onion. I loved every bite of it.

One of the specialties of the café is their hand-dipped milkshakes ($4.25). Each is made with strawberry, vanilla, or chocolate ice cream made by Sunshine Dairy in Portland. Flavorings are added to the ice cream to create house specialties like the O'Henry (chocolate and peanut butter), and Kyle (strawberry and peanut butter). Milkshakes are served in a glass with a tin of extra shake on the side. For a malted shake, add 25 cents. Apparently visitors love the milkshakes. Pat Merrill told me he ends up making most of the milkshakes. Last July they sold 791 shakes. That's a whole lot of shakin' going on!

On Sundays, try the all-you-can-eat spaghetti with meat sauce meal offered for $8.95. Children's spaghetti meals are $5.95. The spaghetti comes with tossed salad and garlic bread.

Before you leave, check out the framed photo in the women's restroom. If you are a male, ask the waitress or another female to guard the door so you can take a look. You will leave the restaurant with a smile.

Address: 3350 Highway 101 N Suite E, Gearhart OR 97138
Phone: 503-738-5505
Hours: 8 a.m.-8 p.m. Tuesday-Sunday, closed Monday
Restrooms: ADA accessible

Pop's Sweet Shop Ice Cream

Cynthia Taft decided she wanted to do something upbeat, so eight years ago she opened an ice cream-scone-candy-fudge-and-coffee kind of place in the lovely coastal town of Gearhart. She named her new enterprise, Pop's Sweet Shop, after a Gearhart store of the same name that had been a bustling business in the 1920s through the 1940s. To simplify matters, Pop's is a take-out only, cash-only business. There are no tables in the shop. There are a few chairs inside, and places to sit and eat in the outside side yard patio. Most people grab their treat to go, and then they are off to their next destination. You will find Pop's is a very friendly place to visit. Cynthia Taft seems to know all of the locals who come in for coffee or ice cream. It is easy to tell that this is a close-knit community. The customers chat amiably and are quick to sing the praises of this proprietor.

You will find 24 flavors of Tillamook ice cream during the summer months and slightly fewer choices during the winter. Single-scoop cones are $3.50, double-scoop cones are $4.75, and a triple cone is $6. Try one of the popular waffle cones that customers say tastes like a big cookie. Waffle cones are $4.50/$5.75/$7. If you want both a cookie and ice cream, order a handmade ice cream sandwich for $6.25. Warm, homemade scones seem to beckon to many patrons. Locally made taffy and caramel corn are big sellers. The fresh caramel corn comes in three sizes that sell for $4.50, $6.25, and $7.75. Pop's sells its own homemade fudge. Coffee drinkers will find a large selection of drinks.

The store is located in an old building that would be hard for a wheelchair to enter. There is a buzzer outside so disabled patrons can ring for service. I have not seen this accommodation anywhere else in the state. It is a nice gesture from a nice owner in a nice community.

Address: 567 Pacific Way, Gearhart OR 97138
Phone: 503-738-8484
Facebook: www.facebook.com/pages/pop's-sweet-shop
Hours: Winter: 7 a.m.-5 p.m. daily
Summer: 7 a.m.-8 p.m. daily
Restrooms: Non-ADA accessible

Manzanita

The Coffee Shop

The first time I walked into the Coffee Shop in Manzanita and ordered a mint chocolate milkshake (the 12-oz. size is $2.95 and the 16-oz. size is $3.95), made with Tillamook Mint Chocolate ice cream, I thought there had been a mistake. "Hey Ross," I whispered to my nephew, "I think something must have been wrong with the machine that made the chocolate pieces for this tub of ice cream. The chunks of chocolate are really large. Maybe the pieces somehow got stuck together at the factory and ended up in this tub." Ross ordered the same flavor of shake and he thought the same thing. We both smiled conspiratorially and enjoyed our shakes even more, thinking we had somehow scored one-of-a-kind shakes no one in the world would ever get again.

It turns out that the joke was on us. The chunks of chocolate in Tillamook Mint Chocolate ice cream are always mostly large enough to clog the milkshake straw. The folks at the Coffee Shop know how to make great milkshakes. They mix ice cream and milk to a perfect milkshake consistency. At the bottom of the shake cup you will discover wonderful lumps of chocolate, with just a tad bit of mint ice cream left over. Eating the chocolate chunks last is the perfect ending to this wonderful shake.

The Coffee Shop is a fun place to stop for baked goods or coffee. The store sells 12 flavors of Tillamook ice cream (single scoop $2.85, single-scoop sundae $3.50). The shop is located on the main street in Manzanita. Two blocks west is the beach. Take your snack from the Coffee Shop and enjoy it while watching the waves from the comfort of one of several benches conveniently located for beachcombers and tourists near the pedestrian entrances to the beach. If you would prefer not walking to the beach, there is also a long bench outside the Coffee Shop that is in a great location for people watching. During inclement weather, there are several tables for customers inside the Coffee Shop. Take time to admire the huge science posters that hang inside the Coffee Shop. The posters were originally displayed in a grade school. Reading each sign and trying to understand each scientific concept will be an education in itself.

When you have finished your treat, check out the wonderful set of shops in Manzanita. You are sure to be impressed by this cute coastal community.

Address: 60 Laneda Ave, Manzanita OR 97130
Phone: 503-368-CAFE
Hours: Winter: Sunday-Thursday 7 a.m.-1 p.m.,
Friday-Saturday 7 a.m.-5 p.m.
Summer: 7 a.m.-8 p.m. daily
Restrooms: ADA accessible

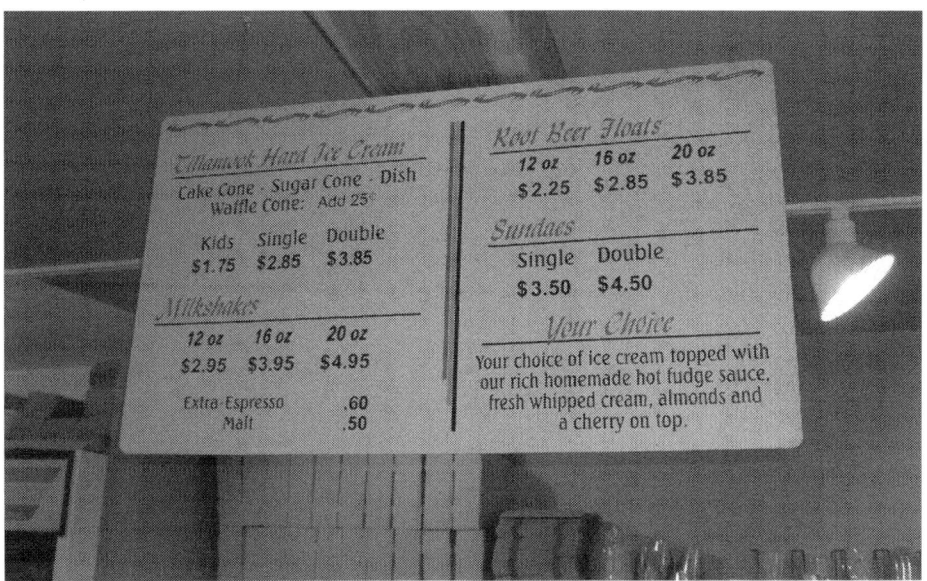

Oceanside

Brewin' in the Wind

You will love spending time in Oceanside. First, park at the Oceanside Beach Recreation Site. With a scenic view of Cape Lookout to the south and Three Arches Rocks out past the breakers, this is a lovely spot for a walk on the beach. Then, visit Brewin' in the Wind, a darling restaurant just steps from the beach parking lot. This cozy restaurant has something for everyone. Whether you want to warm up with an espresso or coffee drink, or you have worked up an appetite and are looking for breakfast, lunch, or dinner, you will find something on the menu to please you. Try dishes such as Mediterranean Quiche ($5.95), Baked Peach-Blueberry French Toast ($6.25), or Turkey Pesto Sandwich ($8.95). Treat yourself to one of several desserts, including Tillamook ice cream. A kids' sugar cone is $2. One scoop in a waffle cone is $2.50. Two scoops are $4.50. Whatever you choose to eat or drink, you are sure to enjoy the casual atmosphere, great food, and remarkable view from this restaurant.

Address:	1610 Pacific Ave NW, Oceanside, OR 97134
Phone:	503-842-1919
Hours:	Daily 7 a.m.-7 p.m.
Restrooms:	Not ADA accessible

FUN FACT
Ice Cream Cone Innovator

In 1913 Frederick Bruckman of Portland, Oregon patented a machine that could roll cones for ice cream.

Seaside

Flashback Malt Shoppe, Collectibles & Gifts

Take a step back in time as you sit in a comfortable booth, relax with an ice cream soda, and listen to Frank Sinatra as his sultry voice fills this cute-as-they-come retro malt shoppe on the Promenade in Seaside. The pride and joy of Robert Crook and Boni Snydercrook, this malt shoppe also teems with collectibles reminiscent of the past. You'll find vintage comic books, over 1000 tin signs, and sections of the store dedicated to Coke memorabilia, Betty Boop, Lucille Ball, and other icons and brands of the past. You will hear songs ranging from 40s swing tunes through songs from the 60s and the Beatles.

You can also enjoy 20 flavors of Cascade Glacier ice cream during the winter season and 30 flavors in the summer season. Try a cone (single scoop $2.95/double scoop $4.45) or a sundae (single scoop $3.45/double scoop $5.75). The sundae comes with whipped cream and a cherry. For nuts, add 25 cents. You may also decide to order one of their many specialty sundaes. A Tin Roof Sundae includes two scoops of vanilla ice cream, one covered in marshmallow topping, one with chocolate topping, and both topped with whipped cream, chopped nuts, and a cherry ($5.95) The Flashback Delight comes with two scoops of vanilla ice cream, covered in raspberry and chocolate syrup, and topped with whipped cream, pecans, and a cherry ($5.95). The list of tasty treats goes on and on. If you are visiting during lunch or dinner, hotdogs ($3), BBQ pulled pork sandwiches ($5), corn dogs ($2), and burritos are on the menu.

What makes this shop most unique is its amazing assortment of sodas from all over the United States and beyond. There are over 180 refrigerated flavors just waiting to quench your thirst or tickle your taste buds. Most bottles are $2.25. Some unusual aluminum-bottled sodas are $2. Flashback also is beginning to bottle their own sodas. So far, they have bottled a traditional root beer, a blue cream soda, and a birch root beer soda. Cherry cola will be added this June. Other flavors will be added in the near future. The birch root beer has an amazing full-bodied flavor, making it one of the best sodas I have ever tasted. Robert Crook says that men who want to impress their dates should order a birch root beer float ($4) because when vanilla ice cream is added to the soda, the ice cream foam turns pink! Yes, it is true. I saw it with my own eyes.

As I sat talking to Robert, enjoying my birch root beer, two 20-somethings dressed in black hoodies came up to the table. One reached out his hand to shake Robert's hand and said, "That was the best root beer I have ever tasted. We will definitely be back." With that comment the two went out the door into the sunshine. Robert Crook smiled and said modestly, "We get that a lot here."

If you like sodas and you like ice cream, try an ice cream float at Flashback Malt Shoppe and you will instantly know why soda fountains used to be all the rage. With the myriad combination of ice creams and soda possibilities to try at Flashback, you can keep your palate entertained for a long time at this shop. Make Flashback a must-taste stop on your trip to Seaside.

Address: 318 Broadway, Seaside OR 97138
Phone: 503-738-6614
Hours: Winter: 10 a.m.-6 p.m. daily
Summer: 10 a.m.-10 p.m. daily
Restrooms: Restroom available in mall. Wheelchairs will fit in the malt shop.

Zinger's Ice Cream

Knowing they wanted to do some kind of work that involved food, Mike and Mona Exinger bought Stogo's book on ice cream making and launched themselves head first into the homemade ice cream business. Their first batch of ice cream, in 2004, was vanilla. Then they started experimenting with flavors, having tasting parties to sort out the winners. They used potato chips so to cleanse tasters' palettes between tastings. Today, at their very successful business, they rotate about 50 flavors of 18% butterfat ice cream during the year. They offer 24 flavors at a time: 12 standard flavors that are always available, and 12 flavors that rotate monthly. Flavors include Banana Pudding (made with real banana pudding and vanilla wafers), Coconut, Licorice, Chocolate Almond, and Toasted Marshmallow. Their best sellers include Mint Chocolate Chip, Oreo Cookie, Marionberry, Very Vanilla, and Just Plain Chocolate.

Single-scoop cones (one flavor) cost $3, double cones (two flavors) are $5, and triple cones (three flavors) cost $7. Handmade waffle cones are 75 cents extra. Sundaes start at $4 with your choice of hot fudge, marionberries, or peanut butter topping. 16-ounce milkshakes cost $5.50. Zinger's is located on Broadway Street, also known as the Promenade, in the coastal town of Seaside.

Address: 210 Broadway, Seaside OR 97138
Phone: 503-738-3939
Email: info@zingersiceCream.com
Hours: Seasonal operation, generally February through September. Call for dates and times.
Restrooms: ADA accessible

Additional information: Cash only. Zinger's has a monthly newsletter at newsletter@zingersicecream.com

Tillamook

Tillamook Cheese Factory

The Tillamook brand is a co-op of over 100 small dairies on the northern Oregon coast that got together and formed the Tillamook County Creamery Association (TCCA). The coastal area is perfect for raising dairy cattle, with lush grass and mild temperatures. The Tillamook brand is most famous for their award-winning cheddar cheese that has been produced for over 100 years. In 1972, Tillamook began making ice cream. It can be found in many grocery stores and scoop shops in Oregon.

For ice cream lovers, the Tillamook Cheese Factory is like going to ice cream heaven. It is the only place in the state that serves all 38 flavors of Tillamook ice cream. The line to get these sweet treats is well worth the wait. A variety of cones and dishes are offered, including freshly made waffle cones and bowls. There are also chocolate-dipped cones, milkshakes, and sundaes on the menu. For small appetites, try a junior dip cone. For larger appetites, visitors can order a 3-scoop sampler cup or a 5-scoop sampler cup. For the ice cream connoisseur with a hefty appetite, or several friends, order all 38 flavors in the "Ice Cream Tour." Be adventurous and check out a flavor or two that are new to you. One of my new favorites is Grandma's Cake Batter. It tastes just like the heavenly cake batter I used to lick off the spoon after my mother whipped up a cake.

The Tillamook Cheese Factory is one of the most visited tourist destinations in the state. At the factory, visitors can go on a self-guided tour to learn the process of turning milk into cheese. Watch the packaging process from windows that look out onto the production floor. You are sure to come away with a new appreciation for the hard work that goes into making cheese, from cow to consumption.

The Creamery Cafe at the Tillamook Cheese Factory serves up delicious, reasonably priced breakfasts, lunches, and dinners. The dining area has lots of seating but may be crowded on busy summer days.

There are lots of Tillamook products available for purchase at the factory. A variety of cheeses, curds and whey, fudge, and Tillamook brand souvenirs are attractively displayed in one section of the factory. In another area is a gift shop with many souvenir items to delight tourists.

If at all possible, visit the factory during the off-season. If you do visit during peak hours, be patient. Tillamook has worked hard to develop a system to keep lines moving and customers happy during their visit.

Address: 4185 Highway 101 North, Tillamook, OR 97141
Phone: 503-815-1300 or 1-800-542-7290
Web: www.tillamook.com
Hours: Labor Day through mid-June, 8 a.m.-6 p.m.
Mid-June through Labor Day 8 a.m.-8 p.m.
Closed Thanksgiving, Christmas
Restrooms: ADA accessible

North Coast Highway 101
Things to See and Do

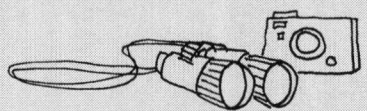

Astoria

Columbia River Maritime Museum

At the mouth of the majestic Columbia River, tons of river water flows west to meet the crashing waves of the Pacific Ocean headed east. Something has to give. The water rushing out to sea collides with the ocean at the mouth of the river at a place called "the bar." This area is also known as the "Graveyard of the Pacific" because many boats and ships have been swallowed by the sea while sailors tried in vain to navigate this treacherous part of the ocean.

The Columbia River Maritime Museum, located right on the Columbia River in the once bustling cannery town of Astoria, is a great place to learn the stories of ships that met their doom. It also explains the remarkable skills of bar pilots who now are required to board ships on the high seas and navigate the vessels over the turbulent bar into the Columbia River. The heroic efforts of the Coast Guard to help troubled boats are depicted in displays that may make you seasick just looking at them.

In addition to the history of ships, glimpse what life was like for the thousands of people who made their livelihood in the fishing and cannery business. Take the wheel of a tugboat and learn how to make a tugboat move. Look at the advances in storm gear for sailors, and enjoy the many nautical displays. Watch fascinating videos. Then walk outside and board the Lightship Columbia, the ship that for years sat outside the mouth of the Columbia River with its beacon lighting the way for ingoing and outgoing vessels. For young and old alike, the Columbia River Maritime Museum has something that will leave you gawking in amazement.

Oh yeah, and have I ever been across the bar? There is not enough Dramamine in the world that would get me into a boat to cross the bar. I know I would get VERY seasick. Yet hundreds of anglers go fishing in this part of the river every year to catch salmon. I'll stick to ice cream, thank-you very much!

Address: 1792 Marine Dr., Astoria, OR 97103
Phone: 503-325-2323
Web: www.crmm.org
Hours: 9:30-5 p.m. daily (closed Thanksgiving, Christmas)
Admission: See website for current prices
Restrooms: ADA accessible
Getting there: Take Hwy 26 to the coast and turn onto Hwy 101 toward Seaside. Continue north on 101 and follow the signs to Astoria. Go through downtown Astoria on Hwy 30 (Marine Drive) and on the left you will see the museum.

Cannon Beach

Cannon Beach Sandcastle Day

Once a year since 1964, the shovels and buckets come out for Sandcastle Day in Cannon Beach. Hundreds of people stroll along the beach in front of Haystack Rock at low tide, watching as groups of kids and grown-ups alike shovel, pummel, scoop, carve, and smooth creations out of the sand. Ranging from traditional sandcastles, creatures from the deep blue sea, whimsical creatures, and sculptures that will just make you laugh out loud, it is a swell way to spend a day at the beach.

For a real treat, get a group of friends or family together and try your own hand at creating a masterpiece. You need to register before the event and the contest is limited to 150 entries. The categories are for Sand Master (groups of 1-10), Business District (5-8 people), Large Group (5-8 people), Small Group (1-4 people), Sand Teens (1-8 people, ages 12-18), Sand Juniors (1-8 people, ages 7-11), and Sand Fleas (1-4 people, ages 6 or less.) There is a $25/person entry fee for Sand Masters. Business District entries are $20/

person. The entry fee is $20/person for both Large Group and Small Group participants. In the younger divisions, there is a $15/person fee for Teens and Sand Juniors, and $5/person for Sand Fleas. Each participant receives a t-shirt that would have cost $15 ($12 for kids) if you just wanted the t-shirt, so it really does not cost much to enter the contest. The fun factor is well worth the effort.

This year I decided to try my hand with three long-time friends, Larry, Janice, and their high school-aged daughter, Suzannah. We had a blast! We went online and found out that the best ratio of sand to water is 8 parts sand to 1 part water. The first thing to do when building a sculpture is to make a big pile of sand that will hopefully stick together when you carve it. It is also important to keep pounding down the sand as you make your pile. Next, using trowels, cookie turners, and putty knives, you carve your masterpiece. Not happy with a particular part? Pound it down and do it again.

We were tickled with our results. What surprised us most was that we all worked well together. We had a vision that evolved as we worked in the sand. In the morning, at the beginning of the event, the beach was fairly deserted except for the groups digging away in the sand. As the day progressed, we focused our attention on the details of our sculptures and began carefully shaping our creation. We started hearing comments from spectators as they walked past us. At first we heard things like, "What is it?" "I think it is going to be a whale." Then a little girl's voice said, "I think that's a cherry on top." BINGO! Then we started hearing comments like, "I'll meet you by the banana split," "I'm getting hungry for ice cream," and best of all, "Nice job." When we finished, we finally stood up and looked around. The beach was filled with thousands of spectators! We were surprised and ecstatic when we won first place in our division and proudly wore our medals to lunch in Cannon Beach. We are already talking about next year.

So go ahead and give it a try. After all it's only sand. Your art piece will be claimed back by the sea in a few short hours. However, your adventure will carve memories that will stay with you for a long time. You will have given others a reason to smile. Besides that, it is fun to play in the sand, no matter what your age!

Address:	Cannon Beach Chamber of Commerce, PO Box 64, Cannon Beach, OR 97110
Phone:	503-436-2623
Web:	**www.cannonbeach.org**
Email:	chamber@cannonbeach.org
Next date:	Call or see website for current dates and times.
Getting there:	The contest is held just north of Haystack Rock, the most prominent feature on the beach.

near Hammond

Fort Stevens State Park

With many thanks to Oregon's environmentally conscious former governor Tom McCall, a "beach bill" was passed in the state legislature in 1967 that guarantees the public" right to free access to Oregon's beaches. Making the coastline even more accessible to the public, a series of states parks have been developed along the coast for the public's enjoyment. Most state parks have day-use areas with picnic tables and restrooms. Many parks also provide overnight camping facilities for campers who use tents, trailers, or RVs. Each campsite has a picnic table and a contained fire pit. Water spigots and garbage cans are located near roadways for easy access. Overnight park facilities offer well-maintained indoor restrooms and shower rooms conveniently located to camping spots. Some state parks also have yurts that can be reserved, making camping an experience available to almost anyone.

At 3700 acres, Fort Stevens is the largest state park on the Oregon coast. There are around 500 camping spots and 15 yurts that can be reserved. Besides a beautiful beach to walk on, the final remaining wreckage of the Peter Iredale can still be seen during low tide. There is not much left of the old ship, but it is still possible to faintly make out its original size from what is left of the iron hull and rusting sides that stick up through the sand. At the north end of the beach is a jetty with a small viewing platform. Watching the waves crash up on the jetty is a great show of nature and the ocean's power.

The park has miles of biking and hiking trails to enjoy. Coffenbury Lake has two swimming areas. We used to take our little two-person sailboat to the lake and had a great time sailing.

Battery Russell is also a fun place to explore. It is what remains of a military post that defended the United States from foreign attack during World Wars I and II. It was the only continental location in the U.S. fired upon during World War II, ironically by the same Japanese sub that I mention in the page on Fort Orford Lifeboat Station. That sub really got around!

Whether you spend a day, a weekend, or a week, Fort Stevens is a special place to spend time on the Oregon coast. Don't forget the ingredients for s'mores!

Address: 100 Peter Iredale Rd., Hammond, OR 97121
Phone: 503-861-1671
Web: www.oregonstateparks.org
Hours: Available year round
Fees : Reservations are accepted for overnight visits. Go to www.oregonstateparks.org. Some sites may be available on a first come, first served basis without a reservation, but don't count on it during the busy summer season!
Restrooms: ADA accessible
Getting there: From Portland, take Hwy 26 west toward the coast. Turn north toward Seaside onto Hwy 101. After Camp Rilea, turn left at Fort Stevens Hwy/OR-104 N. Turn left at Whiskey Rd. Turn left at 18th St/Delaura Beach Lane. Continue onto NW Ridge Road. Turn left at Peter Iredale Road.

near **Manzanita**

Kayak Building On the Oregon Coast

Building a skin-on-frame kayak is a lot like giving birth. You start out with two long boards and slowly build the skeleton one little board at a time. You spend a week of sweat and labor. Cutting here, tweaking and rounding off corners there, the ribs of the frame slowly take shape. Then the "skin" is draped over the kayak. You learn to stitch the cloth around the frame, enclosing it in a tight cocoon. After you waterproof the shell, it is time to take your boat out into the light of the bay. Your first paddle is easily the sweetest. While the waves gently rock you in your kayak, you swell with pride and realize you LOVE your new boat.

If you think you would enjoy the experience of building your own kayak, one that is designed to fit your individual body, Cape Falcon Kayak is a wonderful place to learn. Brian Schulz is a fantastic instructor who gives clear instructions, help when needed, and time to actually enjoy the process of building your boat. Brian works to maintain high standards at each step of the process and he can explain why the boats are built in a particular way. He is a true craftsman who loves the water and is willing to share his love of boat building with others. This is a once-in-a-lifetime experience to remember with fondness and pride.

Address:	PO Box 582, Manzanita, OR 97130
Phone:	503-368-3044
Web:	www.capefalconkayak.com
Email:	capefalconkayak@gmail.com or capefalconkayak@yahoo.com
Hours:	Classes are scheduled in the spring, summer, and fall. Check the website for specific dates and times. 60% of his yearly classes fill up on the first day of registration, January 1.
Fee:	$1200 for the week. Includes instruction and materials to make a kayak and Greenland paddle.
Restrooms:	Port-a-potty located on site
Other information:	Students should bring lunch and or snacks to each class.
Getting there:	The class takes place in a big barn about 11 miles east of Manzanita. See website for specific directions.

Seaside

Seaside Wheel Fun Rentals

Although I do not usually include businesses that belong to national or regional chains, I need to make an exception for Seaside Wheel Fun Rentals. Tourists who use Wheel Fun equipment look like they are having a blast. Pedal-powered activities provide hours of fun for visitors in this coastal community. Tourists can rent various sized bicycle-powered surreys that hold 2-9 people. The colorful surreys with fringe on top can be seen on city streets near the waterfront with passengers pedaling up and down, laughing and giggling with glee. You might see parents (or grandparents) with a couple of kids, groups of teenagers, or all-adult groups of friends, enjoying the camaraderie of working together to propel their surrey along the city streets.

For those who want to spend more time down on the beach rather than on the city streets, Wheel Fun Rents funcycles, which are three-wheeled, low-to-the-ground cycles that give riders a trip to remember as they easily glide over wet sand. The cycles are built for one rider.

Tourists who do not want to work so hard on their adventure can rent a two-seat or four-seat electric car. Motor scooters and a Scoot Coupe are also available for a fee.

Then there is equipment rental for more water-based activities. Boogie boards are available for beach use. Both single and double kayaks can be rented for cruising the body of water that runs through the heart of Seaside. There is also an area here for paddleboats that are built to seat either two or four people. Bumper boats can be rented for some splashing good fun. More sedate visitors may choose to rent a stand-up paddle board to explore the banks of the inlet.

Whatever type of equipment you choose to rent from Seaside Wheel Fun, get ready for an action-packed day at the beach. Seaside Wheel Fun has four locations near the Seaside turnaround, also known as the Promenade.

Address/Phone: Main Hub Store, 407 S Holladay, Seaside, OR 97138, 503-738-8447
Spoke #1, N Columbia, 503-717-4337
Spoke #2, 153 Ave A., 503-738-7212
Convention Center Boat Docks

Web:	www.wheelfunrentals.com/listlocations/64
Hours:	Available year round, weather permitting. Call ahead to check.
	Summer: Open daily 9 a.m.-sunset
	Winter: Monday-Friday 9 a.m.-5 p.m.
	Weekends: weather permitting
Rental fees:	See website for current prices

near Tillamook

Bay Ocean Spit

In 1906, T. B. Potter, a real estate developer, got the brilliant idea to create a tourist destination that would rival the East Coast's Atlantic City. During its short heyday, Bay Ocean Park, as it was named, developed many amenities that would draw in tourists. There was a general store, bowling alley, hotel, and natatorium. City services, providing electricity, water, and telephones, were installed. Six hundred building lots were sold, and many houses were built. Then the Pacific Ocean began to take back the town. Slowly, waves undermined foundations and buildings began slipping into the sea. Francis Mitchell, who bought the first lot in 1907, stuck it out until 1952, when he was the last to leave.

Today, nothing remains of the town, but it is a wonderful place for a hike. The area is home to over 200 species of birds. There are long stretches of beaches to explore. It is now a very peaceful place to contemplate the power of nature and the wisdom of building houses on sand.

Directions:	From Tillamook, take State Route 131(3rd Street westbound) and follow the signs toward Cape Mears. You will see two large signs describing Bay Ocean Spit on your right after you have driven about 7 miles. Use the dike road to cross over to the spit to begin your exploration.
Restrooms:	No

Tillamook Air Museum

Oregon has several museums that preserve aviation history. The Tillamook Air Museum showcases 30 types of aircraft that once defied gravity and took to the sky. Most of the aircraft displayed are still in flyable condition. Visitors can wander around and admire the planes on a self-guided tour.

The museum itself is in a hangar that was once the home of World War II blimps. The gigantic floating blimps were strategically placed on U.S. coastlines to provide escort to convoys and to guard against submarine attacks on U.S. soil. Of the two original hangars built just outside Tillamook, only one remains. Hangar B is an enormous structure that is a feat of engineering. The interior of the hangar is large enough to play six football games. Be sure to watch the video that showcases the story of the blimps and the construction of the hangars. The hangars were commissioned in 1942 and decommissioned in 1948. Hangar B has been a museum since 1994.

Address: 6030 Hangar Rd., Tillamook, OR 97141
Phone: 503-842-1130
Web: www.tillamookair.com
Email: info@tillamookair.com
Hours: Open daily 9 a.m.-5 p.m. except Thanksgiving, Christmas
Admission: Adults $9, Seniors (65+) $8, Youth (6-17) $5, Active Military ($8), Adult Group (10 or more) $7.50, Guppy Admission $3, Family of 4 (2 adults/2 youth) $25
Restrooms: ADA accessible
Gettng there: The museum is two miles south of Tillamook on Hwy 101.

Tillamook Forest Center

The landscape driving from Portland to Tillamook today is a lot different than it was when I was growing up in the 1950s. We often took Highway 6 on weekends in the summer, pulling our little silver trailerhouse behind our station wagon, on our way to a weekend camping at the beach. Going over the coastal mountain range, I took for granted the tall stand of burned trees, a virtual matchstick forest that towered above the seedlings that struggled to stretch themselves up off the forest floor. "When I was a girl," my mother would say as we motored west, "the sky above Portland was so black with smoke that cars had to turn their headlights on in the middle of the day."

She was talking about the Tillamook Burn of 1933. The Tillamook forest first ignited when she was 13. The fire raged through the trees and destroyed 239,695 acres of tall timber and everything else in its path. Its smoke blanketed Portland and ash fell on ships 500 miles out to sea. Yet the fire of 1933 was only the first of four fires that eventually consumed 355,000 acres of Oregon forests. Occurring every 6 years, from 1933 to 1951, it became known as the 6-year jinx.

After the fires, thousands of people, including kids from schools, youth groups, and other organizations volunteered to replant the forest. The replanting went on for 20 years. The deer and elk ate two out of three seedlings that were planted. The replanting still continued. Today, it is hard to imagine that there was once a ravished forest in the coastal range. Thanks to the help of countless Oregonians, the green forest has returned with majestic trees, once seedlings, still stretching toward the sky.

The Tillamook Forest Center is a place for visitors to glimpse the past, learn about the lifecycle of a forest, and appreciate the work it takes to preserve a healthy natural treasure. It is a great place to learn about trees, and it honors those who helped the Tillamook forest return to life. There are engaging displays in the visitor center, an excellent 15-minute movie about the Tillamook Burn that is well worth watching, and outside there's a forest tower you can climb to see what it is like to work as a forest fire lookout. Behind the main building is a bridge that crosses over the Wilson River to hiking trails and a campground. The center has a gift store and friendly staff to answer questions. Most touching is a bulletin board in the visitor center where guests can put up notes. Many are from people who remember re-planting the forest as children. They share their memories with pride. Today, outside, stands the fruit of their labor for all to enjoy.

Address:	45500 Wilson River Highway, Tillamook, OR 97141
Phone:	866-930-4646
Web:	**www.tillamookforestcenter.org**
Hours:	Summer daily 10 a.m.-5 p.m., Fall, winter, spring, Wednesday-Sunday 10 a.m.-4 p.m.
Admission:	FREE
Restrooms:	ADA accessible
Getting there:	Located on Hwy 6 near milepost 22, about an hour's drive west of Portland

Section 8
Off the Beaten North Coast Highway 101

Ice Cream

Westport

The Berry Patch Restaurant

If you love berries and want to experience marionberry milkshake Nirvana, stop at the Berry Patch Restaurant, located in the town of Westport. Westport is on Highway 30, which winds along the Columbia River from Portland to Astoria. Westport is 25 miles east of Astoria.

The delicious jams, jellies, and pies that you will find for sale there are all the inspiration of Stan Egaas, who began making marionberry jam for his friends in his home kitchen. In 1987, he branched out and began his commercial berry operation out of a pole building that he had licensed so he could make jams. In 1990, he purchased the current building that sits next to Highway 30. Even though Egaas had never been in a commercial kitchen before, there was extra space in the new building, so he decided to turn the unused space into a restaurant.

Today, the restaurant serves breakfast and lunch seven days a week. Dinner is served on Friday, Saturday, and Sunday evenings. The menu is full of wonderful home-cooked food at reasonable prices. I had a turkey sandwich with their tasty signature pepper jelly, and a garden salad, with their wonderful marionberry vinaigrette for $7.95. I loved the lunch, but it was the milkshake that I really came for. The marionberry milkshake ($3.50) comes in an old-fashioned tin with an extra glass. It could easily serve two people, though I blissfully drank the whole thing. It is made using Cascade Glacier vanilla ice cream with Berry Patch marionberries added. The milkshake's rich, creamy berry flavor and texture will definitely keep me going back for more!

All of the jams and other Berry Patch products are made in the Berry Patch building. The small staff works in a modestly appointed kitchen, producing thousands of jars of jams, jellies, and other products, one batch at a time. Visitors may view the operation through glass windows. The staff is willing to stop and answer questions. Peggy, the head jam maker, has been making jams and other products here for over 24 years.

The Berry Patch uses an incredible amount of berries yearly. Last year, 10,000 pounds of marionberries went from their kitchen into their jams, jellies, syrups and pies. They sold over a staggering 4,000 pies! They also used 300 gallons of huckleberries. If you have ever seen huckleberries and you know how small they are, you will better appreciate how many berries there must be in those 300 gallons! This coming summer, an estimated 500 gallons of huckleberries will be needed for Berry Patch products.

The products made in the Berry Patch product kitchen are displayed in an area adjacent to the restaurant where customers can browse. You will find 22 types of jams, jellies, syrups, and other Oregon products. Besides marionberries, there are products made with wild blackberries, chokecherries, and huckleberries. There are also pepper jellies. One unusual item is blackberry catsup, good on ham and other meat products.

The company is just in the process of adding two new berry products, a marionberry topping and a huckleberry topping. Both will be perfect on ice cream. Mr. Egaas let me sample the new toppings with vanilla ice cream. I became an instant fan and I am sure they will both become big hits with customers. Each one tastes like fresh berries, and both are not too sweet and not too tart. They are just right!

Also in the works for the Berry Patch are a new line of products that will be sold in a limited number of supermarkets. Razor clam chowder and wild chanterelle mushroom soup will be sold in glass jars. Also new will be two kinds of chanterelle mushroom gravies, one light, and one dark.

While you are visiting the restaurant and store, be sure to take a look at the historical photos that were taken in this part of Oregon. You can also view a 16-minute video that pays tribute to the ingenuity of Simon Benson, a famous Oregonian who made a fortune in the lumber business in the early 1900s. The video is well worth your time. With great food and interesting things to see, make the Berry Patch Restaurant a must-see on your next trip on Highway 30.

Address: 49289 Highway 30, Westport, OR 97016
Mailing Address: 77129 Watach Dr., Clatskanie, OR 97016
Phone: 503-455-2250
Hours: Monday-Thursday 8 a.m.-3 p.m.,
Friday-Saturday 8 a.m.-8 p.m.,
Sunday 8 a.m.-7 p.m.
Restrooms: ADA accessible (ask at the counter)

FUN FACT

Top 10 Ice Cream Flavors in the U.S.

Vanilla, 29%
Chocolate, 8.9%
Butter Pecan, 5.3%
Strawberry, 5.3%
Neopolitan, 4.2%
Chocolate Chip, 3.9%
French Vanilla, 3.8%
Cookies and Cream 3.6%
Vanilla Fudge Ripple, 2.6%
Praline Pecan, 1.7%

Off the Beaten north Coast Highway 101
Things to See and Do

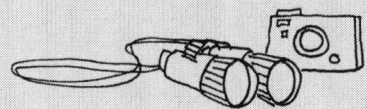

Westport

Westport Ferry

Just down the street from the Berry Patch Restaurant, you'll find the directional sign to the Westport Ferry. Since 1925, this no-frills little ferry has been transporting people and vehicles between Westport and Puget Island, an island in Washington State. The ten-minute ride takes passengers on a short trip on the Columbia River. On the Washington side you will find farmlands, with houses scattered on the island.

On sunny days, many people like to ferry their bikes across to the island. They spend a relaxing day riding on the island's flat roads and then ferry themselves back to the Oregon side. The island is also a great spot for bird-watchers.

The ferry leaves each dock once an hour seven days a week. Even if you just decide to ride the ferry round trip and never get off, you will have a pleasant, if short, outing on the river.

.....

Address: Westport, OR
Hours: Daily. The ferry leaves each dock once an hour.
The ferry holds approximately 12 vehicles.
Admission: No credit cards accepted
Only one-way tickets are available.
Passenger cars, pickups, and tractors under 20 feet, $5.
Passengers in vehicles, FREE
Foot passengers, $1, no kids under 12 years old without supervision.
Bicycles $2, Motorcycles $3
Trucks, motor homes, and specialized equipment under 25 feet, $10 (each additional 5 feet $5)
Tractors under 20 feet $4 (each additional 5 feet $2)
Trailers under 20 feet $4 (each additional 5 feet $2)
Buses $20
Restrooms: Restroom on ferry

Section 9
Central Coast Highway 101

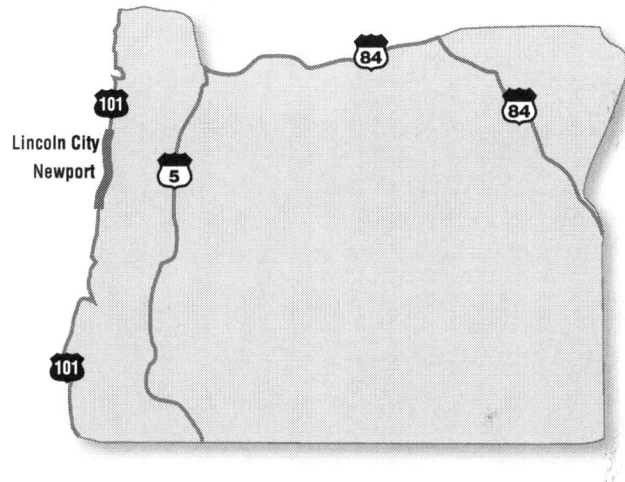

Eleanore's Undertow Cafe and Ice Cream Parlor, Lincoln City

Central Coast Highway 101
Ice Cream

Lincoln City

Eleanor's Undertow Cafe and Ice Cream Parlor

Over 30 years ago, Eleanor Kramer was working at Mo's Chowder Restaurant in Taft when she decided that what the town really needed was a place to go for take-out food and ice cream. She told Mo that she wanted to open her own place and they made a no-competition deal, agreeing that Eleanor would not sell chowder and Mo would not sell ice cream. Eleanor opened her little store next to Mo's, at first serving four flavors of ice cream: vanilla, chocolate, strawberry, and rainbow sherbet. Four years later she built the store that still stands across the street from Mo's, offering ice cream and desserts, as well as lunch items, but no chowder.

It is hard to miss the cafe. It is pink...bright bubble gum pink. The store is known for its homemade quarter-pound chocolate chip cookies ($1.50), homemade cobbler ($4/ala mode $5), and delicious, good, old-fashioned 20-oz. shakes. The store serves 16 flavors of Umpqua ice cream. Single-scoop cones are $2.75, double scoops are $4. Lunch items include 1/3-third pound hamburgers, halibut fish and chips, and more.

Eleanor's is conveniently located near the ocean, where beachcombing, picnicking, or just hanging out watching the waves and the sea lions are just steps away. Lots of parking spots are available near the cafe.

Address:	869 SW 51st St., Lincoln City, OR 97367
Phone:	541-996-3800
Hours:	Daily 11 a.m.-6 or 7 p.m.
Restrooms:	ADA accessible
Getting there:	Eleanor's Undertow is at the far south end of Lincoln City in historic Taft District. Take U.S. Hwy 101 south. Turn west onto SW 51st. The cafe is on the right.

Wildflower Grill

At the northern end of Lincoln City on Hwy 101, the Wildflower Grill is a darling cottage restaurant nestled among a variety of cheerful wildflowers that invite customers to the front door. The restaurant is on a curve in the highway that makes the restaurant easy to miss, but it is worth taking the time to find if you would like a tasty, well-prepared breakfast, lunch, or dinner. The food is wonderful, although not the cheapest in town. A half sandwich and soup is $8.95. A Cobb salad with wonderful marionberry walnut vinaigrette is $14.95 and a French dip sandwich is $11.95. Kid's lunches (for children 12 and under) are $4.95 and include several choices.

The pièce de resistance for me is their mud pie, made with delicious Cascade Glacier Kona ice cream. The ice cream sits on a thick chocolate cookie crust and is topped with a layer of chocolate and whipped cream. Chocolate syrup is drizzled all over the top. A slice of this epicurean delight costs $5.95. I prefer to eat mine slightly thawed, sitting on the enclosed deck at the back of the restaurant, looking out over the pond below where the ducks are paddling around. It doesn't matter the time of year or weather, the coziness and relaxed atmosphere of this restaurant makes me feel like I am treating myself to a special time just for me.

Address: 4250 NE Hwy 101, Lincoln City, OR 97367
Phone: 541-994-9663
Hours: Open daily
Breakfast 7 a.m.-11 a.m.
Lunch 11 a.m.-4 p.m.
Dinner 5 p.m.-9 p.m. Tuesday-Saturday
Restrooms: ADA accessible
Getting there: The Wildflower Grill is at the northern end of Lincoln City on Hwy 101.

FUN FACT

Which U.S. cities eat the most ice cream?

Portland Oregon, St. Louis Missouri, and Seattle Washington.

Newport

Bay Latte

Newport is a wonderful town for window shopping along the bay front, sampling a variety of foods, watching boats returning with their daily catch, and discovering knick knacks and art pieces that you know would look perfect in your house. During the summer take a break at Bay Latte, owned by Don and Fran Matthews, where you can enjoy an expresso, Italian soda, or one of 16 flavors of Tillamook ice cream.

Right outside the ice cream shop, take the time to watch fishing boats coming and going in and out of the harbor. Sea lions sometimes swim close to the dock and can be quite entertaining. While savoring your ice cream treat, enjoy the suspense as people pull in crab pots they have left attached to the railing, hoping for a juicy crab to enter their trap. Did they get any crabs? If so, how many and are they the legal size? You might also see a fisherman or two enjoying a lazy day of casting their line into the watery depths to see what they can attract to their hook. Ah, ice cream and the smell of a salty sea. Does it get much better than this?

Address: 663 SW Bay Blvd., Newport, OR 97365
Phone: 541-265-2208
Hours: Summer: Sunday-Thursday 10 a.m.-8 p.m.,
Friday-Saturday 10 a.m.-9 p.m.
Weather-dependent—if it's pouring, they might close early
Closed November-February but open some weekends
Limited flavors during the winter
Restrooms: Next door
Getting there: Bay Latte is on the ocean side of the bay front in Newport. The bay front is on the north side of the bridge that crosses the harbor on Hwy 101. To get to Bay Latte, take Hwy 101 and then follow the signs to the bay front.

Flashbacks Café

If you are in the mood to go to a retro cafe, Flashbacks may be just for you. Their extensive menu boasts lunch and dinner entrees including burgers, sandwiches, pizzas, calzone, salads, steaks, chicken, and seafood. They serve fountain drinks, sundaes, malts, and shakes, using 18-24 flavors of Cascade Glacier, Umpqua, and Tillamook ice creams. Luncheon sundaes are $3.75, classic sundaes are $4.95, and specialty sundaes range in price from $4.45-$12.50. Old-fashioned milkshakes are $4.45 and malts are $4.75. Ice cream floats and ice cream sodas are $4.25. The casual atmosphere makes this cafe a relaxing place to unwind.

Flashbacks offers two kinds of ice cream parties with advance reservations. The birthday package, ($6.95/person) for a minimum of 10 people, includes vanilla ice cream sundaes with one topping, pitchers of soda, a bouquet of balloons, party favors, birthday hats, games, and dancing. The ice cream party, also for $6.95/person for a minimum of 10 people, includes a hot fudge mountain sundae with "a mountain of chocolate and vanilla ice cream topped with glaciers of hot fudge and marshmallow topping, a cloud of whipped cream, cherries, and sprinkles." The party also comes with pitchers of soda, a bouquet of balloons, games, and dancing.

One of Flashbacks' unique services is delivery, for a fee, to Waldport, Seal Rock, Newport, Agate Reach, Beverly Beach, and Toledo. For more information about this service, please call the cafe.

Address:	3333 South Highway 101, Newport, OR 97365
Phone:	541-867-6901
Hours:	Summer: Sunday-Thursday 11 a.m.-10 p.m., Friday-Saturday 11 a.m.-11 p.m. Winter: Sunday-Thursday 11 a.m.-8 p.m., Friday-Saturday 11 a.m.-9 p.m.
Restrooms:	One of the unisex bathrooms is ADA accessible.
Getting there:	Flashbacks is on the east side of the street on Hwy 101 in Newport

Newport Candy Shop & Ice Cream Parlor

Robert Hoefs learned to make chocolate candies when he was 18 from an elderly German candy-maker. Now 40, he is still making delicious chocolates, caramel corn, and salt water taffy. He recently purchased an ice cream store in Newport when the former owner retired. At that location you will now find caramel corn, 57 flavors of salt-water taffy, mouth-watering chocolates, and 40 flavors of ice cream, including Tillamook brand. Single-scoop cones or cups sell for $2.75. Waffle cones cost $3.75. 16-oz. milkshakes cost $3.75, and 24-oz. milkshakes are $4.75. Sundaes are $3.75 and $5. Banana splits cost $7. Try a mouth-watering brownie sundae for $4.75. A new addition to the line-up of cones will be sugar cones partly dipped in chocolate and then covered with either sprinkles, Butterfinger bits, or other sweet nuggets. These special cones will cost $1.25 more. Also, new waffle machines are now regularly making homemade waffle cones and waffle cups for the store.

Saltwater taffy sells for $6.50/pound. Caramel candy comes in $3, $4, and $5 boxes. Chocolates are $15.99/pound. So the next time your sweet tooth starts singing the blues, go to the Newport Candy Shop & Ice Cream Parlor. You are sure to find something yummy that will satisfy your craving.

Address: 19 North Coast Highway, Newport, OR 97365
Phone: 541-265-2256

Central Coast Highway 101
Things to See and Do

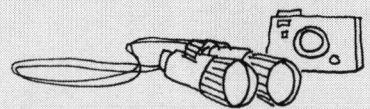

Lincoln City

Finders Keepers Glass Float Hunt
Since the 1900s, Oregon beachcombers have spent many hours searching for Japanese glass floats among the tangled seaweed that washes up on the shore, especially after major storms. The floats they are looking for were originally attached to long fishing nets that stretched for miles in the Pacific Ocean. The buoyant floats held up the fishing nets as they lay suspended in the ocean, waiting for unsuspecting fish to enter. If and when the floats, which were greenish or bluish, separated from the nets, they drifted with the tides, tossing and turning and sometimes becoming entangled in kelp and other seaweed. Eventually, many of the floats washed up onto Oregon beaches. Finding a float is a real thrill. Some people have searched a lifetime with no luck. Now, unfortunately, glass floats have been replaced by floats made of plastic or other materials. These days it is rare to find a Japanese glass float.

Then, someone in Lincoln City got the brilliant idea of having artists create hand-blown glass floats for tourists to hunt. It has become a creative way to get tourists to visit the coast during the off-season. Starting in 1999-2000, 2000 glass floats were tucked into crevices and behind logs along the seven and a half miles of coast between Road's End, north of Lincoln City, and Cutler City, south of the bridge at Taft. Every year, one more float is added, so in 2001 there were 2001 glass floats, and in 2002 there were 2002 glass floats, etc.

The program begins in mid-October and ends on Memorial Day. "Float fairies" daily hide the beautiful, colorful glass floats on the beach for visitors to find. The glass floats are found above the high tide mark and below the cliffs. They are not easy to spot. It often takes a lot of luck and keen eyes to find one. In fact, finding one may become your new lifelong pursuit.

Be safe. Visitors are asked to stay off the cliffs to avoid erosion. Do not turn your back to the ocean. Sneaker waves are unpredictable and often bring water rushing above the tide mark where you might expect the water to stop. It is also important to use caution around logs. Even large logs can move unpredictably and people are sometimes trapped under them. Remember that floats are not hidden during storms.

If you find a glass float, you get to keep it. If you do find one, call the Visitor and Convention Bureau at 1-800-452-2151 or 541-996-1274. Register your float and they will send you a Certificate of Authenticity and information about the artist who created your particular float.

Even if you don't find a float, do not be discouraged. Special drawings for glass floats are held once a month at the Visitor Center. All you have to do is take one bag of beach trash that you have picked up during your beachcombing to the Visitor Center at 540 N.E. Hwy 101. There you will fill out a form for a chance to win a float. You will also have helped keep Oregon beaches clean.

For information: Call the Lincoln City Visitor and Convention Bureau at 1-800-452-2151 or 541-996-1274
When: Mid-October to Memorial Day
Cost: FREE

Jennifer L. Sears Glass Art Studio

Jennifer Sears was one of the visionaries who established the Finders Keepers program in Lincoln City. Her idea was to have artists create one-of-a-kind glass balls that could be hidden on the beach for visitors to search for during the tourist off-season. Since 1999-2000, that program has been a wonderful success story. However, Jennifer Sears did not end her brainstorming there. She also imagined a place where tourists could go to make their own glass balls. That dream was realized when the city bought and remodeled a building in Taft (at the south end of Lincoln City) that bears the name of Jennifer Sears to honor her contribution to the city.

Since 2005 the building has been leased by Kelly Howard, James Benson, Jon Meyers, and Daniel Millen. Their business is called Lincoln City Glass Center. At the center, friendly, helpful artisans help visitors make their own glass balls, just like the ones that are hidden on the beach. The thrill of making one of these art objects includes picking out colors and helping in the blowing and shaping of the glass ball. It is a thrilling experience. After the glass ball is finished, it is placed in a machine called an annealer, where the glass is allowed to slowly cool so the ball does not break. The following day, customers can return to the shop to pick up their project, or the glass ball can be mailed home to the customer.

Besides making a glass ball, customers may choose to make a paperweight, a giant float, a bowl, a heart, or a starfish. Even if you decide not to make your own glass object, tourists are welcome to visit the studio and watch the fascinating process of glass blowing.

Address:	4821 S.W. Highway 101, Lincoln City, OR 97367
Phone:	541-996-2569
Web:	**www.jennifersearsglassart.com**
Hours:	First 2 weeks in January CLOSED. Wednesday-Sunday 10 a.m.-6 p.m. July 4-September 1 open daily 10 a.m.-6 p.m. Cost to make objects: Glass float $65, paper weight $75, heart $85, jumbo float $95, starfish $105, bowl $135
Restrooms:	Not ADA accessible. However, it is possible for other-abled people to make their own glass float; call for information.
Other information:	Call ahead to make a reservation. Walk-ins only if there is room. Do not wear open-toed shoes or fleece when you are blowing glass.

Mor Art

If you have ever been intrigued by fused glass and would like to explore this medium, check out Mor Art in Taft, at the south end of Lincoln City. In one session at this charming studio, you'll be able to create a unique piece of fused glass art, starting at $25 for a 6" x 9" rectangle. Prices go up from there depending on the size of your project. This would be a perfect activity for one of Oregon's rainy days at the beach. In a couple of hours, both kids and adults can create beautiful works of art at this studio. The colorful glasses are fun to assemble into different patterns and pictures. A wonderful variety of textures is possible with this medium. Your finished project will be ready the day after your class after it has been fired in a kiln and then allowed to cool before taken home.

Dan Watts, who has years of experience with fused glass, and his assistant Maurice Martinez, will help you through the process of creating your piece. Both men are enthusiastic and will help make your day at the studio one to remember. Stop by to see some of the wonderful art pieces for sale at the studio.

Address: 4933 SW Hwy 101, Lincoln City, OR 97367
Phone: 541-994-2427
Web: **www.morart.net**
Hours: Tuesday-Sunday 10 a.m.-5 p.m.
Restrooms: Not ADA accessible. However, it is possible for other-abled people to create an art piece. Call for information.

Newport

Oregon Coast Aquarium

Newport has been the home of the Oregon Coast Aquarium since 1992. The fledgling aquarium got a huge boost in attendance and revenue when it became the temporary home of Keiko, the orca whale who starred in the movie, Free Willy. Keiko arrived at the aquarium in 1996. He began training so that he could be freed back into the wild. He left the museum in 1998 and was transported back to Iceland, where he had been born, to continue his transition back into the wild.

Keiko's stay at the Oregon Coast Aquarium meant that a huge tank had to be installed to comfortably hold the whale. When Keiko left the aquarium, the space was remodeled into a new exhibit featuring sharks. Now, visitors can walk through a clear tube into a shark enclosure. Get an eyeball-to-eyeball look at these magnificent predators. Thank goodness the aquarium pipes in calm, soothing music. If they piped in the theme to Jaws, it would be a whole different experience.

The aquarium has a wonderful variety of sea life on display. Some of the aquarium's animals are in the main building and some are in outdoor enclosures. Inside, among other animals, you can watch seahorses and jellyfish. There is usually a special exhibit inside that changes during the year to keep visitors coming back for more. Outside, visitors are sheltered from rain by cleverly placed overhanging rocks in the viewing areas. You can see otters, sea lions, and even an octopus. Staggered feeding times allow visitors to observe the animals when they are fed. Shore birds happily glide through ponds and allow a close-up view. Throughout the aquarium, guides are eager to share information with visitors. If you want a real thrill, check out the regularly scheduled overnight adventure at the aquarium. You will have a chance to sleep in the shark tunnel and enjoy a variety of other scheduled activities during the evening.

There are also opportunities for animal encounters. Have you ever touched an octopus or been kissed by a sea lion? With a little planning, these experiences can happen for you at the Oregon Coast Aquarium.

You're sure to learn something new during each visit to the aquarium. With a comfortable cafe and interesting gift store, the Oregon Coast Aquarium will provide a nice outing for both kids and adults.

Address:	2820 SE Ferry Slip Rd., Newport, OR 97365
Phone:	541-867-3474
Web:	**www.aquarium.org**
Hours:	Daily except Christmas. Summer: 9 a.m.-6 p.m. Winter: (starts after Labor Day) 10 a.m.-5 p.m.
Admission:	See website for current prices
Restrooms:	ADA accessible.
Other information:	For overnight stay or animal encounter, call ahead for dates, times, and reservations.

Section 10
South Coast Highway 101

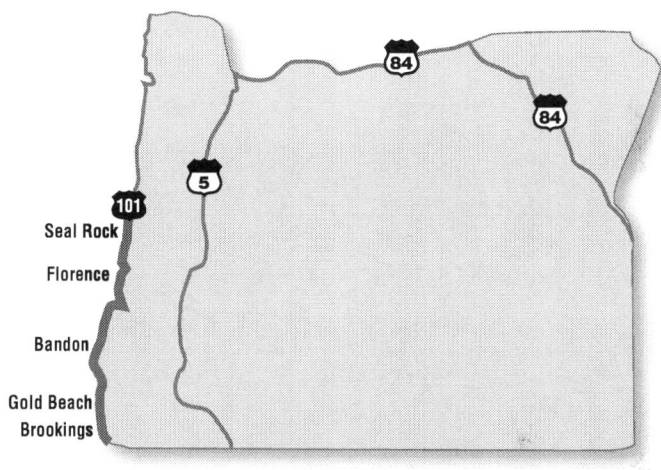

Game Park Safari, Near Bandon

South Coast Highway 101

Ice Cream

Brookings

Slugs 'n Stones 'n Ice Cream Cones

You just have to love a store with a name this cute. The imaginative offerings may make you giggle or at least smile, and isn't that the point of ice cream after all? Listed as "for the brave," the menu includes such offerings as Hanna Banana Slug Split ($4.75 small/$7.25 large)), Uncle Andrew Slug's Belly Acher Special ($15 for 10 flavors with all the trimmings served in your choice of a reusable pie tin or reusable beach bucket), and Dirt and Worms ($4.50). (Don't worry, they use chocolate "dirt" and gummy worms). For those without a sense of direction, there is the Foggy Bottom Sundae ($4.50), a sundae made upside down. Republicans in your group should try the Ultra Conservative Sundae with Mable Beyondallilo Nilla Vanilla and choice of topping, whipped cream, and a cherry on top.

Everyone will love this cute shop located at the Port in Brookings. The shop serves 35 flavors of Umpqua and Cascade Glacier ice cream. They even have sugar-free and milk-free products so people with food restrictions can get in on the fun. Yet even with the choices of ice creams and toppings available, vanilla is still the #1 best seller! Half-scoop ice cream cones are 75 cents and whole scoops are $1.75. Small milkshakes are $3.50 and large shakes are $4.25. Floats, freezes, and fizzes (all 20 oz.) are $4.

Two sisters, Willa Jones and Pat Silveria, opened this quirky shop together 17 years ago. As girls growing up, their family owned a mountain resort. The sisters learned how to deal with the many moods of the public. When it came time to start a business together, smile-making ice cream seemed like the perfect product to sell. Their homey shop has a casual atmosphere with tables and chairs available to better enjoy your ice cream treat. It is also a cozy place to get out of the occasional summer storm and wile some time away with a tasty ice cream dessert or take a break from shopping at the other nearby stores at the Port.

Address:	Port of Brookings
	Mailing: 97950 Holly Lane, Brookings, OR 97415
Email:	slugsandstones@webtv.net
Phone:	541-469-SLUG
Hours:	11 a.m. to dusk daily March 1-October 7
Restrooms:	ADA accessible restroom about four doors down from the shop.
Getting there:	Brookings is on the southern Oregon coast just north of the California border. In Brookings, follow the signs to the Port.

Florence

BJ's Ice Cream

Using a homemade family ice cream recipe originally formulated in Slater, Iowa in 1917, Keith Cole still uses his great-great grandfather's recipe to churn out 48 flavors of homemade ice cream at a small ice cream parlor in Florence, Oregon. Using cane sugar instead of corn syrup, 14.2% buttermilk cream from a dairy in Junction City, Oregon, and fresh berries, fruits, and nuts, Mr. Cole adds flavors by hand, ensuring each batch of ice cream is of exceptional quality. A favorite for many customers is BJ's Oregon Trail. It combines double chocolate, blackberries, and hazelnuts into a delightful treat.

Keith Cole is the fourth generation of his family to make ice cream. His father opened BJ's after he returned from serving in Vietnam. The original idea was to open the store so his wife would have a job while he worked at Safeway. Safeway later asked him to relocate to another location. He loved his home in Florence so he quit his Safeway job and settled in to help develop his wife's store. His son, also named Keith Cole, did not grow up thinking that the ice cream business would become his career. He managed a helicopter logging business for ten years. When the logging industry collapsed, he went to Ashland to try his hand at tourism. There he started his own ice cream store. Eventually he returned to Florence to manage the ice cream making end of the family business. After all these years he still loves ice cream. His favorite flavor is huckleberry.

Single-scoop cones cost $3.25, small hot fudge sundaes are $3.90, and small milkshakes are $4.60. Other sizes are available. Soft drinks start at $1.25. BJ's also makes homemade fudge and wonderful-looking cakes. The only items in their store that are not made by BJ's are the taffy, sorbets, and sherbets. You won't find BJ'S in any grocery stores. For that to happen the stabilizers in the recipe would need to be changed, and BJ's does not want to serve anything but the freshest ice cream with minimal stabilizers.

Address:	2930 Highway 101, Florence, OR 97439
Phone:	541-997-7286
Hours:	Summer: 10 a.m.-11 p.m.
	Winter: noon-10 p.m.
Restrooms:	ADA accessible
Additional information:	Tours of the facility can be arranged by calling ahead of tim

Gold Beach

Cone Amor

For some people, changing jobs can be like changing ice cream flavors, you just have to try something new. Geri Kendall and her husband Donald had had several different jobs in their lives before landing in the ice cream business a year ago. Donald was a firefighter and schoolteacher before co-owning a coffee shop and an ice cream store. Geri has had an even more colorful, or should we say flavorful, life. She was an IBM hardware programmer for 20 years. Then she was a surgical tech for Kaiser Permanente. After that she started a coffee shop in Gold Beach because she was bored in retirement. Soon she realized she needed more storage for her leased coffee shop space. She rented more space in the building and ended up with extra space. An ice cream shop perfectly filled that empty spot and her ice cream customers are certainly glad!

The ice cream store features 16 flavors of Umpqua ice cream. Local favorites are Pralines and Cream, Expresso Madness, Rainbow, Mountain Blackberry Revel, and Oregon 150. Geri's favorite is Pralines and Cream, although she admits to having loved Neapolitan as a youngster. Child single-scoop cones are $2.50, regular single-scoop cones are $3.50, sundaes are $4 and milkshakes are $4.25.

Like several ice cream stores in the state, this one is seasonal and closes in the fall, but not before celebrating with a giant Halloween bash for young and old alike. Even after Halloween, customers desperate for ice cream can go to the clerk at the coffee shop across the hallway and the clerk will walk over and get you your ice cream treat...that is until the last of the season's ice cream is finally gone. After that you will just have to wait until the next summer.

Address:	9975 Harbor Way, Gold Beach, OR 97414
Phone:	541-247-4270
Hours:	May 1-October 31, daily noon-8:30 p.m. Also open during Spring Break
Restrooms:	ADA accessible restroom in the building
Getting there:	Cone Amor is located in the Cannery Building at the Port of Gold Beach. The Cannery Building is located just off Hwy 101 at the north end of Gold Beach in the port boat basin on the waterfront. The port is on the south side of the Rogue River, just south of the bridge.

Seal Rock

Indulge Sweets

Monica Teem has always had a sweet tooth. She also has a winning smile and a quick laugh. She started out as the candy maker in her family. It was not much of a stretch for her to open a candy store in the little ocean side community of Seal Rock. The shop features homemade fudge, brownies, and caramel corn, all made from scratch. She added ice cream to her menu and now finds herself as the stopping point for a faithful clientele of people who come in for their ice cream and sweet tooth "fixes." When asked why they keep coming back to the shop, one customer said, "If I have a gallon of ice cream at home, I eat the gallon of ice cream. I come here to satisfy my craving and to have some control. Also, Monica can make me laugh."

Monica says people come in for their "happy calcium." She has a regular set of customers and she recognizes their cars as they pull into the parking lot. "That is a Tillamook Espresso Madness on a sugar cone," she says as a car pulls into a parking space. Sure enough, that is exactly what the customer ordered. I asked the customer, "What flavor would you choose if she ran out of your favorite flavor?" The customer stopped and thought for several minutes. She then looked up at me, looking a little crest-fallen. "She doesn't even want to THINK about that possibility," jumped in Monica, and with that she handed the ice cream to the customer whose demeanor suddenly brightened.

The store features 20 flavors of ice cream made by Tillamook and Umpqua. How does she choose her flavors? "It has to do with the "whine factor.". How much trauma and drama will probably occur if we run out of a particular flavor. Two flavors we try to NEVER run out of are Tillamook Mudslide and Umpqua Bordeaux Cherry."

Ice cream costs $2.50 for a single scoop, $4.75 for two scoops. Waffle cones are $3.25 for a single and $5.25 for a double. Kids scoops are $1.50 in a plain cup or cone and $2 for a waffle cone. Hot fudge sundaes are $3.50 and 16 oz. milkshakes are $3.50. Also for sale are a variety of coffee, mocha, chai, and latte drinks starting at $2.25 and costing as much a $3.75.

Monica Teem has been in the sweets business since 1999. She recently moved from a little shop a few blocks south to her current bright and cheery location. (Her store was formerly known as S.R. Fudge n' Stuff). Make sure you go to the correct address to indulge in this wonderful variety of sweets and ice cream in this friendly store.

Address:	10645 Pacific Coast Highway, Seal Rock, OR 97376
Phone:	1-877-99-FUDGE or 541-563-2766
Web:	**www.indulgesweetsoregoncoast.com**
Email:	99fudge@casco.net
Hours:	Closed Tuesdays Summer: 10:30 a.m.-6 p.m. Winter: 10:30 a.m.-5 p.m.
Restrooms:	No restrooms on site. The closest one is a short drive or walk south at Seal Rock State Recreation Site.
Getting there:	Seal Rock is between Newport (to the north) and Waldport (to the south) on Hwy 101 (Pacific Coast Hwy) on the southern Oregon coast.

South Coast Highway 101
Things to See and Do

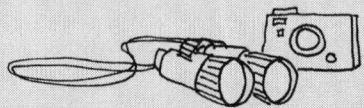

near Bandon

Game Park Safari
"The Original Walk-Thru Safari"
Calling itself "America's largest wild animal petting adventure," I arrived at Game Park Safari a skeptic and left a believer. No sooner had I gone through the concession's gift shop and into the wild beyond, then I came face to feathers with a peacock in full living color, just like the NBC logo, except with a lot more blue. The peacock began quaking his shimmering plumage like a jet engine revving up. Then he ran straight toward me! I turned and ran away, looking over my shoulder at my pursuer. After about five feet the peacock stopped and that was the end of our little pas de deux (which was really more of a quick step). I heard a woman behind me say, "I've never seen one do THAT before!" I don't have a clue why he chose to chase me except that I had on a royal blue fleece. Maybe the color got his attention. Anyway, it was a wonderful beginning to my visit and a good reminder that wild animals are just that...wild. It is a thrill to get close enough to share a moment with them, with no gates or fences between us. It is entirely possible to have that experience, in a controlled environment, at Game Park Safari.

Game Park Safari has over 450 animals, including adult lions, tigers, bears, and other wild animals. Some of the animals are in cages that allow visitors to get close-up views. Other animals, such as peacocks, deer, and goats, roam the grounds freely right along with the human visitors. Animal food, sold in ice cream cake cones, is available for visitors to buy so they can feed the animals. At times visitors can be surrounded by a herd of deer or bumped by a goat, all wanting a little snack. Keep your camera ready because you can take some great pictures. Signs explain what to do if the animals become too aggressive about wanting the food. (Basically, give it to them and retreat!)

Throughout the day visitors are invited to hands-on experiences with a variety of wild animals, supervised by a staff member. I was lucky enough to meet Game Park Safari's two adorable 4-week-old lion cubs, Mumba and Bella. I entered an enclosure for a short but unforgettable up-close encounter. It was magical. Bella sat on my lap making her cute baby lion sounds that will someday turn into a roar but for now sound more like a throaty little conversational squawk. I learned from the assistant that female lions are very talkative and social. Mumba, a male, was more interested in following my shoes around the enclosure as he toddled back and forth, gaining confidence in his ability to move on all four feet.

After touring the grounds, I started to leave only to discover my exit was blocked by the same peacock I met at the beginning of my visit. As I stood trying to decide how I was going to get around him without being attacked, a small child walked right up to him and admired his feathers, which towered over the child's short stature. (No attack.) Then two young men snuck up behind the peacock and peered through his feathers as a friend took a picture of them from the front of the peacock. (No attack.) After seeing this, I just ambled cautiously by him, (no attack) but maybe with a little more respect, and that might just be the whole point of the adventure.

Address:	46914 Highway 101 South, Bandon, OR 97411
Phone:	541-347-3106
Email:	info@gameparksafari.com
Hours:	See website for current days and times
Admission:	Seniors (60 years and older) $15, Adults (13 years old and up) $16, Students (7-12 years old) $9, Children (2-6 years old) $6, Toddlers (under 2 years) FREE
Restrooms:	Not ADA accessible. Located in front of building outside concession area. The floor is uneven in the women's restroom. Be careful.
Additional information:	Great opportunity for photos. The walking surface is somewhat uneven.
Getting there:	Game Park Safari is 7 miles south of Bandon on Hwy 101.

near Florence

Sea Lion Caves

Sea Lion Caves, 11 miles north of Florence on the Oregon coast, has been a popular tourist destination for many years. When I was a youngster, every car visiting the attraction was outfitted with a yellow Sea Lion Caves bumper sticker. I longed for the day when my family could go to the caves so we too could boast a bumper sticker on our car. Today you have to pay for the bumper sticker, and admission to the cave, but the attraction is still a popular destination and an amazing natural wonder.

Billed as "the world's largest sea cave," it is home to hundreds of wild sea lions who either seek shelter in the cavernous cave or loll around on the rocks outside of it. To see the inside of the cave, visitors descend 208 feet in an elevator. The doors open into a passageway that leads to an overlook. Visitors can watch hundreds of sea lions resting below on the rocks while gigantic bulls maneuver and vie for a dominant position within the groups of sea lions. The Pacific Ocean's waves continually roll in and out the mouth of the cave adding to the feeling of perpetual motion. Another passageway leads visitors to a wonderful view of nearby Heceta Head Lighthouse to the north of Sea Lion Caves. Within the passageways are a variety of educational signs explaining what you are seeing.

Outside the cave, visitors can take a short stroll down a well-paved path to a viewpoint to watch the sea lions resting on rocks or hunting for food in the Pacific Ocean. At times the swimming animals swirl in a giant circle, the whole group looking for fish. When one sea lion spots a meal and dives after it, other sea lions may follow the leader to try to catch a bite. Besides the sea lions, there are a variety of birds, including cute pigeon guillemots, whose big orange feet look like they are made for a different bird when they dive into the ocean big-feet last. From Sea Lion Caves, visitors get a fantastic look far out to sea.

Address: 91560 Highway 101, Florence, OR 97439
Phone: 541-547-3111
Hours: 8 a.m.-6 p.m. daily except Thanksgiving, Christmas
Admission: See website for current prices
Restrooms: Restrooms are in the main building down a flight of stairs.

ADA:	The stairs going down to the restrooms and the outside sidewalks going to the viewpoint would make wheelchair use challenging.
Getting there:	Sea Lion Caves is located on Hwy 101 about 11 miles north of Florence or 38 miles south of Newport. The parking for Sea Lion Caves is across the highway on a blind curve so BE CAREFUL CROSSING THE HIGHWAY!

Sand Master Park

Who says you need snow to ride down hills on a board strapped to your feet? If you are willing to think outside the box, sandboarding could be your next adventure. A video showing the thrill of sandboarding plays in the shop. It actually makes the sport look do-able. Boards rent for $10-$25 for 24 hours of thrills and spills. Rental fee includes free board wax and access to the 40 acres of sand trails behind the board shop. When I visited, it seemed like a lot of customers were taking their boards to Honeyman State Park, located three miles south of Florence, where they were camping for the weekend. Others were trying out the 40--foot-long ramp in the front of the shop. It takes a little practice and perseverance, but sandboarding looks like it could be a lot of fun. The only problem? No chair-lifts!

Address:	87542 Highway 101, North Florence, OR 97439
Phone:	541-997-6006
Web:	**www.sandmasterpark.com**
Hours:	Summer: June 1-September 10 daily 9 a.m.-6:30 p.m. Off-season: 10 a.m.-5 p.m., closed Wednesday, Sunday noon-5 p.m. Closed January 15-March 1
Getting there:	Sand Master Park is at the north end of Florence on Hwy 101. Parking is in front of the shop. The ramp is visible from the highway.

Gold Beach

Jerry's Jet Boats and Rogue River Mail Boat Trips

It was a foggy, slightly drizzly morning in July. Starting out at 8 a.m. for the 104-mile trip up and down the Rogue River, I sat in the last row of open air passenger benches, just in front of the captain's perch. I had a heavy tarp (provided for each row of seats) across my lap and my rain jacket zipped up practically to my nose. The weather often changes dramatically just a few miles inland from the ocean so under the rain jacket I wore shorts and a t-shirt in case the sun came out later in the day. We slowly pulled away from the dock and ambled a short way downstream for a look at the historic Hwy 101 bridge that spans the Rogue River. Then the captain said, "Hold on to your hats," (and he meant that literally) and the boat slightly lifted as he gunned the engines and we roared up the river using over 1000 horsepower from the boat's three hydro-jets.

Mail boats have been used on the Rogue River since 1895. At first, one man rowed the boat while another man used a pole to help guide the boat upstream to deliver mail to the town of Agness. As technology changed, so did the mail boats. Today the mail boats still deliver mail, but they are also one of the few ways people of all ages can get to see this rugged stretch of river that has been designated as a Federal Wild and Scenic River.

We zoomed upstream through majestic twists and turns of the river. The captain paused to let us admire the bountiful wildlife that live along the banks. We saw bald eagles, heron, ospreys, turkey vultures, Canadian geese, deer, otters, and more. At one point we discovered an osprey with a 10-12" pike in its mouth, struggling to carry his prey down river to her waiting chicks. When the bird realized we were watching, she hopped to shallow water and pushed the fish underwater, holding it in place with the talons of one foot. Finally she got a good grip and half-dragged and half-flew the squirming fish down river about 30 feet until she had to rest again before struggling with the fish once more. I rooted for the osprey, but the fish wasn't giving up.

We stopped in Agness at the Cougar Lane Lodge to stretch our legs, use the restroom, and get something hot to drink. Then we donned life jackets for the most thrilling part of the ride, going UP the rapids of the Rogue River. It was a crazy, thrilling, hang-on-to-your-seat ride! At the top of several rapids, we reached a deep water hole and the captain pirouetted the boat in a spectacular 360-degree turn that sent water flying everywhere, including on most of us. After that came shouts of joy and 20 or more thumbs rose in the air in unison from the passengers in the front of the boat to show their approval. In front of me, a wide-eyed 7—year- old turned around to give the captain a toothy grin, showing his awe of the captain's ability to maneuver the boat and to show the captain he was having the time of his life.

The mail boat goes up the Rogue River as far as the bottom of Blossom Bar, one of the most famous rapids on the river. It is also one of the most treacherous. We paused to admire the rocks and water tumbling toward us. Several rafters in wet suits scouted the rapid before actually trying to run it. We waited but no rafters came through. I am not surprised the rafters hesitated because after you see Blossom Bar from the top of the rapid, it takes time to calm your nerves before attempting to run it. It is not a rapid in which to make a mistake. It could cost you your life, for it has cost others theirs.

The mail boat turned and began the trip back to Gold Beach, bouncing down the rapids in a wet ride. Several times, after running a rapid the captain turned the boat around at the bottom and we went back up for a second chance to experience the thrill. We again stopped in the area of Singing Springs Resort, Lucas Lodge, and Cougar Lane Lodge, this time for a leisurely lunch (not included in the price of the trip). The sun was shining and from the outside deck of the restaurant, we could look down on the majestic Rogue River. Two young deer ventured to the water's edge for a drink. I was glad I had worn shorts. Then, after lunch, it was back to Gold Beach for the end of the trip. It had been the perfect way to spend a perfect day in nature.

Address: Mailing Address: PO Box 1011, Gold Beach, OR 97444
Physical Address 29985 Harbor Way, Gold Beach OR 97444
Phone: 1-800-451-3645 or 541-247-4571
Web: **www.Roguejets.com**
Email: Jerrys@Roguejets.com
Hours: There are 4 different trips available: one is 64 miles long, two are 80 miles long and one is 104 miles long. The 64-mile trip and 104-mile trip are available from May through October 15. The other two trips start later in the season and end earlier.
Call for reservations.

Admission:	64-mile trip: Adults $45, Children (4-11) $20, under 4 free 80-mile trip: Adults $65, Children (4-11) $30, under 4 free 104-mile trip: Adults $90, Children (4-11) $40, under 4 free
Restrooms:	ADA accessible restrooms at office and in Agness.
Getting there:	Jerry's is located just off Hwy 101 at the north end of Gold Beach in the port boat basin on the waterfront. The port is on the south side of the Rogue River.

near Langlois

Floras Lake Windsurfing and Kiteboarding

Oregon is famous for Gorge windsurfing, but if you want to learn to windsurf or kiteboard, there is no better place than Floras Lake, a shallow, little-known body of water tucked behind sand dunes on the southern Oregon coast. At Floras Lake Windsurfing and Kiteboarding, you can take lessons, rent or buy equipment, and talk all things windsurfing and kiteboarding. You can even rent kayaks and stand-up boards and paddles.

Will Brady, owner of the windsurfing/kiteboarding business, has been quietly operating in this location for 21 years. The youngest windsurfing student he has taught was 4 and the oldest student was 87. He has developed a mellow clientele of enthusiasts who come year after year to windsurf, and more recently kiteboard, on the lake.

With your own equipment, windsurfing/kiteboarding on the lake is free. Three-hour beginner windsurfing lessons, gear included, usually begin at 10 a.m. and 1:30 p.m. and cost $60. Other times can be arranged by appointment. For students, a jet ski is available to come to your rescue if you are blown downwind and you cannot get back to your starting spot.

Kiteboarding lessons are more complicated, using a different kind of board. Learning initially involves being dragged around the lake by your kite before you progress to getting up on a board. Kiteboarding lessons are $575 for six hours, usually spread out over several sessions, or $110/hour.

Although harder to learn initially, once you get the hang of it, kiteboarding becomes easier than windsurfing. Kiters can experience some incredible mid-air jumps.

For visitors wanting a more relaxed visit in this area, the beach is a short walk from the lake over a sand dune. Part of this beach area is the protected nesting site of the snowy plover. The rest of the beach is one of the most isolated places on the Oregon coast, with huge waves crashing into the shore. Soft sand makes long walks tedious, but sitting, watching, and listening to the waves crash is almost hypnotizing. Just don't turn your back on the ocean.

Address: 92870 Boice Cope Rd., Langlois, OR 97450
Phone: 541-348-9912
Web: **www.floraslake.com**
Hours: May-September
Restrooms: ADA restroom in Boice Cope County Park, adjacent to Floras Lake Windsurfing and Kiteboarding. It is a 3-5-minute walk to the restroom.
Getting there: Floras Lake Windsurfing and Kiteboarding is a little difficult to find because it is located adjacent to and south of Boice-Cope County Park. There is a path on the southwest corner of the campground that leads down to the lake and school site.

Coming from the south on Hwy 101, the turnoff to Floras Lake is about 15 miles south of Bandon after you go through the little burg of Langlois. Take a right at the little sign that says "Floras Lake-Boice Cope Park." Drive about a mile and then take a right on Floras Lake Road. In about 1.5 miles, the road bends sharply to the left. Take the first right, which is Boice-Cope Road. At the end of the road on the left is the bed and breakfast run by Will and his wife Liz. From there you will see Boice-Cope County Park. Day parking is available for a small fee in the park, or you may park on Boice-Cope Road.

Coming from the north on Hwy 101, about 9 miles north of Port Orford, look for a small brown sign on the right side that says "Floras Lake-Boice Cope Park." Turn left at the sign and go about a mile and turn left onto Floras Lake Road; then follow directions above.

Port Orford

Port Orford Lifeboat Station

Gutsy is the only way to describe the brave U.S. Coast Guardsmen who, from 1934-1970, went out in all kinds of weather to rescue people from boats and ships in distress off the southern Oregon coast. Their motto was "You have to go out, but you don't have to come back."

Visitors to the lifeboat station can get a clear glimpse of what life was like for the daring crewmen. In the building that used to be the crew quarters, you can see memorabilia from the lifeboat station's heyday, watch a film depicting rescues, and get an idea of the perils the Coast Guardsmen faced. One interesting exhibit explains the working of a Lyle gun, a sort of cannon that shot out rope from the shore to a vessel in distress within 700 yards of shore. After the line was secured to the vessel, passengers could be rescued using a sort of make-shift basket consisting of a buoy and rope.

The Coast Guardsmen must have had incredible stamina. To get to the boathouse 280 feet below the main station, crewmen needed to race down 532 wooden and concrete steps. Fuel was taken down to the boats in 5- gallon containers. Although the original boathouse burned down, the sheltered cove where the boathouse and concrete breakwater were constructed is a picturesque natural marvel. It is easy to imagine the difficulty of setting the rescue boat out into an angry sea.

A gently rolling short .35-mile hiking trail leads to spectacular views of the ocean from the cliffs above. The footings of the station's observation tower are still visible on one of the trails. From this vantage point, crewmen used to look out to sea to search for vessels in trouble. At times the weather was so bad that the crewman in the tower needed to stand on the opening door, which was in the flooring, so it would not blow open.

The Lifeboat Station also has information about a truly remarkable event during World War II. A Japanese submarine, called the I-25, surfaced near Cape Blanco on Wednesday, September 9, 1942. On board was a plane whose wings could be assembled on-deck and then catapulted from the submarine. Japanese pilot Nubuo Fajita flew over the coast near Brookings and dropped incendiary bombs, hoping to catch the woods on fire. The bombs did not ignite, thanks to the dampness of the coast, but the submarine was discovered by a U.S. bomber and slightly damaged. It quietly rested on the bottom of the ocean near Port Orford until it could repair itself and then the sub traveled up the Oregon Coast. Today, Nubuo Fajita is still the only man to ever drop bombs on the continental United States.

An unusual souvenir can be made at the Lifeboat Station. See how a dog tag maker works while it cranks out a custom dog tag just for you, or maybe your dog? The tags are $5 each or two for $8.

....

Address:	PO Box 1132, Port Orford, OR 97465
Phone:	541-332-0521
Web:	**portorfordlifeboatstation.org**
Hours:	Visitor center open Thursday-Monday 10 a.m.-3:30 p.m. April-October Grounds open year round.
Admission:	Donations welcome
Restrooms:	Outhouse
Getting there:	Port Orford Lifeboat Station is located in the town of Port Orford. It is a few blocks off Hwy 101 at 9th Street. It lies within the Port Orford Heads State Park.

Seal Rock

Seal Rock State Recreation Site

At low tide, Seal Rock State Recreation Site is a perfect place to view a treasure trove of sea life, all clinging to temporarily exposed rocks as the ocean recedes for a few hours before returning to once again bathe the marine life in salty water. Starfish, barnacles, sea anemones, and mussels are just a few of the creatures that compete for space and food in this rich sea environment. Look closely in the tide pools surrounding the rocks and it might be possible to catch a glimpse of a crab or tiny fish, as they dart out for a dash across the water to a new hiding place. Farther out in the ocean you may see a sea lion. This site is also a wonderful place to relax and soak in the natural beauty of the rocks, ocean, and ever-changing sky. It is just waiting to be explored.

Address: Seal Rock, OR
Phone: 1-800-551-6949 (information)
Hours: Day-use area
Fee: FREE for public use
Restrooms: ADA restrooms. It would be difficult to get a wheelchair down the bluff to the sandy beach, but there is a nice picnic area adjacent to the parking lot.
Getting there: Seal Rock is between Newport (to the north) and Waldport (to the south) on Hwy 101 (Pacific Coast Hwy) on the southern Oregon coast.

Section 11
Mt. Hood / Shaniko / Kah-Nee-Ta Triangle

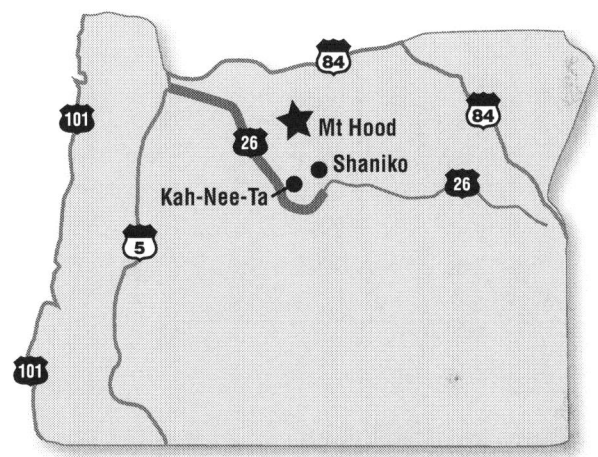

Rafting at Deschutes River, Maupin

Mt. Hood/Shaniko/Kah-nee-Ta Triangle

Ice Cream

Maupin

Imperial River Company

During the summer, the Imperial River Company, located near the bridge in Maupin, offers a selection of guided rafting adventures that vary in length from a few hours to a few days. The trips begin and end on their property. For other boaters floating down the Deschutes, the green lawn at the Imperial River Company must look like a desert oasis, beckoning them to come ashore and take a break from riding the adrenaline pumping rapids on the Deschutes River.

At the Imperial River Company you will find both casual and formal dining, cold drinks and welcome shade from the hot desert sun. For those rafters who are tired of sleeping on the ground, the Imperial River Company has 25 rooms for lodging, most rooms with two beds.

You don't have to be a rafter to enjoy this pristine get away. Bike riders, hunters, fishermen, and tourists looking for a relaxing spot to spend some time will love this place. Just sitting by the water, watching the Deschutes River flow by is hypnotic. Sit, or relax on a blanket and enjoy a good book while savoring some of the freshest air in the state.

If you are hungry for ice cream, order The Thing. The Thing is big enough for four people to enjoy. It consists of a warm, gooey, moist brownie with hot fudge on top. The brownie is piled with Tillamook Vanilla Bean ice cream and whipped cream. It is topped with chocolate sauce and slivered almonds. This delightful desert dessert is $6.50.

For smaller appetites you can order Tillamook ice cream in a variety of flavors for $1.25 per scoop.

Address:	304 Bakeoven Rd, P.O. Box 130, Maupin, OR 97037
Phone:	541-395-2404 or 1-800-395-3903
Web:	www.deschutesriver.com
Additional info:	Call or go to web for reservations for lodging, dining, rafting trips.

LLC Whitewater Photo and Ice Cream

So after you have churned, pirouetted, splashed, swam, and slid your way downstream on the Deschutes River, stop by for some ice cream at the store with the kayak hanging at the top of the roof and the sign that says "Photos, Pizza, and Ice Cream" located on the east side of the bridge that crosses the Deschutes River in Maupin. There you will find 13 flavors of Umpqua Ice Cream (single scoop $3.50, small dish $4, root beer float $2.50). While enjoying your ice cream, you can look over the whitewater shots that have been taken of groups that have rented equipment from the sister store next door, Deschutes U-Boat Rental/Guides. If you or your group has had their picture taken, you can buy a copy either as a print, CD, or jpeg on the website.

So what are the favorite flavors of boaters and kayakers at this store? Huckleberry Cheesecake, Cookies and Cream, and Cookie Dough top the list. Mountain Blackberry Revel is also a big hit. No matter what flavor you choose, on a hot day in central Oregon nothing hits the spot like ice cream.

Address:	409 Bakeoven Rd., Maupin, OR 97037
Hours:	Memorial Day-September 30 Monday-Thursday noon-7 p.m., Friday noon-9 p.m., Saturday 9 a.m.-9 p.m., Sunday 9 a.m.-7 p.m.
Getting there:	From Portland, take Hwy 26 past Mt. Hood toward Bend. After you enter the Warm Springs Reservation, turn left on Hwy 216, toward Maupin. Go about 30 miles to Hwy 197. Turn right onto Hwy 197 and go 2 miles to Maupin. You will see the ice cream store after you cross the bridge over the Deschutes River. Coming from the Columbia Gorge on I-84, take Exit 87 and proceed south on Hwy 197 about 39 miles until you reach Maupin.

Shaniko

Shaniko and Goldie's Ice Cream Parlor

Shaniko is one of Oregon's last remaining ghost towns. In the 1800s this part of Oregon was famous for its wool, cattle, and wheat. Shaniko grew up at the end of a railroad spur built to transport those goods to market. The town briefly flourished and then was largely abandoned in the early 1900s when alternative railroad lines were built. The population of Shaniko has greatly fluctuated over the years, from a high of 600 to a low of 7. Today Shaniko boasts a population of approximately 25.

Visitors can wander around town and see many buildings that look straight out of a Hollywood western, including a schoolhouse, bank, and water tower. In addition, there are a number of old-time vehicles for the curious tourist to see. Great opportunities for photography abound in this straight-out-of-a-western town.

Dr. Robert Pamplin, an Oregon businessman, bought the Shaniko Hotel in 2000 and redecorated it to its original beauty. He envisioned eventually redoing the whole town to make it a tourist destination. Unfortunately, Dr. Pamplin and Shaniko residents became deadlocked over water rights. Dr. Pamplin died in 2009 and the hotel is now locked up with a for sale sign posted on the front door.

Despite this turn of events, parts of the town have businesses that continue to operate, mostly from the spring to early fall, before the weather makes it iffy for travelers to get to Shaniko. An old-time saloon, bookstore, jewelry shop, art gallery, and candy store and t-shirt shop are several of the businesses in Shaniko.

Goldie's Ice Cream Parlor is operated by Goldie Roberts, who also happens to be the town's mayor. She sells Eberhard's ice cream as well as lunch items. Her store is open 10 a.m.-5 p.m. seven days a week from April 1-October. She is a wealth of information and does a bustling business on warm days. Sundaes, ice cream sodas, and ice cream floats all sell for $4. Milkshakes cost $4.50. Single-scoop cones are $2.50, and double-scoop cones are $3.50. Add fifty cents if you would prefer a waffle cone. Goldie's also sells snowcones ($1.50) and sodas ($1.25-$1.85).

The town hosts a variety of special events during their short season to encourage tourism. I happened to visit during the Annual Wool Gathering event in September on a beautiful fall day. I had a wonderful time. There were vendors selling beautiful woolen goods (I still regret I didn't buy a wool hat there), and lots of gorgeous yarn and weaving supplies. Sheep-shearing demonstrations were scheduled during the day. Sheep-herding dogs demonstrated their skills to the delight of the crowd. I will definitely go back again for this event.

Other summer events include Pioneer Day in June, Transportation and Incorporation of Shaniko in July, Shaniko Days in August, the Tygh Valley Bluegrass Jamboree at the end of September, a Ragtime and Vintage Music Festival in October, and a Spookhouse in October.

Goldie's Phone: 1-541-489-3443
Shaniko Events Phone: 1-541-3434
Email: rlgroberts@rconnects.com
Hours: 10 a.m.-5 p.m. daily
April 1-October 31
Restrooms: ADA accessible
Getting there: From Portland, drive east 104 miles on I-84 to Biggs Junction. Turn south on Hwy 97. Drive 58 miles to Shaniko.

Mt. Hood/Shaniko/Kah-nee-Ta Triangle
Things to See and Do

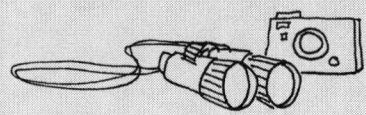

Government Camp

The Adventure Park at Skibowl

During the winter, Skibowl is one of Mt. Hood's premier ski parks for downhill skiers who flock to the slopes. In the summer, it is transformed into an "adventure park" with over 20 fun things to do for adults and kids, including the Northwest's only half-mile dual alpine slide. The slide begins with a ride to the top on the ski lift. Then it's downhill on a plastic sled that has a lever to brake and accelerate. The first time down you may feel a little tentative, but the second ride can cause whoops and shouts of delight as you gain confidence and speed.

At the park there are also go-carts, a climbing wall, miniature golf, bungee trampoline, 18-hole frisbee golf, batting cages, and more. You can pay for individual attractions or get 2-hour, half-day, or all-day adventure passes. On the east side of the highway is a 100-foot bungee tower, 500-foot zipline, and Indy carts that are included in the "East Side Extreme Package." Whether you stop for a short break on your way to or from Mt. Hood, or choose to go for the day, the Adventure Park has a little something for everyone.

Address: Mailing: PO Box 280, Government Camp, OR 97028
Physical: 87000 E Hwy 26, Government Camp, OR 97028
Phone: 503-222-2695
Web: www.skibowl.com
Hours: Monday-Friday 11 a.m.-6 p.m., Saturday-Sunday 10 a.m.-7 p.m.
Admission: See website for current prices
Restrooms: Available

Additional information:	Snacks are available for sale on the site. You may bring your own picnic lunch and lawn chairs.
Getting there:	Skibowl is clearly marked on Hwy 26 at Government Camp.

near Government Camp

Hawk Watch International at Bonney Butte

Breathtaking. Majestic. Awe-inspiring. Spiritual. These describe both the views from Bonney Butte and the raptors who glide through the corridor on Mt. Hood's eastern flank on their yearly fall migration. Since 1994, Hawk Watch International has been recording the numbers of migrating raptors to help understand population trends and conservation needs of these amazing birds. Golden eagles, bald eagles, sharp-shinned hawks, Cooper's hawks, red tail hawks, turkey vultures, and many more can be observed during the annual bird count that runs from the end of August to October 31 each year, weather permitting. During the season, 2500-4500 birds are counted each year.

Visitors are welcome to share in the observation and identification of these birds as they slowly glide and flap their way through the corridor. Binoculars in hand, watching a bird come into view, you can become part of a lively discussion of how you can tell a sharp-shinned hawk from a Cooper's hawk. A running tally is kept on site by the friendly, trained observers who scan the skies for birds each day from 9 a.m. to 6 p.m. Some of the birds are caught and banded, before being released to continue their journey, in order to better understand migration patterns. If you are lucky enough to be there when one of the raptors is being released, you can get a close-up view of the bird.

Even when there are no birds to count, on a cloudless day the view from Bonney Butte is one of the best in Oregon. Mt. Hood, Mt. Adams, and Mt. Jefferson are all visible from this location. On the south side of the butte you can clearly see where the forests end and the beginning of the dry side of the state begins. In the fall the changing colors are spectacular, and the air is crisp and clean. Hawk Watch International at Bonney Butte is one of Oregon's little-known gems.

Web:	www.hawkwatch.org
Hours:	Daily from 9 a.m.-6 p.m. from the end of August to October 31, weather permitting. If it is pouring down rain, the observers do not observe. They are staying dry and I hope the birds are too.
Restrooms:	Outhouse at the bottom of the hill before the climb to the top. No facilities at the top.
Getting there:	Okay, this is the hard part. You need to have a car that has clearance. Part of the road is primitive, with big potholes. Also, go on a sunny, dry day to avoid driving through mud. After Government Camp. travel 4 miles east of Hwy 26 on Hwy 35. After you cross the White River, you will see the White River East Snow Park. Turn south here on Road 48. Go 7 miles and turn left onto paved Forest Road 4890. Go 3.75 miles and turn left onto Forest Road 4891, which has a sign to Bonney Meadows Campground. (This is where you will discover the 4-mile road with some rough, rocky spots, but take heart, the whole road is not as bad as it seems at about mile two.) After this 4-mile stretch, you will reach Bonney Meadows Campground. Instead of turning right into the campground continue on the main road about a ¼ of a mile beyond. You will see a parking area on the right and on the left a blockaded road with a Hawk Watch sign pointing toward the viewpoint. There is an outhouse just beyond the sign. The walk to the top is about ¼-mile over rocky ground.
Warning:	Bees were numerous. If allergic, take your EpiPen. I found that dryer sheets also kept the bees at bay, as did bug repellent.

Trillium Lake

If you are looking for a postcard-perfect lake with a breathtaking view of Mt. Hood, Trillium Lake is the place to visit. During the summer, it is wonderful for a picnic or an overnight family camping trip. Many people enjoy sitting by the water's edge with a fishing pole in the water, enjoying the view and the lake's serenity while hoping to catch their next meal. Others sit back, relax, and read a good book. Canoes and non-motorized boats silently glide through the water or rock gently as the wind stirs ripples on the lake. Swimming and playing in the water are fun in the afternoon when the air heats up a bit. There is a flat, easy 2-mile path around the lake that leads the hiker through meadows, marshes, and the water's edge, with boardwalks constructed over the muddy parts. During the summer, there are a variety of wildflowers to see and enjoy.

During the winter, Trillium Lake is a popular day-trip destination for cross-country skiers. Cars park on the highway. Skiers begin their descent down to the lake on the snow-covered road that is left unplowed. The trip is fairly easy because the road does not have a lot of sharp twists and turns. It is a good place for beginners, especially once they get past the first downhill by the highway. I call the first part "Killer Hill" but that is only because I have never mastered the art of stopping on skis!

I love Trillium Lake and have a lot of wonderful memories. I hope you will fall in love with this lake too.

Phone:	503-622-3191
Web:	www.recreation.gov
Admission:	Day use fee of $6/vehicle. Overnight camping is $18, $19, and $36/pull-through spot. Some spots are accessible. Reservations must be made at least 4 days in advance. They can be made 6 months in advance. Campsites fill up so reserve as soon as possible.
Restrooms:	ADA accessible outhouses
Additional info:	Sno-park permits are needed on vehicles from November 1-April 31. They can purchased at the Mt. Hood Meadows or Mt. Hood Country Store in Government Camp. For fishing permits: **www.takemefishing.org**
Getting there:	Coming from Portland, take Hwy 26 east and turn one mile past Government Camp. Follow the signs two miles to Trillium Lake.

in Kah-Nee-Ta

Kah-Nee-Ta Resort

Ah, the smell of sagebrush, fresh air, and the anticipation of a warm swim are all lures capable of getting me to hop in my car and drive to Kah-Nee-Ta, a resort on the Warm Springs Indian reservation about a two- hour drive from Portland. Boasting sunshine through much of the year, it is a great place to slather on the suntan lotion, grab a towel, a good book, and perhaps your inflatable mattress or pool float. Treat yourself to a blissful day in the sunshine by the pool at the village.

The double Olympic-size hot springs-fed pool is fairly warm. No need to work your way into the depths, one painful body part at a time. Just take the leap. Then when you get out notice how you feel cool, even on a sweltering hot day. After going back to your book or conversation, and warming up in the sun or shade, it's back to the pool. Then repeat. Can it get much better than this? If you want a little more excitement, there are always the two waterslides to enjoy.

Dining at Kah-Nee-Ta ranges from convenient hamburgers and other casual fair by the pool area to fine dining in the upper lodge. The food is tasty. Be sure to try the delicious Indian Fry Bread with huckleberry jam.

If you would like to stay longer, spend the night at Kah-Nee-Ta. RV camping is one option. Staying in a teepee, complete with concrete floor, barbecue, and fire pit is another (ring your own bedding). There are 30 hotel type rooms for rent in the village compound. Up the road a bit is a stylish lodge with 139 guest rooms. There is a separate swimming pool up there for lodge guests.

Swimming is just one activity at Kah-Nee-Ta. Horseback riding, guided kayaking, guided fishing, and golf are all options during your summer trip. Whether you go for the day or overnight, Kah-Nee-Ta will make its mark in your memory. The Confederated Tribes of Warm Springs have created a wonderful desert oasis complete with a natural backdrop straight out of a big screen Western.

Phone:	541-553-1112
Web:	**www.kahneeta.com**
Email:	mschnider@kahneeta.com
	Reservations@kahneeta.com
Admission:	Call or go to website for current prices
Restrooms:	ADA accessible
Additional information:	There is a $5 parking fee for the lot by the village.
Getting there:	From Portland, take Hwy 26 east toward Bend. Turn left at the sign for Simnasho. At Simnasho, turn right and follow the signs to Kah-Nee-Ta.

Timberline

Timberline Lodge

Standing on the steps of Timberline Lodge on a clear day makes you feel like you really are "on top of the world." In the distance Mt. Jefferson can be seen to the south. Trillium Lake is nestled below in trees just a few miles from the base of the mountain. Miles and miles of green forest lay before you on top of undulating hills, peaks, and valleys. The air is crisp and clean and the grandeur of the space makes you want to think grand thoughts.

On September 28, 1937, President Roosevelt came to Oregon to dedicate the completion of Timberline Lodge, constructed during the Depression by the Works Progress Administration (WPA) and the Civilian Conservation Corps (CCC). The project had provided much needed jobs to over 500 men and women during the difficult days of high unemployment. The imagination and skill of those craftsmen created a true Oregon treasure. Their creative use of iron, stone, wood, and the arts can still be seen throughout the lodge, from the railings on the stairs to the glass mural in the Blue Ox bar to the magnificent beams in the structure. Timberline was added to the National Register of Historical Places in 1972.

The exterior of Timberline was featured in the movie The Shining, starring Jack Nicholson. Supposedly, the moviemakers could not use the interior of the building (maybe so staying at the lodge would not creep out future tenants?) but I could swear I recognized the carpet in the hallways upstairs from the movie. We had a lot of fun saying, "Heeere's Johnny!"

The lodge has three dining areas: a formal restaurant, a casual dining area, and a bar. A gift store is located on the main floor.

Visitors can explore the lodge during the day. They may opt to pay and stay overnight in one of several hotel rooms. If you are able to spend the night, you may notice the lodge takes on a calm serenity as the sun goes down. Shuffleboard and ping-pong are available for guests. Sitting next to the fireplace playing cards is a peaceful way to pass the time. There is an outdoor swimming pool and sauna. On television several documentaries detail the construction of Timberline. Also, if things seem too quiet, guests may check out DVDs of The Shining.

Besides the main lodge there is a day use area called WyEast just steps from the lodge. It was built in 1981. Skiers and snowboarders use the day use area there to hang out, buy snacks, and change into and out of their skiing attire.

Timberline is a year-round tourist destination. There is snow skiing and snowboarding in the winter, and Mt. Hood is one of the few places in the U.S. to ski during the summer. Kids from all around the country to attend skiing and snowboarding camps during the summer. Some of those campers have gone on to become Olympians. During the summer, hiking is also a popular activity at Timberline.

Timberline is located on the Pacific Crest Trail, a 2600-mile trail from Mexico to Canada. For the casual day hiker, there are lots of wildflowers and short day hikes in the area. Whether you come for a short while to admire the view, stay for a meal, ski, hike, bike, or just sit in the sun, Timberline is well worth a visit.

Address: Timberline, Timberline Lodge, OR 97028
Phone: 503-272-3311
Web: www.timberlinelodge.com
Email: info@timberlinelodge.com
Hours: Open for public visits from 7 a.m.-11 p.m.

Admission: Visiting the lodge is free. Call for rates for skiing, dining, and overnight lodging.
Restrooms: ADA accessible
Getting there: Coming from Portland, take Hwy 26 east and just past Government Camp follow the signs to Timberline Lodge.
Additional information: Sno-park permits are needed on vehicles from November 1-April 31. They can purchased at the WyEast Lodge at guest services.

Maupin

Rafting on the Deschutes River

With names like Boxcar, Buckskin Mary, and Oak Springs, the class II-IV rapids on the Deschutes River provide a thrilling white-water ride enjoyed by hundreds of adventure seekers each year.

There are many ways to float down the river. Being a passenger on a raft with a rowing frame, oared by a single experienced person, is probably the least stressful way to travel. All you have to do is sit back and enjoy the ride. For those who want to be more of a participant, paddle rafting is exciting. In this case everyone has a paddle and everyone is expected to use it with gusto when directed by the boat's captain, who sits at the back of the raft and steers. However, when you actually come to a rapid, some people may stop paddling, either from fright or because they are thrown up in the air by a wave. They grasp onto the safety rope for dear life. When that happens, the raft careens through the rapid cock-eyed, like a car with a flat tire. The captain tries to keep the boat going down the rapid right side up. Most of the time they are successful.

Other boaters may want to depend on themselves during the trip. They prefer to take fate in their own hands. For these folks, inflatable kayaks offer an exciting, up-close view of the water. Finally, some rafters use hard-shelled kayaks. Usually, these are experienced boaters who know how to "roll" their kayak back over if they flip and they know how to get out of the kayak during an emergency.

No matter how you decide to travel down the river, the most important thing is to go with someone who knows what they are doing so you are safe. There are a variety of outfitters in Maupin who offer guided float trips and boat rentals. I have not used any of the outfitters in Maupin, so shop carefully and pick the trip that offers the most fun for a reasonable price. Day trips are available as well as overnight adventures.

My best advice is to ALWAYS wear a life jacket. Remember that it is just as easy to fall IN the boat as OUT. If you do fall out, assume the position, sitting facing downstream with your feet poised to help you bounce off rocks. You will have a wonderful time. Floating down the Deschutes River is an Oregon adventure you will remember forever.

Web: Google "Deschutes River Rafting"

Additional information: Reservations should be made in advance if possible.

Getting there: From Portland, take Hwy 26 past Mt. Hood toward Bend. After you enter the Warm Springs Reservation, turn left on Hwy 216, toward Maupin. Go about 30 miles to Hwy 197. Turn right onto Hwy 197 and go 2 miles to Maupin. You will see a variety of outfitters as you enter Maupin, and more after you cross the bridge over the Deschutes River.

Coming from the Columbia Gorge on I-84, take Exit 87 and proceed south on Hwy. 197 about 39 miles until you reach Maupin.

Section 12
Bend Area

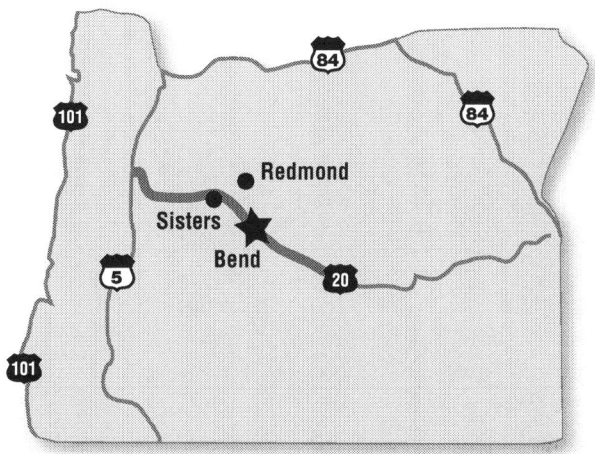

High Desert Museum, Bend

Bend Area
Ice Cream

Bend, Redmond, Prineville, Sunriver

Goody's Soda Fountain & Ice Cream

You can't help but be giddy at Goody's. Walking into Goody's, you will feel like a kid in a candy store, because, well, you ARE in a candy store, as well as a popular ice cream parlor that serves delicious Oregon brand Goody's ice cream. Inside the store is a feast for the eyes. Mouth-watering Goody's homemade chocolates fill display cases and will keep chocoholics coming back for more. Jars of colorful candies line the walls and display area. Lots of candies will remind you of your childhood days. If you are a boomer, you will remember the candy wax lips you used to buy and wear to amuse your friends. The candy necklaces you used to eat in class are there, too. Neccos? Goody's has them. You will be delighted to find these and many more of your long-lost favorites at Goody's.

Goody's also stocks an incredible variety of stuffed animals. During the Beanie Baby craze, people were known to follow the car of the store's buyer so they could be the first to get their hands on a special animal!

Then, there is the ice cream. With 16% butterfat, it is some of the richest ice cream you'll find anywhere. A regular sugar cone or dish costs $2.95 for a single scoop or $4.25 for a double scoop. Homemade cones are $3.95 for a single scoop and $5 for a double scoop. Single-scoop sundaes are $4.25 in a dish or $4.95 in a waffle dish. Old-fashioned banana splits are $5.95. Did I mention that Goody's makes their own hot fudge for sundaes? Yum. Shakes cost $5.95 and come in 16 flavors!

Goody's is the creation of Marn and Marion Palmateer. They started out with a candy store in Sunriver at the Sunriver Village Mall. In 1984, they added a soda fountain. They decided to create their own brand of ice cream to add to their store's uniqueness. The six original flavors are still served today. They include vanilla, Oreo Cookie, coffee, chocolate, Chocolate Almond, and strawberry. Other flavors are rotated into the line-up. Goody's actively searches out new flavors to delight ice cream lovers. Customers are welcome to suggest their ideas.

In the early days, when there was just one store in Sunriver, Goody's sponsored a "mooing" contest to celebrate the store's anniversary. A farmer brought in a cow and then three age groups of moo-ers, (kids, teens, and adults) competed to see who could moo most like a cow. Everyone won a prize.

Over the years Goody's has expanded. The downtown Bend location opened in 1989. The Bend Forum shop opened in 1999.

In 2007, Mrs. Palmateer retired and the business was purchased by Dane and Jvon Danforth. Both are retired educators; Dane was a principal, and Jvon was a school counselor. They loved the idea of having a company that would be fun to operate and where they could still be around kids. They started the Redmond Goody's in 2007. A brand new Prineville franchise store will open in 2011.

The inside scoop from Goody's is their plan to open a factory store in Bend, starting mid-June 2011. The new factory will include a factory tour that will be open to the public. Visitors will be able to see the process of making chocolates and how ice cream is made. Six samples will be given during the tour, including freshly made ice cream. The tour will cost $3 to cover the cost of gloves, containers, and taster spoons. At the factory, there will be a section where visitors can hand-dip their own ice cream bar.

Going to Goody's will surely become a family tradition. Once you have been to Goody's, you will be hooked on their creamy, rich ice cream. It is no wonder Goody's has been voted by customers as Bend's best sweet spot for a sugar high.

Goody's Downtown Bend Location

Address:	957 NW Wall St., Bend, OR 97701
Phone:	541-389-5185
Hours:	Summer: 10 a.m.-10 p.m. daily
	Winter: Sunday-Thursday 10 a.m.-9 p.m.,
	Friday-Saturday 10 a.m.-10 p.m.
	Closed Thanksgiving, Christmas, Easter
Restrooms:	Not-ADA accessible

Goody's at the Forum

Address: 2680 NE Hwy 20, Bend, OR 97701
Phone: 541-388-6965
Hours: Summer: 10 a.m.-10 p.m. daily
Winter: Sunday-Thursday 10 a.m.-9 p.m.,
Friday-Saturday 10 a.m.-10 p.m.
Closed Thanksgiving, Christmas, Easter
Restrooms: ADA accessible

Goody's at Sunriver

Address: 57100 Mall Dr., Sunriver, OR 97707
Phone: 541-593-2155
Hours: Summer: 10 a.m.-10 p.m. daily
Restrooms: ADA accessible

Goody's Downtown Redmond

Address: 521 SW 6th St., Redmond, OR 97756
Phone: 541-923-1806
Hours: Summer: 10 a.m.-10 p.m. daily
Winter: Sunday-Thursday 10 a.m.-9 p.m.,
Friday-Saturday 10 a.m.-10 p.m.
Closed Thanksgiving, Christmas, and Easter
Restrooms: ADA accessible

Goody's franchise in downtown Prineville

Address: 346 N.W. Deer, Prineville, OR 97754
Phone: 541-286-4173
Hours: Summer: 9 a.m.-9 p.m. daily
Restrooms: ADA accessible

Goody's Factory Store

Address: 1111 SE Division, Bend, OR 97702
Contact phone: 541-385-7085
Hours: Daily 10 a.m.-5 p.m.
Cost: $2/person
Restrooms: ADA accessible

Bend

Hardy's Burgers, Salads, and Ice Cream

Hardy Lussier has owned and operated Hardy's for seven years. An Oregon transplant via Florida, California, and Colorado, his restaurant is known for its chicken wings and burgers. About 95% of his business are returning customers. That will come as no surprise once you have tasted one of his delicious burgers. Choose from one of 12 mouth-watering choices that range from $5.95 to $7.95. You will not leave hungry! Pair your burger with Hardy's unusual golden crispy French fries with catsup or sauce and you will be in burger heaven. If you like wings, they are sold by the piece. Six wings are $6.95. Ten wings are $9.95. Fifty wings are $39.95. (That's like a whole flock!)

Hardy says that he has always had a sweet tooth. Last year he added an ice cream bar so his customers could see which of eight Eberhard ice cream flavors they wanted to enjoy. He always stocks vanilla, strawberry, chocolate, and rainbow sherbet. The four other flavors change periodically. Hardy says the best milkshake combination he has made so far uses one-half chocolate ice cream and one-half mint chip ice cream. He also says that rainbow sherbet makes a good milkshake. A single cup or cone is $1.95. Double scoops are $2.95. Triple scoops are $3.95. Milkshakes are $4.95. An ice cream sandwich is $1.95. A chocolate chip OR brownie sundae is $4.95 and includes whipped cream, nuts, and a cherry. Once you discover Hardy's, you will go back for more!

Address: 238 NE. 3rd St. Bend, OR 97702
Phone: 541-382-6962
Web: www.HardysHotwings.com
Hours: Tuesday-Saturday 11:30 a.m.-7:30 p.m.,
Sunday 11:30 a.m.-4:30 p.m.
Closed Mondays
Restrooms: ADA accessible

Pine Tavern

For a fabulous treat that you will long remember, try a piece of Sky High Mud Pie ($8) at the Pine Tavern in Bend. Big enough and rich enough for two to share, this mouth-watering masterpiece uses Eberhard Coffee Almond Fudge ice cream heaped on an Oreo cookie crust. It is covered with a wonderfully rich fudge layer and then topped with toasted almonds and whipped cream. The pie will be at its peak of perfection if you allow it to stand at room temperature for a few minutes before eating. I know waiting will not be easy, at it looks so yummy, but trust me, flavors blossom when the ice cream is just slightly soft.

The Pine Tavern has been in business since 1936. It offers fine dining and is on the expensive side compared to other eateries in this book. However, you can go to the Pine Tavern just to enjoy a piece of mud pie. The pie makes a wonderful midday treat or wonderful dessert before going to the Tower Theater, just down the block, for one of their fabulous live theater offerings. After sharing a piece of this pie, and just before going on stage at the Tower Theater, Marvella McPartland, bass guitar player for the hit show, HotFlashes The Musical, told me, "That's the best thing I have ever eaten in my life." I could not have said it any better.

Address:	967 NW Brooks Street, Bend, OR 97701
Phone:	541-382-5581
Web:	www.pinetavern.com
Hours:	Winter: 11:30 a.m.-9 p.m., lunch 11:30 a.m.-2:30 p.m., lounge menu from 2:30 p.m.-5 p.m., dinner 5 p.m.-9 p.m. Summer: 11 a.m.-10 p.m., lunch 11 a.m.-2:30 p.m., lounge menu from 2:30 p.m.-5 p.m., dinner 5 p.m.-10 p.m
Restrooms:	ADA accessible

FUN FACT

Lickability

Supposedly it takes approximately 50 licks to eat a single scoop cone. Try it out for yourself and see if it is true.

Redmond

History of Eberhard Ice Cream

The Eberhard creamery, located in Redmond, first opened in 1951 as a place where dairy farmers could take their fresh cream. Eberhard would then sell the cream to make butter. Eberhard started churning its own butter in 1953. Dry milk production was added in 1955. The company was content to offer this limited number of products until 1964 when they became a full-line processing dairy. They slowly started adding to their line of high-quality dairy products. Eberhard cottage cheese was introduced in 1965. Fresh Eberhard milk hit the markets in 1967. Ice cream was also introduced in 1967.

In the beginning, the ice cream making was a labor-intensive business. Using a small-batch freezer, two and a half gallons of ice cream mix yielded five gallons of delicious ice cream. One batch could be produced every 10-12 minutes. So every hour, Eberhard employees could make 25 gallons of ice cream. Compare that to their operation today. Using a triple barrel freezer, Eberhard can now crank out 450 gallons of ice cream an hour!

The original Eberhard flavors were vanilla, strawberry, chocolate, maple nut, and peppermint. Bob Eberhard, a second-generation descendent of the company founders, and Mark Eberhard, a third-generation descendent, are particularly proud of the Eberhard brand vanilla ice cream made with vanilla beans that come from Madagascar. The beans have been made into a pure bourbon vanilla extract. When added to Eberhard's ice cream mixture, it produces a rich, flavorful ice cream that is well loved by the public. The cocoa beans in Eberhard's chocolate ice creams come from Africa.

Today, you can buy Eberhard's Ice Cream in 13 flavors. There are three flavors of vanilla: vanilla, Vanilla Bean, and French Vanilla. The other flavors are chocolate, strawberry, Rocky Road, Death By Chocolate, Dulce de Leche, Maple Nut, Mountain Blackberry, Mint Chocolate Chip, Huckleberry, and Peppermint Candy.

You will find Eberhard's Ice Cream in scoop shops and grocery stores within a radius of about 150 miles from Redmond. You are sure to love the new shape of the ice cream container that was introduced in 2009. Eberhard's calls it an "easy scoop carton." The slanted sides of the carton mean getting fewer gooey fingers dishing out the ice cream. After this new carton was introduced, ice cream sales increased 30%. So go ahead, buy local when you are in the Bend/Redmond area. Try delicious Eberhard's Ice Cream.

Phone: 541-548-5181

Sisters

B.J.'s Ice Cream

As I was window-shopping in Sisters, I did a double take when I saw the sign. "Hey, wait a minute, that sign wasn't here the last time I drove through town," I thought, "B.J.'s ice cream in Sisters? How could that be? B.J.'S homemade ice cream is made in Florence, one hundred and seventy miles west, on the Oregon coast." I stepped inside and asked, "Is this the same B.J.'s as the B.J.'s ice cream in Florence?" "Yes," came the reply. I whooped with delight. I was thrilled.

B.J.'s in Sisters is owned and operated by Crystine Cole, the granddaughter of Keith Cole, the owner of B.J.s in Florence. For a little less than a year, this darling shop smack dab in the middle of Sisters has been serving 32 flavors of B.J.'s delicious homemade ice cream. I ordered a cone with Cappuccino Fudge ice cream, a new flavor for me, and I thought that it was a taste-tickling combination of coffee and fudge with just the right punch to magnify its flavor. Crystine's favorite flavor is Kahlua Crunch. The public's current favorite pick is Chocolate Peanut Butter. Jr. scoops are $2.65 and double Jr. scoops are $3.60. A regular single scoop cone is $3.50. Add 50 cents for a waffle cone. Milkshakes are $4.75/$5.35. Hot fudge sundaes are $4.25/$5.90.

There are other items for sale in this store. Homemade fudge, made by B.J.'s in Florence, is for sale in a variety of flavors for $11.99/lb. I noticed saltwater taffy was also for sale, but it is not made by B.J.'s. You will also find an unusual assortment of non-ice cream merchandise in a corner section of B.J.'s. Blown glass objects, handbags, bud vases, and wooden bowls are all attractively displayed. But go for the ice cream. Once you have tried B.J.'s ice cream, you will be back for more.

Address: 170 W Cascade Av, Sisters, OR 97759
Phone: 541-549-6394
Hours: Winter: daily 11 a.m.-7 p.m.
Summer: daily 10 a.m.-9 p.m.

Sno Cap Drive-In

Driving through Sisters during Spring Break was a little eerie this year. Where was the throng of people who usually stroll up and down the streets of this cute tourist town window-shopping? Okay, granted, there was a stiff wind blowing dust up and down the street, and anybody in their right mind would have run for cover, but still, where were the people?

We discovered many of them at the Sno Cap Drive In. The six booths inside were packed. The tables outside were also crowded with people, and the waitresses looked like they had just run a marathon. This is a popular stop for tourists looking for the homemade ice cream that comes in at least 14 flavors. During the summer, people sometimes line up for forty-five minutes to sample this legendary ice cream. Single scoops are $2.75 and doubles are $3.75. A single-scoop waffle cone is $3.25 and a double-scoop waffle cone is $4.25. Soft-serve ice cream (not homemade) is also available for shakes, starting at $3.75.

Besides a variety of ice cream concoctions, the drive-in serves good old-fashioned burgers, hotdogs, fish and chips, chili, and other lunchtime delights. Deluxe burgers are $6.15 with chips and $6.85 with fries. Fish and chips are $8.95. Whether hungry for lunch or for an ice cream treat, the Sno Cap Drive-In is a great place to stop for a bite to eat.

Address: 380 W Cascade Ave, Sisters, OR 97759
Phone: 541-549-6151
Hours: 11 a.m.-7 p.m. Summer: 10 a.m.-10 p.m.
Restrooms: Not ADA accessible

Bend Area
Things to See and Do

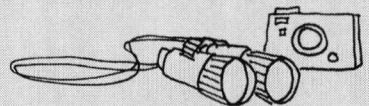

near Bend

High Desert Museum

If you have ever wanted to see a bald eagle, porcupine, or bobcat up close, check out the High Desert Museum just outside Bend. These animals, along with many other creatures native to the high desert, are all on display, both inside the museum and outside in special enclosures. The High Desert Museum also has exhibits devoted to three major cultural groups who lived and settled here: pioneers, Native Americans, and Chinese immigrants. Each played an important role in shaping the West as we know it today. Life-size dioramas depict each group's daily life in the untamed West. The living quarters, tools, and implements of each culture clearly show the ingenuity of using available materials. The customs and traditions of each culture are also explored.

Outside there is a sawmill that is, at times, still operational. You will also be able to walk around a pioneer farm and its outbuildings. Many hiking trails are available for guests to explore the grounds.

Special exhibits also travel to the High Desert Museum. When I visited, there was a spectacular exhibit on butterflies. It had an incredible walk-in area where guests could wander among dazzling, colorful, live works-of-art of nature.

Be sure to check the listing of special talks and daily presentations that will enhance your visit. Also, don't miss the wonderful sculptures that are both inside and outside the museum. There is a gift store at the museum and a cafe where you can sit down and enjoy a nice lunch or snack.

Address: 59800 South Hwy 97, Bend, OR 97702
Phone: 541-382-4754
Web: **www.highdesertmuseum.org**
Hours: Summer: May 1-October 31, 9 a.m.-5 p.m. daily
Winter: November 1-April 30, 10 a.m.-4 p.m.
Closed Thanksgiving, Christmas, New Years
Admission: See website for current prices
Restrooms: ADA accessible

Additional information: Stroller rental $3, Wheelchair FREE
Cafe hours: Summer 10 a.m.-4 p.m.
Winter 11 a.m.-3 p.m.
Pets are not allowed in the museum (except service animals) Airline-type kennels are available so pets can relax in the shade and not be cooped up in a hot car.

Section 13
Southeastern Oregon

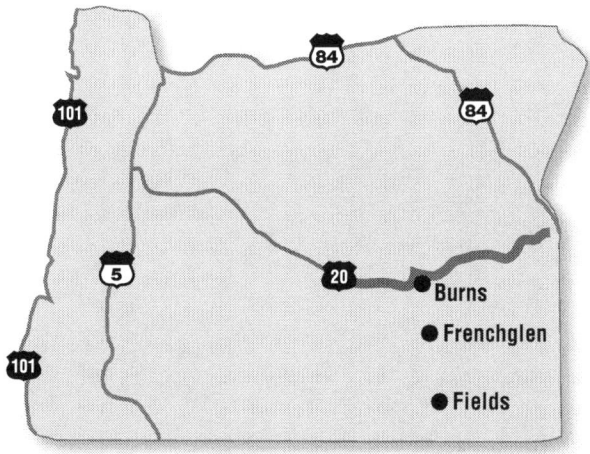

Alvord Desert, in the Field's area

Southeastern Oregon
Ice Cream

Fields

The Fields Station

About as far in southeastern Oregon as a person can get without being in Nevada is the Fields Station. It was established in 1881 as a roadhouse for the stagecoach line that ran from Burns, Oregon to Winnemuca, Nevada. Known for its thick milkshakes, the Fields Station is a welcome relief for travelers passing through the miles and miles of this isolated landscape.

How isolated is it? It is so isolated that planes sometimes land on the state highway in front of the station to grab a quick something-to-go.

Tammy Downs and Kris Tingue scoop up milkshakes ($4.75) that are so thick that when one accidentally fell over during our taste test, not a drop fell out of the cup. The milkshake reputation has grown steadily by word of mouth. The scoopers say that during the summer, buses from as far away as Portland call ahead for 120 milkshakes to be ready when they arrive. Coming in 25 flavors, our group tried several and loved the Oreo milkshake best of all. The milkshakes are so large that two people can easily share one.

Posted on the wall in the cafe is the tally of how many burgers and shakes have been sold during the year. The totals for 2010 were 3,763 burgers and 4,854 shakes. These numbers beat the 2009 record.

Breakfasts and lunches are also served in the cafe. Breakfasts cost between $7.95 and $9.95 while burgers with chips start at $7.50. The most expensive burger is a double bacon cheeseburger with fries for $14.50. All burgers are 1/2 pounders.

Besides the cafe, the Fields Station consists of a small store, gas station, and post office. The Fields Station boasts one of the smallest liquor stores in the state with a booming business!

For overnight guests, there is an RV park ($20/night). There is a motel ($50/single, $65 for two queen beds/two singles or two couples.) There is an old hotel with three rooms. One of the rooms has two queen-sized beds. Two rooms each have one queen-sized bed. Each hotel room rents for $90/night.

Memorial Day Weekend is the major weekend of the year for the Fields Station. For the last six years during their four-day event, 25 cents from the sale of each milkshake is donated to the Injured Marines Semper Fi Fund. They also accept donations to this worthy cause. Last year they raised $596.79.

Address: 22276 Field's Dr., Fields, OR 97710
Phone: 541-495-2275
Web: **www.fieldsoregon.com**
Hours: Monday-Saturday 8 a.m.-5 p.m., Sunday, 9 a.m.-5 p.m.
Restrooms: ADA restrooms are going to be built soon.
In March 2011, outhouses were available across the street from the station.

Southeastern Oregon
Things to See and Do

near Burns

Crystal Crane Hot Springs

"This is like a dream come true!" exclaimed my nephew Nicholas after he swam across the steaming length of the outdoor hot spring pond at Crystal Crane Hot Springs. "I've always wanted to have a hot tub I can swim in, and here it is!" With that he floated on his back, relaxing as he admired the clear blue sky and the birds circling overhead.

Crystal Crane Hot Springs is built up just enough to provide options for a variety of different experiences to suit people's needs. Admission for hot springs day use is $3.50. For those who like a little more privacy, enclosed spas are available for one or more people for $7.50 per person per hour, or $4 per hour for children 6 and under. Attached to the enclosed hot tubs is a bathhouse with restrooms, changing rooms, and showers.

Simple cabins can be rented for overnight guests (starting at $45/night with shared bathroom). RV spaces are available (starting at $18) as is tent camping ($15/night for double occupancy.) Pets are charged $3/night/pet. A bunkhouse cabin with half-bath is $60/night. A "round-up room" for group get-togethers can be rented for up to 50 people for $50. Kitchen facilities are on site for the use of guests. Free high speed Internet is available.

Address:	59315 Highway 78, east of Burns, OR 97720
Phone:	541-493-2312
Web:	www.cranehotsprings.com
Hours:	Daily 9 a.m.-9 p.m. Reservations recommended.
Additional information:	There are no in-and-out privileges to the facility.
Restrooms:	ADA accessible
Getting there:	From the north, coming through Burns, drive 25 miles east on Hwy 78.

in the Field's area

Alvord Desert

I had been intrigued by the Alvord Desert for a long time, ever since my sister told me the story of her family and their trip to this barren (as in there is absolutely NOTHING here) place in southeast Oregon. As the story goes, her younger son Ross, 8, had been complaining that his older brother Bryce, 11, ALWAYS got to drive the car when they were out in the middle of nowhere. He did not think it was "fair."

So my brother-in-law and Bryce got out of the car, set up a couple of lawn chairs, and told Ross to go have a good time. (For years I thought Ross was the only person left in the car but thankfully my sister had the good sense to go along for the ride.)

Anyway, after a marvelous 15-minute drive on a perfectly flat surface with no rocks, weeds, trees, shrubs, other people, animals of any kind, or cars anywhere in sight, Ross decided it was time to turn around and go pick up his dad and brother. The problem was there was no one in sight. He had driven so far on this desert floor that the U.S. Bureau of Land Management says is six miles wide and eleven miles long that he could not see anything or anybody but flat desert floor all around. Well, the story has a happy ending, because Ross, with his trusty mother as scout, were able to follow the faint tire prints they had left in the dried, cracked surface back to where they had started. From that time on I wanted to see this place.

I was not disappointed. There really is nothing growing in the Alvord Desert, but it holds all kinds of possibilities for things to do. Part of the year the desert is a muddy mess and driving is impossible, but from July to November, the ground is often dry enough for a car to drive across the vast open space. The U.S. Bureau of Land Management says that the desert is used for land sailing, glider flying, and camping. There are no restrooms, potable drinking water, cell phone service, or shade, so visitors must come prepared to take care of themselves.

On this trip my brother had his own ideas of fun planned. He wanted to put a paper bag over his son's head and tell him to walk in a straight line. Supposedly, if you walk far enough, you will start to follow the curvature of the Earth. (I thought he would end up walking in a big circle.) Then he wanted to put the car in first gear, jump on the roof, and let the car carry him across the desert. I was concerned about how he was going to get back into the car. As for me, I wanted to play Ultimate Frisbee.

In the end, we simply walked out onto the desert floor and admired the view. It was a little too muddy to drive a car. Besides that we found little pieces of barbed wire that had apparently flown loose from a fence in a wind storm and then had broken into pieces. It would have been terrible for car tires. It was a little too windy for Ultimate Frisbee. It was perfect for standing around, occasionally throwing the frisbee, chatting with friends, and marveling at one of nature's oddities.

Restrooms: No
Best time of year to visit: July to November are usually the driest months of the year.
Getting there: Coming from the north through Burns, take Hwy 78 southeast about 72 miles. Turn right onto East Steens Road and travel about 43 miles to the Alvord Desert.

Coming from the south through Fields, go north on East Steens Road.

Alvord Hot Springs

Adjacent to the Alvord Desert is Alvord Hot Springs. Although privately owned, people are usually permitted to use the two rustic, concrete hot tubs that are about 200 yards from the road. To find the springs, look for a little enclosure with corrugated tin walls on the east side of the road. The tin forms three walls that surround one of the two tubs. The other tub is in the open air. One tub is slightly warmer than the other. Park your car just off the main road and then take the path to the hot tubs. Be careful of the water in the springs leading into the tubs. It is hot!

Admission:	It seems to be free so far. Please be courteous and keep the area litter-free and glass-free so it may be enjoyed by others.
Restrooms:	No
Time of year to visit:	Any time of year
Getting there:	From Fields, Oregon take East Steens Road north for approximately 23 miles.

Frenchglen

Frenchglen Hotel

In the southeastern part of Oregon, way out in the middle of sagebrush and cattle country and far from city crowds is the picturesque Frenchglen Hotel, located in the heart of the town of Frenchglen, population 11. The hotel is an Oregon State Heritage Site, originally built in 1916 and then torn down and rebuilt in 1923. It was then remodeled by the Civilian Conservation Corps in the 1930s.

The hotel is managed by John Ross and his staff. They also do most of the cooking for the hotel that pretty much has the corner on the dining market since the closest town, Burns, is 61 miles north. The restaurant part of the hotel, which doubles as the main entry and lobby of the hotel, seats 24 people at three large, heavy wooden tables with benches on two sides. Breakfast, lunch, and dinner are served there.

Breakfasts can be selected from a menu, ranging from $4.50-$9.50 and served from 7:30 a.m.-9:30 a.m. Delicious homemade cinnamon rolls are on the breakfast menu. Lunch has selections priced from $5.00-$10.00 and is served from 11:30 a.m.-2:30 p.m. Sack lunches are also available for purchase. For dinner, a daily special is served family style. It includes a salad, rolls, vegetable, potatoes or rice, a meat dish, and a dessert. The hotel is noted for its marionberry cobbler with vanilla ice cream. Reservations are needed for dinner, which costs $20 and begins promptly at 6:30 p.m.

The eight rooms in the hotel are all upstairs. Each tiny room has a bed or two, a nightstand, a chair, a neatly folded stack of bath towels, and just enough room to move around the bed but not much more. Also in each room is a small bowl of peppermint candies and a journal that guests are invited to read or to add their own thoughts and comments. Separate men's and women's bathrooms down the hall are shared by all the hotel guests. By modern standards the hotel accommodations are minimalist. There are no room keys, television, or telephones in the hotel. One lonely pay phone booth is outside, across the street and about a half of a city block away, standing at the ready but looking out of place in this postcard-perfect town locked in time to the early 1900s while frequented by people trying to find solitude yet wielding cell phones and GPSs

So what is the allure of the Frenchglen Hotel? There is the peace and quietness of the location. Time somehow slows down here and you can relax, miles away from your hometown life and responsibilities. The Frenchglen Hotel is the perfect spot for bird-watchers to stay while they explore and marvel at the abundance of birds and other wildlife that migrate and/or live in the Malheur National Wildlife Refuge.

Next, Frenchglen is at the gateway to the majestic Steens Mountains. The amazing Alvord Desert is also nearby, as are hot springs, hiking, caves, and interesting geological formations. This part of the state includes many "roads less traveled" and you too can feel the thrill of early explorers as you "discover" a small piece of the planet not often visited by hordes of tourists. In short, a visit to the Frenchglen Hotel can be your start to a great adventure right here in Oregon's backyard!

....

Address: 39184 Highway 205, Frenchglen, OR 97736
Phone: 541-493-2825
Email: fghotel@yahoo.com
Hours: The hotel is open from March 15 to November 1. Food is only served during specified dining hours.
Rates: Double bed $70/night
One double and one twin $75/night
Restrooms: The hotel rooms are upstairs and the bathrooms are not ADA accessible.
Types of payment: Checks, Visa/Master/Discover cards
Area information: **www.or.blm.gov/steens**
www.harneycounty.com

Frenchglen area

The Round Barn and Visitor Center

The Pete French Round Barn, built in the 1880s to train horses during the bitterly cold winter months in southeastern Oregon, is actually more of a corral than a barn. It is a beautifully designed wooden structure with big, weathered beams. Looking up at the ceiling from inside the barn is like looking at the inside spokes of an umbrella. The barn is unusual mostly because it is round and not rectangular like most barns. It was listed on the National Register of Historical Places in 1971.

A short distance away is a nondescript building that is the Round Barn Visitor Center. The simple outside is deceiving because inside is a wonderfully decorated visitor center. A wide assortment of pamphlets about things to see and do in this part of the state are on one wall. Throughout the center are many browsing opportunities for souvenirs: Western art, books, greeting cards, jewelry, and more, all tastefully displayed and suited to many price ranges. There are also specialty items like silver horse bits, tools for repairing barbed wire fences, and spurs that, yes, jingle jangle so cowboys do not get kicked by their horses or cows.

The real gem in this center, though, is Richard Jenkins, who operates the visitor center. Not only is he a longtime resident of the area, local history expert, and wonderful story-teller, he is a welcoming host who helps visitors feel at home while they are in the center. On a blustery day when 19 of us descended on him unannounced, he brought out three cardboard tables and suggested that we eat our picnic lunches inside the center rather than outside in the wind where there were no tables. It became a special lunch to remember, mostly because of Richard Jenkin's generous hospitality.

One area of the visitor center houses several exhibits donated by the Jenkins family that offer a glimpse into their family's early life in this rural area.

In addition to running the visitor center, Jenkins also offers tours of the area, which we did not take, but if you are interested in a tour, contact Jenkinstours@centurytel.net.

Address:	51955 Lava Bed Rd., Diamond, OR 97722
Phone:	888-493-2420
Email:	Jenkinstours@centurytel.net
Admission:	FREE
Hours of operation:	Daily 9 a.m.-5 p.m. Seasonal hours in January and February
Restrooms:	ADA accessible
Getting there:	Coming from the north, take Hwy 78 from Burns. After 35 miles, take Lava Bed Road 404 at New Princeton. Follow signs to Pete French Round Barn (14 miles).
	Coming from the south on Hwy 205, turn east on South Diamond Lane, turn left on Lava Bed Road 404 after 7 miles, and follow the signs to the Pete French Round Barn (9.5 miles).

near Frenchglen

The Sage Grouse Strut and Bird Watching in the Malheur National Wildlife Refuge

It was before dawn and I had been quietly sitting in a parked car on the side of the road with three friends for about 15 minutes, becoming more skeptical as time passed. Three other cars full of my friends and family with binoculars and spotting scopes were parked both in front and behind us, all of our engines and headlights off, sitting in our makeshift bird blinds. We had caravanned from the Frenchglen Hotel, where we had been given specific directions to go to a certain road, turn left, and then go 9.1 miles; not 9.0 or 9.2, but 9.1. We had been told that we would find the birds on the left side, not the right side, of the road. We needed to get to this spot by 5:45 a.m. Oh, yes, and we were told NOT to get out of the car because a) it would scare the birds and mess up their mating ritual, and b) because we might be shot for messing up said ritual by other disgruntled bird-watchers.

What we were hoping to see was the annual "sage grouse strut," the courtship dance that male sage grouse perform in the spring to attract mates. Supposedly, sage grouse gather and display themselves in the exact same location every year. I was beginning to have my doubts. Through my monocular I saw barren rocks and sagebrush on the left side of the road and I saw equally barren rocks and sagebrush on the right side of the road.

At the stroke of 5:45 a.m., Ardy, sitting in the backseat, said, "I see something white." The sun's rays became just a little brighter and it was like some giant director in the sky yelled down, "It's showtime, boys! Action!" As if on cue, male sage grouse began to reveal themselves from behind all kinds of rocks and brush, puffing up their chests to form huge, ripply, impressive displays of white feathers, while at the same time their tail feathers spread into beautiful black fans. Then they began their proud, spectacular strut. It was truly a jaw-dropping experience.

It was much harder to spot the coy females who stayed partially hidden in the brush. After about 10 minutes of the males' amazing show, a hawk glided over and sage grouse flew up and away for cover from all kinds of rocks and brush. I was disappointed, thinking the hawk had ended the action, but slowly more males began revealing themselves and we enjoyed Act II. After about 45 minutes, the show ended and we went back to the Frenchglen Hotel for breakfast and to get ready for the rest of the day in the Malheur National Wildlife Refuge.

The Malheur National Wildlife Refuge is a birdwatcher's paradise. It was designated as a wildlife refuge by President Theodore Roosevelt in 1908 to protect birds that were being killed for their colorful feathers. It is now the home for over 320 species of birds and other wildlife. Today, birders can take one of several car loops around the refuge, or hike, to watch an amazing assortment of waterfowl, songbirds, raptors, and other birds who either migrate through the refuge or who call the refuge home. Every day, bird-watching is a new adventure, full of surprises and interesting bird encounters. Fall and spring are the best seasons to view the birds.

Phone:	U.S. Department of Agriculture, Malheur Wildlife Refuge at 541-493-2612
Web:	**www.fws.gov**
When to visit:	Spring and fall are the best seasons to visit. Some hotels and vendors are not open during the winter. Check in advance.

Area information: An excellent pamphlet about the kinds of bird species in the refuge, how common they are, and when during the year they can be seen is available from the U.S. Fish and Wildlife Service. It is called, "Malheur National Wildlife Refuge: Watchable Wildlife." For more information about the refuge, call 1-800-344-WILD or go to **www.fws.gov**

Getting there: The Refuge is between Burns and Frenchglen.

Section 14

Ice Cream and Attractions in Multiple Locations

Ice Cream

Burgerville

Technically a Washington State company, no book on Oregon Ice Cream would be complete without mentioning Burgerville. A fast food restaurant with a commitment to using locally grown ingredients whenever possible, Burgerville, can be found in 39 locations in both Oregon and Washington. The original Burgerville site was in Vancouver, Washington, just across the bridge from Portland.

Burgerville buys its ice cream from the Sunshine dairy, located in Portland. Burgerville milkshakes are superb. Besides offering a standard menu of milkshake options, like Strawberry, Chocolate, and Vanilla, there are specialty milkshakes, including Northwest Cherry Chocolate and Mocha Perk. Milkshakes come in three sizes, 12 oz., 16 oz., and 24 oz.

Then there are the seasonal flavors, each usually featured on the menu for approximately one month. Many are loaded with fresh berries or hazelnuts grown and harvested from Oregon farms. My all time favorite milkshake is Burgerville's Chocolate Hazelnut milkshake ($3.19-$4.99). It is hard to beat this marvelous masterpiece. Pairing chocolate and hazelnuts together makes a mouth-watering combination. This seasonal favorite is usually found on the menu in January. But no matter what time of year you visit Burgerville, you will find a milkshake to tickle your taste buds.

And then there is the food. Burgerville offers a wonderful assortment of burgers, salads, and fries that are fresh, flavorful, and filling. Whether you are in the mood for beef, chicken, fish, or a nice salad, Burgerville has something to please everyone. You will be happily surprised by this unique Northwest chain.

Web: www.burgerville.com

Attractions
in Multiple Locations

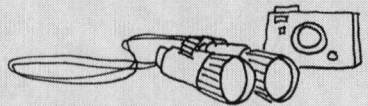

Covered Bridges

Many Oregon bridges built for cars, trucks, and trains during the early 1900s were made from wooden beams cut from Oregon's vast forests. To keep the rain and other elements from quickly rotting the timbers and rotting the decks of the bridges, engineers cleverly covered the bridges with structures that look like barns with openings at either end. At one time, Oregon boasted 450 covered bridges. That number has shrunk to 50 standing covered bridges today. Most of those early bridges have been replaced over the years with structures made of metal and concrete. A very few covered bridges are still used by motor vehicles. Some of the covered bridges are now used only for pedestrian traffic. Others stand upright but abandoned next to functioning newer bridges. Whatever their current condition, Oregon's covered bridges are picturesque and worth a stop for a photo opportunity.

The Cottage Grove area is called the "Covered Bridge Capital of the West." Visitors can see six covered bridges very near the town. Within Lane County, which includes Cottage Grove, there are 20 covered bridges that can be visited in one day. In fact, Lane County maintains the most covered bridges in Oregon, 16 of them listed on the National Register of Historical Places. Fourteen are still used in some fashion.

The six bridges nearest to Cottage Grove are Chambers Railroad Bridge, Stewart Bridge, Dorena Bridge, Centennial Bridge, Currin Bridge, and Mosby Creek Bridge. When you drive into Cottage Grove, look for road signs that lead to the covered bridges route. For more information about the Cottage Grove bridges, contact www.cottagegrove.net/history/covered_bridges/

For more information about other Oregon covered bridges in the state, go to **www.oregon.com/covered_bridges**. There you will find an interactive map that gives directions to their locations.

Oregon Lighthouses

In the late 1800s, lighthouses were built along the Oregon coast. Their job was to shine beacons of light out to sea to help ships safely navigate along the Oregon coast and into harbors without being smashed to smithereens by the wild Pacific surf and rocky shores. Especially during long dark stormy nights, the lighthouses were a welcome sight to ships surrounded by angry, pitch-black seas.

The lighthouses were run by dedicated light keepers. For years, they braved all kinds of weather to ensure that the lights atop the towers did not fail. With the advent of modern technologies, the need for manned lighthouses became antiquated. Plans were made to shutter many of them. However, several lighthouses have survived, in one form or another, because of the outpouring of community support to save these beautiful, romantic structures that are an important part of Oregon history.

Today, the lighthouses that remain provide some of the most dramatic views of the Oregon Coast. You will find wonderful photo opportunities. Many lighthouses have preserved their important history and welcome guests to explore. Each has its own tale to tell. Starting from the northern most part of Oregon, here is a list of the remaining lighthouses and their location.

For fantastic in-depth information about the history of each lighthouse and other facts, be sure to check out www.lighthousefriends.com. For information about state parks, go to **www.oregonstateparks.org**.

Tillamook Rock Lighthouse

Known as "Terrible Tilly," this lighthouse is perched on a rock off the coast of Tillamook Head. It was eventually made into a "columbarium," a place for funeral urns to be interred. The lighthouse is not open to the public, but it can be seen from Ecola State Park. Ecola Park is just north of Cannon Beach. Follow the signs to Indian Beach. A short hike will lead you to glimpses of the lighthouse from the trail. Alternatively, follow the signs to the viewpoint. A short walk to the viewpoint ends with a great view of the lighthouse. Day use permits for parking are $5.

Cape Meares Lighthouse

Meares Lighthouse is a rather stocky, short lighthouse. It is located eight miles west of Tillamook and two miles off the 3 Capes Scenic Tour. (The other capes are Cape Lookout and Cape Kiwanda.) The park is open daily, 7 a.m.-dusk. A short walk from the parking lot takes visitors right to the lighthouse. From the cliffs, visitors have spectacular scenic views. The wildlife refuge has walking trails and wonderful bird-watching. To schedule a tour, call 503-842-2244.

Open April 1-October 31, 11 a.m.-4 p.m. daily. FREE
For more info: **www.capemeareslighthouse.org**

Yaquina Head Lighthouse

Yaquina Head Lighthouse is the tallest lighthouse on the Oregon Coast. It is located three miles north of Newport. The lighthouse is part of a natural area operated by the U.S. Bureau of Land Management. You will find an interpretive center and gift store located next to one of the main parking lots. A short film there introduces guests to tide pools and birds that can be seen at the park.

Outdoors, there are acres of park to roam, great ocean views, and an up-close view of the lighthouse. From the interpretive center, you can take an easy, 10-minute walk to the lighthouse or you can drive past the interpretive center and park closer to the lighthouse.

Try to visit on one of the days when the lighthouse is open for visitors. At those times, guests are allowed in small groups to climb the spiraling staircase all the way to the top floor of the lighthouse. At the top, visitors are allowed, one or two at a time, to climb a steep set of seven or eight stairs to get a look at the faithful light that still operates day and night. It is amazing to think that this small light, together with its fresnel lens, creates a beacon that can be seen by ships 19 miles out to sea.

During low tides, you'll find amazing tide pools to explore at Cobble Beach. Respect the sea creatures you find and try not to step on them or pull them off the rocks. It is common to see harbor seals, whales (in season), and a variety of seabirds here. Take time to listen to the sound as the ocean waves pull back from the rocky shore. It also sounds like an appreciative audience clapping. After visiting Cobble Beach, you're sure to agree that the place is something to applaud! At Quarry Cove, disabled guests can obtain entrance to the lower observation desk by asking for the key at the interpretive center.

Park grounds:	Open at sunrise or 6 a.m., whichever is later; closes at sunset.
Interpretive Center hours:	Summer, 9 a.m.-5 p.m., Fall 10 a.m.-5 p.m., Winter 10 a.m.-4:30 p.m. Call for days and times when the lighthouse is open to the public.
Lighthouse hours:	Summer 9 a.m.-4 p.m., Fall 10 a.m.-4 p.m., Winter 12 p.m.-4 p.m.

Parking fee required. $7/3-day pass for one vehicle with 1-9 passengers. They also accept an Oregon Pacific Coast Passport. It has a 5-day limit good for day use at 15 federal and state parks, including Yaquina Head. The cost for this pass is $10.

For more info: **www.blm.gov/or/resources/recreation/yaquina/index.php** or **www.yaquinalights.org/**

Yaquina Bay Lighthouse

This lighthouse is situated on the north side of the Yaquina Bridge in Newport. It had a brief working life between 1871 and 1874. In recent times it has been renovated into a privately funded working lighthouse that is a navigational aid to ships. Unlike the design of other lighthouses, this one has the living quarters attached to the lighthouse. It is listed in the Register of Historic Places. Visitors are welcome to visit the watch room. The light tower is off-limits to the public. On your visi,t be sure to watch the video about the lighthouse and browse the gift store.

Open to the public every day except major holidays such as Thanksgiving, Christmas, and New Years. Summer hours (from Memorial Day to September 30): 11 a.m.-5 p.m. Winter hours (October 1-Memorial Day): 11 a.m.-4 p.m. Entrance fee to lighthouse by donation. The lighthouse is in Yaquina Bay State Park.

For more info: **www.blm.gov/or/resources/recreation/yaquina/index.php.** or **www.yaquinalights.org/.**

Cape Perpetua Lighthouse

This lighthouse was built in 1976 by Jim Gibbs, a former lighthouse keeper. He wrote extensively about lighthouses and shipwrecks. This lighthouse is not open to the public, but it can be glimpsed from the pullout at milepost 166 on Highway 101. This pullout is 1.8 miles south of Yachats. The turnout for parking and the road's shoulder is narrow at this spot. It is not safe to pull over and get out to see the lighthouse on days with heavy traffic.

Heceta Head Lighthouse

The light from Heceta Head Lighthouse, located 13 miles north of Florence on Highway 101, can be seen 21 miles out to sea and is the most powerful beacon of any Oregon lighthouse. It is part of the Oregon State Parks Heceta Head Lighthouse State Scenic Viewpoint. This lighthouse is the most photographed lighthouse in the state. Dramatic pictures can be taken from many locations in the area, including Sea Lion Caves. Free guided tours of the Keeper's House and the Lighthouse are available. Donations are gladly accepted. The Interpretive Center is located on the first floor of the Keeper's House. Upstairs, six rooms are available for a luxurious bed and breakfast experience. The waiting list to reserve one of the rooms can be at least three months in advance.

The Keeper's House Tours are available from Memorial Day weekend through Labor Day weekend, Thursdays-Mondays from noon-5 p.m.
To arrange tours at other times, call 866-547-3696.

Lighthouse Tours are daily from March-October from 11-5 p.m.
To arrange a tour at other times, call 800- 551-6949.

The observation area at the lighthouse is open every day during park hours.

Gift shop on site is open daily from Memorial Day weekend-September, during Christmas open house, and select weekends.

There are also hiking trails and bird-watching opportunities starting at the scenic viewpoint.

There is a day-use parking fee of $5.

For more info: **www.hecetalighthouse.com/**

Umpqua River Lighthouse
At the entrance to Winchester Bay, six miles south of Reedsport is this charming lighthouse. Tours for up to eight people are scheduled daily from 10 a.m.-4 p.m. from May 1-October 30. It is operated by the Douglas County Parks and Recreation Department. For more information and fees, call 541-957-7007.

For more info: **www.umpqualighthouse.org/**

Cape Arago Lighthouse
The light at Cape Arago Lighthouse was turned off in January 2006. In 2008, Cape Arago itself was returned to several confederated native tribes who have ancestral burial sites in the area. An agreement was reached that the lighthouse will become available for the general public to visit. Currently, the lighthouse is closed to the public. You can get a good view of the lighthouse from Sunset Bay State Park which is located 12 miles southwest of Coos Bay.

Coquille River Lighthouse
Two miles north of Bandon, you will find the Coquille River Lighthouse located within Bullards Beach State Park. A short, squatty lighthouse, it is adjacent to sandy beaches that are perfect for exploring and bird-watching. The lighthouse has staff on duty from May through October. They are there to explain the history of the lighthouse. For more info, contact the State Parks Info Center at 800-551-6949.

Cape Blanco Lighthouse
Cape Blanco is 9 miles north of Port Orford. Tall and majestic, Cape Blanco has a spectacular view of the Pacific Ocean. It is located adjacent to Cape Blanco State Park. There you will find many acres of beach to explore and trails to hike. Lighthouse tours are given from April to October. The cost for the tour is $2/adult, $1 children under 12, or $5/family. There is also a well-preserved Victorian house nearby that offers tours of the home.

Lighthouse tours are available April-October 31, Tuesday-Sunday, 10 a.m.-3:30 p.m. The last tour starts at 3:15 p.m. and the gates close at 3:30 p.m.

The Hughes House tours are given April-October 31, Tuesday-Sunday 10 a.m. -3:30 p.m. Donations are gladly accepted for the house tour.

Oregon Rodeos

For a real Western experience, try to attend one of Oregon's wild-west rodeos. There is a lot to see in an afternoon of bucking broncs, bull-riding, and roping that will keep you stomping your feet and clapping in approval. Daring young buckaroos challenge themselves and common sense as they race for the best score in calf-roping, saddle bronc-riding, bull-riding, and more. Watch thrilling rides, incredible spills and near disasters as each cowboy tries to claim a share of prize money. Even the ladies get a turn as they lead their horses in barrel racing for the fastest time.

There are over 50 rodeos in Oregon each year. Most are held during the summer. Each rodeo has its own personality. Here are a few of my favorites. Call for specific dates and times.

St. Paul Rodeo	St. Paul, Oregon 503-633-2011	July 1-July 4
Chief Joseph Days	Joseph, Oregon 541-432-1015	July
Pendleton Round-Up	Pendleton, Oregon 1-800-457-6336	September

Live Theater and Musical Venues

Oregon is rich with places to go for live music and theatrical events. Here are my top 20 sites worth exploring.

Ashland

Oregon Shakespeare Festival

Famous for both Shakespeare productions and contemporary theater. Three theaters, including an outdoor Elizabethan stage, and two indoor venues, the Angus Bowmer Theater and the New Theater.

Address:	Oregon Shakespeare Festival, 15 South Pioneer Street, Ashland, OR 97520
Box Office:	541-482-2111 or 1-800-219-8161
Web:	**www.osfashland.org**
Email:	boxoffice@osfashland.org or administration@osfashland.org

Bend

Tower Theater

A beautiful theater in downtown Bend, the Tower Theater presents a wide variety of local and national live entertainment.

Address:	Theater address: 835 NW Wall St, Bend OR 97709
	Mailing address: P.O. Box 1378, Bend, OR 97709
Phone:	541-317-0700
Web:	**www.towertheatre.org**
Box Office Hours:	Monday-Friday 10 a.m.-5 p.m.

Cannon Beach

Coaster Theater Playhouse

Theater performances and educational workshops in the coastal town of Cannon Beach.

Address:	Theater address: 108 N Hemlock St., Cannon Beach, OR 97110
	Postal address: P.O. Box 643, Cannon Beach, OR 97110
Box Office Phone:	503-436-1242
Web:	**www.coastertheatre.com**

Eugene
Hult Center for the Performing Arts
Silva Concert Hall seats 2,500 people and Soreng Theater seats 500 people, making Hult Center for the Performing Arts an attractive venue for a wide range of events and shows.

Address:	One Eugene Center, Eugene, OR 97401
Phone:	541-682-5746
Web:	www.hultcenter.org
Email:	HultCenter@ci.eugene.or.us

Jacksonville
Britt Festival
The Britt Festival, still going strong after 49 years, features world famous performers during a series of summer concerts. From pop, country, bluegrass, blues, jazz, and classical music, the summer concerts are some of the best in the state. The concerts are held on the Britt Grounds in the beautiful town of Jacksonville. The stage is covered and the audience sits in a beautiful natural outdoor amphitheater. Guests may sit on the grass and enjoy a picnic dinner, or tickets are available for bench type seating.

Address:	Postal address, P.O. Box 1124, Medford, OR 97501
Phone:	541-779-0847
Web:	**www.brittfest.org**

Medford
Craterian Ginger Rogers Theater

Address:	23 S Central Ave, Medford, OR 97501
Box Office:	541-779-3000
Web:	**www.craterian.org**

Newport
Newport Performing Arts Center
Fabulous theater space in Newport.

Address:	Theater address, 777 W Olive St., Newport, OR 97365
	Postal address: P.O. Box 1315, Newport, OR 97365
Phone:	541-265-2787
Web:	**www.coastarts.org**

Portland

Aladdin Theater & Performance
This theater has seating capacity of 600 and is a popular venue for musical groups and other entertainers who want a venue smaller than the giants downtown. A broad range of acts perform here.

Address: 3017 SE Milwaukie Ave, Portland, OR 97202
Phone: 503-234-9694
Web: www.aladdin-theater.com

Do Jump! Extremely Physical Theater
Think part acrobatics, part comedy, part trapeze act, with juggling, dancing, acting, music, and imagination thrown in for good measure, and you have a hint at what this innovative, off the grid, mind twisting, physical show is all about. This award-winning group is a wonder to see.

Address: Echo Theater, 1515 SE 37th Ave, Portland, OR 97214
Phone: 503-231-1232
Web: www.dojump.org
Email: dojump@dojump.or

Gerding Theater at the Armory
Originally built in 1891 as an armory for the Oregon National Guard, the Armory was transformed into the Gerding Theater at the Armory in 2006 to be the home for Portland Center Stage. Besides wonderful theatrical productions, you will find a variety of classes and workshops offered during the year.

Address: 128 NW 11th Ave, Portland, OR 97209
Phone: 503-445-3700
Web: www.pcs.org
Email: boxoffice@pcs.org

Ladybug Theater
Ladybug Theater is a great introduction to theater for young children. Since 1965, Ladybug Theater has been a Portland tradition for young families.

Web: www.ladybugtheater.org

Northwest Children's Theater and School
Delightful theatrical presentations featuring adult actors and young actors-in-training. For budding actors, follow your star and learn acting skills for live theater. There are classes geared to kids from 3 ½ years old to 18 years old.

Address:	1819 NW, Portland, OR 97214
Info Phone:	503-222-2190
Box Office:	503-222-4480
Web:	www.nwcts.org

Oregon Repertory Theater

Address:	1516 SW Alder Street, Portland, OR 97205
Box Office:	503-241-9807
Web:	www.artistsrep.org
Email:	boxoffice@artistsrep.org

downtown Portland
Portland Center for the Performing Arts
Includes: Keller Auditorium, Dolores Winningstad Theater, Schnitzer Concert Hall, Newmark Theater

Address:	Mailing Address/box office is 1111 SW Broadway, Portland, OR 97205-2913
Phone:	503-248-4335
Web:	www.pcpa.com
Email:	info@pcpa.com
Box Office:	Monday-Saturday 10 a.m.-5 p.m. Box office is closed on federal holidays

Salem
Historic Elsinore Theater
A lovely, historic performing arts center in Salem.

Address:	170 High St. SE, Salem, OR 97301
Phone:	503-375-3574
Web:	www.elsinoretheatre.com

Sisters
Sisters Folk Festival
The Sisters Folk Festival is a three-day event held on the weekend after Labor Day. Hear a variety of music from blues to bluegrass.

Address:	Postal address P.O. Box 3500, PMB 304, Sisters, OR 97759
Box Office:	541-549-4979
Web:	**www.sistersfolkfestival.org**
Email:	info@sistersfolkfestival.org

Tigard
Broadway Rose Theater Company
See fabulous live professional summer theater. Drama camps, teen workshops, and technical theater internships are also available. Some summer productions take place at Deb Fennell Auditorium, at Tigard High School. Other productions are at the New Stage Auditorium.

Address:	New Stage Auditorium, 12850 SW Grant Ave, Tigard, OR 97281
	Deb Fennell Auditorium, 9000 SW Durham Rd., Tigard, OR 97224
Box Office:	503-620-5262
Web:	**www.broadwayrose.org**
Email:	boxoffice@bwayrose.com

Acknowledgements

There are so many hard-working business owners and employees to whom I am indebted for giving me their time and the inside scoop about their businesses. Please forgive me if I have forgotten to mention your name.

Don Baldwin, Lon Beale, Elizabeth Beekley, Harry Beres, Eva Bernhard, Will Brady, Rebecca Bond, Leb Borgerson, Marianne Brogan, Tyson Brown, Liam Burke, Becky Burnett, Mary Burns, Patti Burns, Tracey Cadonau McKinnon, Leslie Carnes, Jodi Chapa, Carrie Clayton, Lee Clinton, Jennifer Cobos, Crystine Cole, Keith Cole, Alyce Cornyn-Selby, Tim Croghan, Robert Crook, Robin Crowell, Jvon Danforth, Lee Dawson, Reid Decker, Marilyn DeVault, Sandra Downs, Chad Draizin, Michael Drannow, John Dundas, Bob Eberhard, Stan Egaas, Lew Evans, Mike Exinger, Steve Feldkamp, Sydney Fisher, Katharine Flanagan, Jay Fonville, Michelle, Forster, Lisa Freeman, Stephanie Gibson, Julie Gleason, Bertha Gomez, Ryan Hagen, Cathie Hanthorn, Ian Hay, Jerry Hayes, Nancy Higgins, Wendy Hoag, Robert Hoefs, Bob Horning, Jane Horning, Kelly Howard, Richard Jenkins, Geri Kendall, Jennifer Kent, Jennifer Kevil, Terri Klouda, Roy Koback, Eleanor Kramer, Denise Kryger, Sarah LaCompte, Nick Laflin, Suzy Lambert, Marilyn Lasseigne, Pat Love, Justin Luber, Hardy Lussier, Emily MacKay, Auxilio Maldonado, Rhett Martin, Victoria Martindel, Maurice Martinez, Don Mathews, Therese McMichael, Pat Merrill, Jane Minnick, Sarah Minnick, F.E. Kidd, Karen Norton, Mike Ooley, Jim Osburn, Jeff Parker, Ken Paul, Malcolm Phinney, Myra Plant, Nikki Price, Shane Reaney, Jeffery Reiter, Amanda Rhoads, Tammy Rickerd, Goldie Roberts, Jim Robertson, Steve Roemen, John Ross, Bob Russell, Carissa Sauer, Norma Sax, Dennis Schrag, Earl Scott, Pamela Severe, Pat Silveria, Vicki Sink, Terry Smoke, Carla Sorweide, Randi Stupfel, Cynthia Taft, Monica Teem, Brian Tenney, Jack Triperinas, Nancy Walsh, Joe Wassink, Dan Watts, Stacy Webb, Bruce Weimer, Mike Wellins, Justin White

I am very lucky to have a wonderful family and friends who support me and all my crazy ideas. They are always game to try a new ice cream place or go on a new adventure. Thank-you for all your encouragement and ideas.

Many thanks to the ice cream tasters: Alexander Arnis, George Arnis, Nick Arnis, Sonya Arnis, Sandy Auld, Jeanne Bevis, Phil Coquillette, Rebecca Easton, Suzanne Easton, Lynda Eng, Elena Hoffnagle, John Hoffnagle, Nicholas Hoffnagle, Penny Holeman, Rocky Johnson, Sue Johnson, Bryce Kellogg, Dan Kellogg, Lynn Kellogg, Ross Kellogg, Linda Layfield, Nancy Lee, Deborah Kimokeo, Kimo Kimokeo, Carolyn McBee, Marvella McPartland, Connie Moen, Jennifer Pietka, Janice Philbrick, Kate Philbrick, Larry Philbrick, Susannah Philbrick, Sue Plaisance, Annalee Purdy, Diann Rockstrom, Nancy Salas, Nancy Walsh, Ardi Winters.

Also, thanks to Kate Loggan for her binocular/camera icon.

Index

A

Active Culture, 68
Adair, 152, 153
Adventure Park at Skibowl, 222, 223
Agness, 210
Albany, 135, 136
Albany Brass Ring Historic Carousel & Museum, 135, 136
Alden's Natural and Organic Ice Cream, 4, 121, 122
Alderton, Charles, 14
Alf's Ice Cream & Burgers, 64
Alma Rose, 77
Alpenrose Dairy, 8
Alpenrose Dairyville, 9
Alpenrose Easter Egg Hunt, 8
Alpenrose Ice Cream, 4, 64, 67, 160
Alpenrose Opera House, 9
Alpenrose Stadium, 8
Alpenrose Storybook Lane, 9
Alpenrose Velodrome, 8
Alvord Desert, 247-249, 250
Alvord Hot Springs, 248, 249
Annual Wool Gathering, 221
Apple Valley Country Store and Bakery, 86
Artificial freezer, 3
Artichoke Music, 46
Ashland, 118, 137, 138
Ashland Chamber of Commerce, 138
Ashland City Band, 137
Astoria, 172, 173
Audubon Society of Portland, 53

B

Baby Gramps, 156
Baker City, 94, 95
Bandon (near), 206, 207
Banks, 72, 73
Baskin-Robbins, 4
Baur, Jacob, 14
Bay Latte, 190
Bay Ocean Park, 179
Bay Ocean Spit, 179
Bella Union Restaurant and Saloon, 124
Bend, 232-236, 240, 241
Benson, James, 195
Benson, Simon, 184
Beres, Harry, 73
Bernhard, Eva, 12
The Berry Patch Restaurant, 183-186
BigFoot, 18
B.J.'s Ice Cream, 4, 118, 202, 238
Blossom Bar, 211
BluePlate Lunch Counter and Soda Fountain, 10, 11
Boardman, 84, 85
Boice Cope County Park, 213
Bonneville, 95, 96
Bonneville Fish Hatchery, 95, 96
Bonney Butte, 223, 224
Boring, 33
Boxcar, 229

Bradham, Caleb, 14
Brady, Liz, 212, 213
Brady, Will, 212, 213
Brewin' in the Wind, 166
Bridal Veil, 98, 99
Britt Festival, 124
Brogan, Marianne, 46, 47
Brookings, 200, 201
Brothers, 137
Buckskin Mary, 229
Bud's Ice Cream Shop, 119
Bullwinkle's Restaurant, 149, 150
Burgerville, 4, 256
Burnett, Becky, 26
Burns (near), 246
Burns, Mary, 110
Burnside Bridge, 33
Bute, Eric, 18
Butte Creek Mill, 140, 141

C

C & D Drive-In and Bakery, 84, 85
Cadonau family, 8
   Cadonau, Henry, 8
Campbell, Duncan, 75
Cannon Beach, 160, 161, 173-175
Cannon Beach Sandcastle Day, 173-175
Cape Falcon Kayak, 177
Carver, 60
Cascade Glacier Ice Cream, 4, 10, 18, 31, 43, 62, 65, 67, 68, 79, 89, 92, 110, 122, 134, 160, 167, 183, 189, 191, 200
Central Point, 139, 140
Chapa, Jodi, 108
Chapman School, 53-55
Charm Trail, 102
Children's Course, 75, 76
Chocolate, Strawberry, and Vanilla: A History of American Ice Cream, 3
Civilian Conservation Corps (CCC), 227, 249
Clinton Street Theater, 16
Ciao Bella, 4, 122
Coca Cola, 14
The Coffee Shop, 164, 165
Cole, Crystine, 238
Cole, Keith, 202, 238
Columbia River, 100, 186
Columbia River Gorge, 98
Columbia River Maritime Museum, 172, 173
Cone Amor, 203
Confederated Tribes of Warm Springs, 226
Cool Moon Ice Cream, 4, 12, 13
Cooper family, 142
Correction Connection, 103
Cornyn-Selby, Alyce, 34
Costco, 4, 122
Cottage Grove, 256
Cougar Lane Lodge, 210
Covered Bridges, 256
   Centennial Bridge

Chambers Railroad Bridge
Currin Bridge
Dorena Bridge
Mosby Creek Bridge
Stewart Bridge
Cozy Room, 106
Crater Lake National Park, 154, 155
Crater Rock Museum, 139
Croghan, Tim, 23
Crook, Robert, 167, 168
Crystal Springs Hot Springs, 246
Culinary Institute of America (CIA), 128
Curling, 37

D
Danforth, Dane, 233
Danforth Jvon, 233
Dari-Mart, 125, 126
Del Campo, Jorge Martin, 31
Dentzel family, 135
Dentzel III, Bill, 135
Deschutes River, 218, 219
DeVault, Marilyn, 20, 21
Disc Golf, 44, 80
Discovery Golf, 75
Doernbecker Children's Hospital, 45
Downs, Tammy, 244
Dr. Pepper, 14
Draizin, Chad, 16
Dundas, John, 112
Dutch Girl Ice Cream, 121

E
Eagle Cap Wilderness, 113, 114, 116
Eagle Creek Hike, 96, 97
Eagle Point, 140, 141
Eastbank Esplanade, 33
Eastern Oregon Correctional Institution, 103
Eastern Oregon Fire Museum & Learning Center, 101
Eberhard, Bob, 237
Eberhard, Mark, 237
Eberhard's Ice Cream, 4. 220, 235, 236
Eberhard's Ice Cream,
 history 237
Egaas, Stan, 183, 184
Einstein, Albert, 142
Eleanor's Undertow Café and Ice Cream Parlor, 188
Elephant Garlic Festival, 68, 69
Elvis, 64
Eugene, 119, 120
Evans, Jeanne, 25
Evans, Lew, 25
Evans, Lew Jr., 25
Evans, Marian, 25
Evergreen Aviation and Space Center, 78, 79
Excelsior Inn and Restaurant, 126
Exinger, Mike, 169
Exinger, Mona, 169

F
Fairley's Pharmacy and Soda Fountain, 14, 15
Family Fun Center, 149, 150
Federal Wild and Scenic River, 210
Feldkamp, Ormond, 132
Feldkarmp, Steve, 133
Fields, 244, 245
Fields (near), 247-249
The Fields Station, 244, 245
Fifty Licks, 16
Finders Keepers Glass Float Hunt, 193, 194
Firehouse Five, 137
Fishing, 80
Flashback Malt Shoppe, Collectibles & Gifts, 167, 168
Flashback's Café, 191
Floras Lake, 212, 213
Floras Lake Windsurfing and Kiteboarding, 212, 213
Florence, 202
Florence (near), 208, 209
Food Innovation Center, 26
Fort Stevens State Park, 175, 176
4th of July in Ashland, 137, 138
Fort Orford Lifeboat Station, 176
Fox, Dan, 68
Fred Meyer, 26
Free Willy, 197
Freeman, Lisa, 18
Frenchglen, 249-250
Frenchglen (near), 251, 252-254
Funderburg, Anne Cooper, 3
Furst-Puckler-Eis, 120

G
Gallery of Trees, 56
Game Park Safari, 206, 207
Gaston, 73, 74
Gearhart, 162, 163
Gearhart Junction Café, 162
Gibson, Buzz, 125, 126
Gibson, Gladys, 125
Gibson, Howard, 125
Gibson, Jock, 125
Gibson, Mike, 125
Gibson, Pat, 125
Gibson, Scott, 125
Gladstone, 75, 76
Glass blowing, 143, 194, 195
Glass Forge, 143
Gleason, Alden, 121
Gleason, Jerrad, 121
Gleason, Julie, 121, 122
Gleason, Tom, 121, 122
Gold Beach, 203, 210, 211
Gold Hill, 141, 142
Goldie's Ice Cream Parlor, 220, 221
Gomez, Bertha, 70
Gomez, Daniel, 70
Gomez, Victoria, 31
Goody's Soda Fountain & Ice Cream, 232-234

Government Camp, 222, 223
Grants Pass, 123, 143
Grants Pass Pharmacy, 123
Graveyard of the Pacific, 172

H
Halloween, 88, 203, 221
Hammond (near), 175, 176
Hamley and Company, 104
Harding, Tonya, 37
Hardy's Burgers, Salads,and Ice Cream, 235
Harriet the Frog, 136
Harry and David Tour, 144, 145
Hat Museum, 34
Hawk Watch International at Bonney Butte, 223, 224
Hawthorne Bridge, 33
Heceta Head Lighthouse, 208
Heppner, 108, 109
Herlinger, Lisa, 26
Herschell-Spillman Carrousel, 39
Higgins, Nancy, 152
High Desert Museum, 240, 241
Hillsboro, 76, 77
Hoefs, Robert, 192
Hollywood Theater, 16
Honolulu Coffee Roasters, 160
Hood River, 86-88
Hood River (near), 100, 101
Hood River Fruit Loop, 100
Hop Sing's Chinese Laundry, 105
Horning, Bob, 80
Horning's Fishing and Picnic Hideout, 80, 81
Horning, Jane, 80
Horning, Richard, 80
Horses From Dream Stables, 60
Hought's 24 Flavors, 89, 90
House of mystery at the Oregon Vortex, 141, 142
Howard, Kelly, 195
Hughes, Howard, 78

I
Ice box,3
Ice Crystal Classic, 37
Imperial River Company, 218
Indulge Sweets, 204, 205
Injured Marines Semper Fi Fund, 245
International Rose Test Garden in Washington Park, 35

J
Jacksonville,124
Jamba Juice, 4, 122
Jamison Square Park, 12
Jamocha Jo's Java and Ice Cream, 152, 153
Japanese Submarine I-25, 176, 215
Jefferson, Thomas, 2
Jem 100 Ice Cream Saloon, 67
Jenkins, Richard, 251
Jennifer L. Sears Glass Art Studio, 194, 195
Jerry's Jet Boats and Rogue River Mail Boat Trips, 210, 211
Johnson, Nancy,3
Jones, Willa, 200
Joseph, 110-112
Julie's Organic Ice Cream, 4, 121, 122
Junction City, 125, 126

K
K-R Drive In, 130, 131
Kah-Nee-Ta, 226, 227
Kaiser, Henry 78
Kamakawiwo'ole, Iz, 46
Kayak Building on the Oregon Coast, 176, 177
Keiko, 197
Keizer, 127
Kelly, Tom, 120
Kendall, Donald, 203
Kendall, Geri, 203
Kidd, F.E., 36
Kidd Toy Museum, 36, 37
Kidopolis, 149
Kiteboarding, 100, 212
Kitts, Mike, 87
Kokanee Salmon, 113-115
Kramer, Eleanor, 188
Kreuzer, Maurice, 143

L
LaGrande, 89, 90, 101
Ladd-Reingold house (1910), 34
Lake Oswego, 62
Lake Oswego Ice Creamery and Restaurant, 62
Lake Oswego (near), 63
Lamb's, 63
Langlois (near), 212, 213
Lasseigne, Marilyn, 121
Lavender Festival, 60, 61
Lazerextreme, 149
Lewis Farm, 72
Lewis and Clark Centennial Exposition, 56
Lighthouses, 257-262
   Cape Arago Lighthouse, 261
   Cape Blanco Lighthouse, 261
   Cape Meares Lighthouse, 258
   Cape Perpetua Lighthouse, 260
   Coquille River Lighthouse, 261
   Heceta Head Lighthouse, 260
   Tillamook Rock Lighthouse, 257
   Umpqua River Lighthouse, 261
   Yaquina Bay Lighthouse, 259
   Yaquina Head Lighthouse, 258, 259
Lightship Columbia, 172
Lincoln City, 188, 189, 193-195
Lincoln City Glass Center, 195
Linfield College, 64
Lithia Park, 118, 137
Litster, John, 142
Little Leaguers, 8
Little League Softball World Series, 8
Livingroom Theaters, 16

Index 273

LLC Whitewater Photo and Ice Cream, 219
Lloyd Center Ice Rink, 37, 38
Lochmead Ice Cream, 4
Lochmead Dairy, 119
  history of 125, 126
Lovely's 50-50, 17
Luber, Justin, 63
Luber, Pasha, 63
Lussier, Hardy, 235
Lucas Lodge, 211

M
Mack, Tassie, 87
Mad Mary's Soda Shop, 110
Mail Boats, 210
Malheur National Wildlife Refuge, 252, 253
Manzanita, 164, 165, 176, 177
Maps
  Bend Area, 231
  Central Coast Highway 101, 187
  Columbia River Gorge and I-84, 83
  I-5 Freeway, 117
  Mt. Hood/Shaniko/Kah-Nee-Ta Triangle, 217
  Near Portland, 59
  North Coast Highway 101, 159
  Off the Beaten I-5 Freeway, 151
  Off the Beaten I-84 Track, 107
  Portland, 7
  South Coast Highway 101, 199
  Southeastern Oregon, 243
Marching Macaronis, 137
Market of Choice, 63
Martin Luther King Weekend, 149
Martinez, Maurice, 196
Matthews, Don, 190
Matthews, Fran, 190
Maupin, 218, 219, 229, 230
McCall, Tom, 175
McMinnville, 64, 65, 78, 79
McPartland, Marvella, 236
Medford, 144, 145
Merlin, 145, 146
Merrill, Pat, 162
Meyers, Jon, 195
Midvalley Rehabilitation, Inc., 65
Mike's Ice Cream, 87, 88
Millen, Daniel, 195
Minnick, Jane, 16
Minnick, Sarah, 16
Mission Market, 91
Mitchell, Francis, 179
Mo's Chowder Restaurant, 188
Moose Munch, 144, 145
Mor Art, 196
Morrison Bridge, 33
Mt. Hood, 222, 223, 225
Mt. Hood Ice Cream Company, 63
Mt. Howard, 113, 116
Mountain Rescue Association, 63
Multnomah Falls, 98, 99

N
National Historic Landmark Community, 124
National Registry of Historical Places. 76, 129, 140, 227, 251
New Seasons, 16, 26
Newberg, 67
Newport, 190-192, 197, 198
Newport Candy Shop & Ice Cream Parlor, 192
Nicholson, Jack, 227
1904 World's Fair, 3
North Plains, 68, 69, 80, 81
Nubuo Fajita, 176, 215

O
Oak Springs, 229
Oakland, 128, 129
Oaks Amusement Park, 33, 39, 40
Oaks Park Skating Rink, 40
Obama, President Barack, 119
Obama, Michelle, 119
Oceanside, 166
Oceanside Beach Recreation Site, 166
OMNIMAX, 41
Oregon Coast Aquarium, 197, 198
Oregon Country Fair, 156, 157
Oregon Dairy Association, 55
Oregon Health Sciences University (OHSU), 45
Oregon Heritage Site, 249
Oregon Ice Cream Company, 4
  history of 121, 122
Oregon Miniature Aircraft Squadron (OMAS) Annual Show, 72, 73
Oregon Museum of Science and Industry (OMSI), 33, 41, 42
Oregon Trail Interpretive Center, 94, 95
Oregon State University, 26
Oregon Wildlife Heritage Foundation, 95
Oregon Zoo, 42, 43
Oregon's Parthenon, 56
Osburn, Jim, 160
Osburn's Ice Creamery, 160, 161

P
Pacific Crest Trail, 228
Paletaria El Paisanito 70, 71
Palmateer, Marion, 232
Palmateer, Marn, 232
Pamplin, Dr. Robert, 220
Paparo, Maurizio, 126
Parker, Jeff, 128
Paul, Ken, 38
Peculiarium, 18, 19
Pendleton, 91, 102-105
Pendleton Chamber of Commerce, 102
Pendleton Private Collection of Indian Artifacts, 105
Pendleton Round-Up, 104
Pendleton Underground Tour, 105, 106
Pendleton Woolen Mill, 105
Pepsi, 14
Pete French Round Barn, 251

Peter Iredale, 175
Peters, Christy, 134
Peters, Daryl, 134
Piece of Cake, 20, 21
Pier Park, 44
Pine Tavern, 236
Pioneer Day, 221
Pix Patisserie, 22
Plant, Myra, 128
Pope House Bourbon Lounge, 23, 24
Poppy's Pizza, 84, 85
Pop's Sweet Shop Ice Cream, 163
Port Orford, 214, 215
Port Orford Lifeboat Station, 214, 215
Portland Aerial Tram, 45
Portland Civic Theater, 9
Portland Expo Center, 48
Portland Quarter Midget Racing Association, 8
Portland Rose Festival, 55
Portland Ukulele Association, 46, 47
Portland Ukulele Festival, 46
Potter, T. B., 179
Powell's Bookstore, 47, 48
Prince Hermann Ludwig Heinrich von Puckler-Muskau, 120
Prince Puckler Ice Cream, 87, 119, 120
Prineville, 232-234
Prison Blues, 103
Puget Island, 186

R
Ragtime and Vintage Music Festival, 221
Reaney, Shane, 60
Redmond, 232-234, 237
Reed, Mark, 56
Regina Pneumatic Cleaner Model B, 52
Reiter, Jeff, 10,
Rhoads, Amanda, 29
Rhodochrosite, 77
Rice, Helen, 76
Rice Hill, 130, 131
Rice N.W. Museum of Rocks and Minerals, 76, 77
Rice, Richard, 76
Robertson, Jim, 119
Rocky and Bullwinkle Show, 149
Rodeos, 262
   Chief Joseph, 262
   Pendleton Round-Up, 262
   St. Paul Rodeo, 262
Roosevelt, President Franklin, 227
Roosevelt, President Theodore, 253
Roseburg, 132, 133
Rosenburg, Samuel, 144
Rose City Classic Dog Show, 48, 49
Rose City Grand Floral Parade, 50
Roses Restaurant, 25
Ross, John, 249

Roth's, 63
Round Barn and Visitor Center, 251, 252
Ruby Jewel Ice Cream, 26, 27
Ruddy Duck, 87

S
Sage Grouse Strut and Bird-Watching, 252-254
Sand Master Park, 209
Saturday Market (and Sunday too), 51
Schulz, Brian, 177
Scoop Organic Ice Cream, 28, 29
Sea Lion Caves, 208, 209
Seal Rock, 204, 205, 216
Seal Rock State Recreation Site, 216
Seaside, 167-169 178, 179
Seaside Wheel Fun Rentals, 178, 179
Sellwood Bridge, 39
Sellwood Moreland Improvement League (SMILE), 30
Sellwood Park, 30, 33
Serendipity, 65, 66
Severe, Duff, 106
Shakespeare Festival Theaters, 118
Shaniko, 220, 221
Shaniko Days, 221
Shari's Restaurant, 102
Sheafor, Nathan, 143
The Shining, 227, 228
Shriner's Hospital, 45
Siddon, Dave, 146
Silver Falls State Park, 147, 148
Silveria, Pat, 200
Silverton, 134, 147, 148
Silverton Coffee Station, 134
Silver Falls State Park, 134, 147, 148
Singing Springs Resort, 211
Sisters, 238, 239
Skibowl, 222, 223
Slugs 'n Stones ' Ice Cream Cones, 200, 201
Smoke, Jodi , 92
Smoke, Terry, 92
Smokey Bear, 57
Sno Cap Drive-In, 239
Snydercrook, Boni, 167
Soft drinks, 14, 167, 168
Somewhere Over the Rainbow, 46
Sorweide, Carla, 89
Springfield Creamery, 157
Springwater Corridor, 33
Spruce Goose, 78
St. Patrick's Day, 108
Stark's Vacuum Cleaner Museum, 52
Steele Bridge, 33
Steens Mountains, 250
Stogo, 169
Sturgeon, 95
Sublimity, 147, 148

Sullivan, Herb, 132
Sundae in the Park, 30
Sunriver, 232- 234
Sunshine Dairy Ice Cream, 4, 14, 86, 162, 256
Sweet Productions Ice Cream Parlor & Diner, 108, 109

T
Taft, 188, 196
Taft, Cynthia, 163
Taylor, Til, 103
Teem, Monica, 204
Thai Lotus, 127
The First Tee, 75
3-D Center of Art and Photography, 52, 53
Tillamook, 170, 171
Tillamook Air Museum, 180
Tillamook Burn, 181, 182
Tillamook Forest Center, 181, 182
Tillamook Cheese Factory, 170, 171
Tillamook County Creamery Association, 170
Tillamook Ice Cream, 4, 14, 62, 86, 108, 160, 163, 164, 166, 170, 171, 190- 192, 204, 218
Tillamook (near), 179-182
Timber Temple, 56
Timberline, 227-229
Timberline Lodge, 227-229
Tin Signs, 112
Tingue, Kris, 244
Tiny Tim, 46
Tolly's Restaurant & Soda Fountain, 128, 129
Tonalli's Donuts and Ice Cream, 31
Tower Theater, 236
Tree to Tree Adventure Park, 73, 74
Trillium Lake, 225, 227
Troutdale, 92, 93
Troutdale General Store, Ice Cream Parlor & Confectionary, 92, 93
Two Tarts Artisan Sweets for the Soul, 32

U
Ukulele Band Camp, 46
Umatilla Indian Reservation, 91
Umpqua Ice Cream, 4, 67, 84, 91, 128, 129, 130, 131, 188, 191, 200, 203, 204, 219
  history of 132, 133
U.S. Bureau of Land Management, 247
U.S. Coast Guard, 214

V
Valley Bronze of Oregon, 111, 112
Vaux's Swifts at Chapman School, 53-55
Veneta (near), 156, 157
Veterans Administration, 45

W
Wahkeena Falls, 98
Walk Through the Tulips, 46
Wallowa Lake, 113-116
Wallowa Lake Tramway, 116

Warm Springs Indian Reservation, 226, 227
Washington, George, 2
Washington Park, 43, 56
Wassink, Lee, 143
Waterfront Park, 33
Watts, Dan, 196
Wellins, Mike, 18
Westport, 183-186
Westport Ferry, 186
Westmoreland Milk Carton Races, 55, 56
Westmoreland Park, 55, 56
Wildflower Grill, 189
Wildlife Images Rehabilitation & Education Center, 145, 146
Wilsonville, 149, 150
Willamette River, 33, 39, 45
Windsurfing, 100, 212
Wizer's, 63
Whole Foods, 26
Woodburn, 70, 71
World Forestry Center, 56, 57
Works Progress Administration (WPA), 227
Wurlitzer pipe organ, 40

Y
Your Country Store, 112

Z
Zinger's Ice Crream, 169
Zoey's Café, 118
Zoolights, 42
Zooliner, 43

Save $6.50

Buy One Public Skate Admission and Get The Second Public Skate Admission FREE at Lloyd Center Ice Rink *(Does not include skate rental)*

953 Lloyd Center Portland, OR 97232 • 503-288-6073

www.LloydCenterIce.com

Coupon Valid Until December 1, 2012.
Good with original coupon only.

Oregon Ice Creams and The Inside Scoop On Fun Things To See and Do

---

Save 20-30%

Do you feel lucky, Pardner?

Mention seeing this ad and draw for a store discount on one Prison Blues item.

363 S Main Street, Pendleton, OR 97801 • 541-276-1169
www.correctionconnectionprisonblues.com
Coupon Valid Until December 1, 2012. Good with original coupon only.

Oregon Ice Creams and The Inside Scoop On Fun Things To See and Do

---

Save $1.00

Enjoy $1 off your purchase of $5 or more at Sweet Productions Ice Cream Parlor and Diner

233 N Main Street, Heppner, OR 97836 • 541-676-8022
www.sweetproductions.homestead.com
Coupon Valid Until December 1, 2012. Good with original coupon only.

Oregon Ice Creams and The Inside Scoop On Fun Things To See and Do

A $10-$15 Value
This is one HOT offer!

Purchase $25 or more at The Glass Forge and get one FREE ornament.

501 SW G Street, Grants Pass, OR 97526 • 541-955-0815 • www.glassforge.com
Coupon Valid Until December 1, 2012. Good with original coupon only.

Oregon Ice Creams and The Inside Scoop On Fun Things To See and Do

---

A Great Deal!

Buy any one menu Item at Serendipity Ice Cream and get any second menu item *(of equal or lesser value)* **FREE**

502 NE 3rd Street, McMinnville, OR 97128 • 503-474-9189
Coupon Valid Until December 1, 2012. Good with original coupon only.

Oregon Ice Creams and The Inside Scoop On Fun Things To See and Do

---

$2.25 Value
Good for 1 FREE single scoop

Ice Cream Cone At Jamocha Jo's Java and Ice Cream

6020 NE William R. Carr Street, Adair, OR 97330 • 541-745-2050
Coupon Valid Until December 1, 2012. Good with original coupon only.

Oregon Ice Creams and The Inside Scoop On Fun Things To See and Do

---

YUM!

Buy 1 piece of pie and get the second piece of pie *(of equal or lesser value)* at ½ price

49289 Highway 30, Westport, OR 97016 • 503-455-2250
Coupon Valid Until December 1, 2012. Good with original coupon only.

Oregon Ice Creams and The Inside Scoop On Fun Things To See and Do

$2.75 Value

Good for 1 FREE single scoop

Ice Cream Cake Cone at Eleanor's Undertow Café & Ice Cream Parlor *(with any $5 purchase)*

Eleanor's Undertow is at the far south end of Lincoln City in historic Taft District.
869 SW 51st Street, Lincoln City, OR 97367 • 541-996-3800
Coupon Valid Until December 1, 2012. Good with original coupon only.

Oregon Ice Creams and The Inside Scoop On Fun Things To See and Do

---

$5-$12.50 Value

Rent 1 Board at the regular price and get the second day OR second Board ½ off at Sand Master Park

87542 Hwy 101, North Florence, OR 97439 • 541-997-6006 • **sandmasterpark.com**
Coupon Valid Until December 1, 2012. Good with original coupon only.

Oregon Ice Creams and The Inside Scoop On Fun Things To See and Do

---

www.HardysHotwings.com

$1.95 Value

Buy 1 single scoop ice cream cone and get the second single scoop ice cream cone FREE

238 NE 3rd Street, Bend, OR 97702 • 541-382-6962
Coupon Valid Until December 1, 2012. Good with original coupon only.

Oregon Ice Creams and The Inside Scoop On Fun Things To See and Do

Made in the USA
Charleston, SC
08 July 2011